Crossings 43

It's Saturday
You Left Me
and I'm So Beautiful

IT'S SATURDAY YOU LEFT ME AND I'M SO BEAUTIFUL

Emanuele Pettener

translated by Giorgio Tarchini

BORDIGHERA PRESS

Published by Bordighera Press, an imprint of the John D. Calandra Italian American Institute of Queens College, The City University of New York.

25 West 43rd Street, 17th Floor, New York, NY 10036

All rights reserved. Parts of this book may be reprinted only by written permission from the publisher, and may not be reproduced for publication in media of any kind, except in quotations for the purposes of literary reviews.

Library of Congress Control Number: 2025942438

The Italian language original *È sabato mi hai lasciato e sono bellissimo* was published by Corbo Editore in 2009.

The edition features two quotations from Charles Baudelaire and Søren Kierkegaard, the sources are cited below:

Charles Baudelaire, "I Adore You as Much as the Nocturnal Vault..." in *The Flowers of Evil*, translation by William Aggeler, Fresno, CA: Academy Library Guild, 1954.

Søren Kierkegaard, *Either/Or: A Fragment of Life*, translation by Alastair Hannay, London, England: Penguin Classics, 1992.

The cover image is "Abandonment (The pair)" by Henri de Toulouse-Lautrec.

© 2009, Emanuele Pettener
© 2025, Giorgio Tarchini, English translation

Crossings 43
ISBN 978-1-59954-234-8

Table of Contents

1. JUNE	9
2. JULY	24
3. AUGUST	40
4. SEPTEMBER	62
5. OCTOBER	76
6. NOVEMBER	95
7. DECEMBER	117
8. JANUARY	137
9. FEBRUARY	158
10. MARCH	181
11. APRIL	194
12. MAY (TWO YEARS LATER)	208
Acknowledgments	229
About the Author	231
About the Translator	233

1. June

I was twenty.

Twenty, said like that, it sounds so easy. But that's not how it is. It's not that simple.

I was twenty and fairly aware of how dense you can be at that age, of "the raw vulnerability of immaturity," as I used to say to feel cultivated—more to myself than to anyone else, because being an ignorant twenty year old unnerved me, that filthy aspect of being twenty, a verbal foulness first of all, with the vocabulary of a birdbrain, physical foulness too, the prickly stubble, the guitar player's thickened fingernails, the swagger of a provincial French writer, and so on.

I was twenty, and I had a vertical furrow between my eyebrows. I was twenty, and, as they say, I had my whole life ahead of me. Something was off. The summer was still young, poking its head out like a cute country mouse, like the idea for the novel of the century that comes to you on a luminous June morning and making you glide over the sidewalks—light with happiness and pride—and then dissipates around noon. There was something in the air like impending thunderstorms; the heat rose from the fresh asphalt, and the nights were full of desire. There were friends and a few women, of course, whom fate had placed together in an architecture inlaid with coincidences and nearly perfect metaphors (fate is a meticulous artist), although I would know it only much later.

After all, I was twenty, and I really didn't know much.

And actually, I wasn't twenty yet; I had eight months to go. But two weeks earlier, the rancorous Latin scholar who was president of the committee for the 1990 final exams at Franchetti High School in Mestre had asked me after the test:

"So, what will you do now?"

And suddenly I thought of high school and the peach blossoms just outside the window and my mother's caffè latte and the black stockings worn by the Greek teacher, who asked me about Polybius. *It's all gone*, and I looked into the gray eyes of the sullen Latin scholar, one of those women you can't tell if she's old and seems young or if she's young and seems old, women who are not easily embarrassed. But my silence did embarrass her:

"Because it's now, you know, that you decide on your future," but what about the springtime light on those peach blossoms? And what about the careful setting of a cup of caffè latte on my night table at seven in the morning, its aroma, the rustling of opening curtains, and my mother quietly leaving my room? And above all, *above all* – what about those black stockings?

"You know, these choices will steer your life," but the sunlight streaming into the classroom warmed my face and reminded me of past summers, and, of course, I would have liked to come up with a wise reply, with a whole series of subordinate clauses, but I stared into her gray eyes, which seemed vaguely satisfied that my youth was quickly slipping away, and I was tired, and now I saw my twenties rush at me like a herd of threatening buffalo, heavy and dumb, ("What's wrong? Are you frozen?" she said, by now a little irritated) but I was speechless, like an idiot in the spotlight, mortified, and maybe my silence did affect my final grade.

"As if she had asked you what Truth is!" said Rebecca coldly.

Niso defended me, "In my opinion you did the right thing, but after that you should have French kissed her."

"Too ugly," France argued.

Alcapone capped it off with: "I want some toast."

This was how we spent our evenings in late June. Alcapone ate; we drank beer. I preferred whiskey—it boosted my self-confidence, but it was so expensive, and at my age I felt a little embarrassed drinking it. Paul

Newman could drink whiskey, but could I? I often imagined drinking with my old buddy Paul Newman. I could vent my resentment, and he listened to me. He had a way of looking at people I wished I had, and when he glanced around at the patrons in the bar—he took them in, he took everything in—and you noticed his total control. He was a man; the others were *people*, people who had not been individuals, not even when taken one by one. No, each one alone on a desert island or in a suddenly unpopulated world, each one would still be just regular *people*. A mass of idiots. All of them feeling important with a cigarette dangling between their index and middle fingers, all of them casually laughing, showing toothy smiles—but what's so funny? All working like dogs during the week and braying like mules on the weekend, all of them getting wasted and talking about bikes and women, all of them shoving into each other all sweaty and gross—horribly pubescent—in the carnal abandon of nightclubs.

All happy.

Arthur Rimbaud, a guy Niso was always talking about, had already stopped writing at twenty, at twenty he was already in Africa trafficking guns or selling slaves, who knows, but nonetheless he had already lived a lifetime, at twenty he had become the greatest European poet—and meantime all these guys are dancing!

"Tell me, Arthur, how did you do it?"

"I was drunk," he said with his guttural French *r*.

Paul Newman laughed and poured all three of us another finger of scotch.

Paul Newman and Rimbaud: two guys who had made it.

Anyway, June was unraveling in untouched whiskey, anger, and longing, and we went to the beach, the Lido in Venice. We took the #1 *vaporetto*, which crosses the Grand Canal, sluggish, and we found space astern, in the fresh air. We sat down (next to a tiny old lady and some kind of Rasputin with a long black beard), and the sun washed over us and we felt its scorching warmth on our eyelids, in our bones, and we breathed in the smell of the watermelon rinds and diesel fuel coming from the greenish-golden lagoon, and the wind tousled our hair with salty water. Left and right, buildings of ivory and apricot colors, orange and ruby red buildings stood out, majestic against the blue sky, and went on and on, carried only by their breathtaking beauty, with their little windows with lace curtains and their ancient stone balconies dripping with clusters of purple wisteria and white gardenias. On one of these balconies, I saw a young woman arranging her hair, then I turned around and glanced at the little bone hair stick holding the old lady's bun together, and for a moment I felt complete. None of us spoke. The beauty overwhelmed us, each of us was lost in oblivion—immersed in the golden mist of the 1700s—and yet I know each of us felt as never before the lively beating of our twenty years. The sheer splendor of those buildings sinking into the thick water was brought on not only by the Byzantine delicacy of Venetian marble or the pride of the lions nestled in the Titian-red walls, or the iron gates corroded by algae, but also by the thousand feelings they triggered and the History they oozed. Thus, behind the violet reflections of those windowpanes, you could glimpse little ladies playing the harpsichord and powdered wigs and Casanova seducing a servant girl and Iago sneering in the shadows and the ghosts of doges and popes and thieves and painters and drunks and the plague, the Crusades, Napoleon . . .

And as the eras of History (including the bloodiest) produce a kind of mysterious longing for the thousand possibilities that we have not lived, so too, like never before, we sensed the thousands of possibilities in our future and in being twenty. And it didn't matter that these thousand possibilities (exactly like the ghosts of History) maybe didn't exist, because we smelled their perfume and it numbed us. I looked at my friends: France, who looks at everything, every detail, every gondola, every seagull, as he continually turns his big head left and right, amazed like a child, and in the deafening noise of the *vaporetto*, in the sunlight bouncing off the water, he already sees himself as a judge who's gotten rid of the Camorra once and for all and drives a Cadillac, has bought Naples's soccer team and is engaged to Karin, a Swedish supermodel. Then we have Alcapone, with his fat red cheeks and his baby-blue eyes looking up at the sky, seeming happy and carefree in some hemisphere; he'll be the head chef at the best restaurant in Paris and maybe he's seeing Karin, France's fiancée.

Niso bites his lips instead. On his dark glasses, the sun reflects the ivy-covered buildings, the bricoles, the pink stucco of the *Ca' d'Oro* with its spires and tea tables in the back gardens, and at one point he says:
"Venice is a masterpiece. But I didn't make it. Too bad!"

The sand was burning hot, and the sky was an endless blue fabric, pierced in the middle by an angry sun, and the sea shimmered and the women swarmed, full, firm breasts in tiny, colorful bikinis, soft, pure asses, thighs that got paler toward the groin for our agonizing desires. It was hot. The towels spread out on the sand were already soaked with our sweat, the sun burned our skin and our scalps, but nothing in the world could stop us from playing soccer, so we formed teams: Niso, the poetic soccer player, was paired up with Alcapone, absolutely incapable of any sports activity; France and I, two tenacious mastiffs, reestablished our historic winning duo. The playing field was the beach, bounded by water on one side and the bodies of sunbathers on the other, about 65 feet long and 20 to 25 feet wide. One of my shoes and an empty water bottle served as goalposts on one side, the other goalposts were my other shoe and the bag of groceries that Alcapone had already emptied: Let the games begin!

Right away, Niso shows off all his tricks, heel kicks among other fancy moves, but France, confident in his skills, protects our goal so that Niso can't get through; on the other hand, a few times I catch the ball from my teammate on the counterattack, but getting around the pachydermic Alcapone is no mean feat: No one scores. The scorching sun beats down on us, and we all lose a few pounds except for that walrus Alcapone, who stands still guarding the goal, but at least sometimes the ball ends up in the water, and the chase to retrieve it is a feast of cooling sprays. Then it happened, the turning point: Rebecca shows up and starts watching the game. Then you see Niso spring into action like a bolt of lightning as he burns right through me, passing the ball between France's legs, and landing it between the shoe and the bottle, running toward Rebecca and kissing her on her cute nose. That bastard! Although humilated, we can't help smiling, to the point that Alcapone, stomping like an elephant, reaches the two lovebirds and lifts them up, rejoicing. But just then we stop laughing, because Niso, on defense, retrieves the ball and lobs it right over me, leaving me standing there like a chump, another lob goes past even the poor France; then—the show-off—alone in front of the goal, decides not to score, turns back toward France, circles him, fakes him out to make him open his legs, then he slips the ball between them so that it finally lands between the shoe and the bottle. Alcapone laughs uncontrollably, Rebecca laughs as well, and Niso bows down thanking the imaginary crowd that goes wild.

But here is where team spirit shone: France and I looked at each other, and our comeback was sealed. We launched our attack, hearts, lungs, and brains fully engaged, our plays perfection; we both chased Niso, dogging him, leaving him with nowhere to go. Our first goal stemmed from a corner kick taken from the water's edge. The ball, heavy with water, flew into the air, Niso jumped in vain, Alcapone anchored himself firmly in the sand, motionless, but France soared between them like a condor and scored with a header that grazed the bag of groceries. No time for celebration. With determined faces, we recovered the ball and brought it to the center of the makeshift field while Niso wasted his time insulting Alcapone.

"Move your fat ass!" screamed France (with a hint of a Neapolitan accent). "Quick!" I screamed, too. We resumed. Niso passed the ball back to Alcapone. That's when I sprang into action, running toward him like a madman, knowing he would be taken aback. Alcapone miskicked the ball, and France, faster than Niso, caught it before it landed in the water and kicked it forward toward me. With Alcapone outside the goal, scoring was child's play. Speechless, Niso looked at Alcapone, who made some lame excuses. Rebecca clapped. Fickle woman . . .

But France and I didn't pause to celebrate: Now we wanted to win.

With only five minutes left in the game, Niso was clearly pissed, and so we achieved our masterpiece. France had the ball, and Niso pressured him, but France was still able to pass it to me. Then he sprinted forward, leaving Niso behind, and I passed the ball back to him as I ran parallel. As Alcapone blocked his way forward and Niso was about to kick him from behind, France passed me the ball. And I, from a difficult angle but with an unguarded goal, scored to take the lead. The crowd went wild. France pointed his index finger at me, and I did the same, in a conventional gesture of great psychological significance, and we didn't hug each other only for fear of getting too emotional. (Rebecca jumped up and down on the sand, her small breasts bouncing in her green bikini top, but in that moment our triumph born out of virile friendship couldn't take into account any feminine details.)

Unfortunately, in the last second of the game, damned Niso dribbled past both France and me and found himself all alone with the tying shot two feet from the water bottle and the shoe. But he either hesitated for a second, or he kicked the ball with excessive self-confidence, or maybe the sand slowed down his shot. In any case, in a desperate attempt, I slid across the imaginary goal line, and with the tip of my foot I deflected the ball just enough to prevent it from going in.

(There I lie spread-eagled like a dead man on the sand, under the sun, out of breath, filthy and sweaty—and yet I open my eyes and the sky is so blue. I raise my fists in the air. What a thrill! What a victory! I feel like Juan Alberto Schiaffino at the 1950s World Cup! France jumps on top of me and this time we hug each other, almost in tears – we beat Brazil on its home turf, Uruguay was the World champion, no one could believe it! In the meantime, Niso leaves the field swearing – there were a lot of suicides among the Brazilian fans, at the time – and Alcapone is already soothing himself with a sandwich).

Few are the pleasures more exquisite than diving into the sea, sweaty and exhausted, after winning the World Cup. Even Rebecca decided that it was time for her to take a little swim, and maybe we would finally realize how hot she was: her bikini was mint green, and she wore it with great self-awareness; she knew how good she looked. Her smile encapsulated so much of that June day, and even her eyes were perfectly green, and her dimples looked as if painted by some Flemish miniaturist from the sixteenth century. But we had been classmates for five years now and you know how that goes—she took no interest in us. So, we swam around her wildly so as not to stare at her; still, we couldn't help crudely gushing over her. We were compelled to make her the sole object of our games, our jokes, our foolish frenzy:

"What wonderful tits!" quipped a stunned Niso. "May I?" France asked casually as he lightly grazed her hard nipples through her bathing suit. "Hey, cut it out!" she pulled back petulantly, splashing him on the face. "I would eat them up!!!" burst out a blushing Alcapone. "Of course, you would think about eating," she said without missing a beat. And we laughed, we laughed like crazy, and we splashed around like dolphins in heat for a good half hour, dizzyingly diving to annoy her underwater, soaring like crazed Tritons uprooted from the sea floor to reach for the heavens, clamoring like a bunch of school kids, splashing each other with armfuls of water, and all joining forces to splash Rebecca, and so on.

At night, exhausted, we went back to Mestre. It was around seven o'clock. I got home, and my mother asked me, "Did you have fun?"

Yeah, I had fun.

My future could wait. Yes, my friends and I would enroll at the university. We would extend our youth for a long while. Women, wine, coffee, a long winter with friends going to the movies or playing pool, women. Waiting for spring, the first set of exams, warm croissants, women. Endless soccer games, beers with friends, completing a four-year degree, women, women, and still more women. Something didn't add up, I knew it, a sneaking sense of futility, of things done to forget there was nothing to do, the lack of any great ambition. Maybe they didn't make sense, either, but only the women conferred a feeling of reality. But we had time. First summer, then college, which would give some semblance of propriety to our lives. I stepped into the shower, and I was twenty. I could feel my twenty years pulsating in my neck and in my back muscles, the ice-cold water poured down my skin and washed away all the sand and sweat, together with that feeling of becoming normal. I got out of the shower, and I smelled an intense aroma coming from the kitchen:

"Mom, what's for dinner?"

A large, rare steak and French fries were waiting for me. I was relieved.

The city was peaceful that summer evening. Its dormant state was broken only by the lights still on in the windows of late diners and by the faint melody of the nightly news theme song. I was full and my bones ached. My muscles felt denuded, in the middle of my chest lay the lungs of a bull. I took the car, and I could barely manage to step on the pedals. The weight of the afternoon sun bore down on me, all the energy in my upper legs had been depleted by kicking a soccer ball on the sand, while the whistling wind still echoed in my ears. It was heavenly. I was in no hurry to get to the Sbruffon. I stopped to get some gas, even though I didn't need any: I like the smell of gasoline, it is intoxicating. I was so tired that I felt proud, as if I had moved a mountain, but what kind of pride is there in moving a mountain? It was as if I had worked so hard that now I was spent. Then I left the gas station, rolled down the window and caught a whiff of the hot dust, the voluptuous smell of the fast-approaching night. I studied the roses and the deserted streets, the streetlights teeming with gnats, and I glimpsed a few couples taking a walk holding ice cream cones. Romance filled the air. It was all very romantic, and I should have guessed that something big was going to happen. I arrived at the Sbruffon, parked, but stayed in the car for a few minutes. Happy. I had my elbow resting on the open window as I watched the stars, stupendous stars, incandescent, Californian stars, and an old Cole Porter swing tune was playing on the car radio, the husky voice of the deejay informed me, transporting me to an enigmatic America. I felt so great that I had to go to the bathroom. But I suddenly jumped up, got out of the car, and went into the Sbruffon.

The Sbruffon was the same in the summer as in the winter, about twenty billiard tables, around which everybody felt like Paul Newman in *The Hustler* with the smoky room, the clacking sound of the colored balls. There was always some woman who had seen too many movies, dressed in a tight skirt with a slit up the back, so that, when someone bent over the billiard table for a tricky shot, we all took in an interesting sight by standing behind her. The place had a decidedly macho vibe, and the few women were intentionally more sexy. At the pool table, everyone was willing.

I played with Alcapone, who acted very professional but was a blowhard. A pool table was the only place where he felt like the top dog, and his baby-blue taillight eyes shone with impudent pride each time a ball ended up in a pocket. Rebecca, moved, clapped for him as she sat perched on a high wooden stool in a cream-colored mini skirt, crossing her firm, beautiful, and naked sunburned legs. Oh Rebecca, you are perched on a stilt, and you feel invincible, you feel like you're the only one, look at how strange life is! At that moment we heard a shrill voice:

"Can we play with you?"

She was a crane. A fantastic crane, by God, but the first impression I had of her was that she was a crane. Long, sinewy legs ending in feet encased in elegant red high heels, a micro mini skirt, a checkered blouse unbuttoned in the front. And underneath, a very tight black T-shirt silhouetted the two-pointed bayonets of her breasts. She was with a friend, whom almost no one noticed, in jeans, with curly black hair and a frozen smile. Rebecca just about fell off her stool, huffy, halfway pissed off, all but forgotten. She was most certainly thinking, "What a little slut!"

For sure. In the meantime, France opened his mouth, and it would have taken centuries for him to close it. I felt extremely embarrassed, like I always did when I found myself near a woman of such incredible beauty. Alcapone mumbled something and displayed his most expressive face. As usual, Niso was sharper than all of us.

"Sure, sweetie," he said, not even looking at her. He went on playing, as if nothing had happened. Then, he slowly lifted his eyes and, seemingly lost in thought, smiled at her.

"You play with me," and with that he showed who was in charge, almost brazen: basically, the uncontested leader of the group.

Seeming a bit frightened, she looked at him: "Whatever you say . . ." She murmured softly, like a submissive lamb about to be slaughtered by a wolf.

I hated both. In a split second, they had already excluded us. Rebecca, to hide her escalating rage, forced an unconvincing and meaningless smile. All right, I assessed the situation: Only four of us could play, two would be left out. Since the crane and Niso had already arrogantly taken their spots, it was better to excuse myself right away rather than to be left out by them. Although I would have liked to grab a pool stick and wipe the floor with both of them, I knew I would lose—I certainly didn't have Niso's unflappable composure.

"Here," I said affably to the curly-headed girl with the steadfast smile and handed her my pool stick.

She thanked me with an impertinent look. I figured they had already split the spoils: I would go to the curly-headed girl, Niso to the crane. That damned Niso!

Even France, with his mouth still agape and after some delay, understood that it was better to get out. He put down his pool stick and announced to everyone that he was going to the bathroom.

The crane cried, "Hold on!" France stumbled, livid with tension. "My name is Angelica," said the crane, and France mustered up all his courage to tell her his name, averting his eyes, not even looking at her at all. He was wrapped in a smoke curtain that disoriented him, and an uncontrollable, subtle anxiety made him blush deeply. Angelica the crane, aware of her venomous smile, turned toward Rebecca and shook her hand; their lips widened, reaching disturbing dimensions, emitting a strident gurgling of delight as they pronounced each other's names, treacherous like Judas.

Alcapone just introduced himself, but his large face couldn't conceal anything. You could tell that he would have gobbled her up right on the spot, but that didn't seem to bother her at all; she kept on smiling. When it was Niso's turn, he kissed her hand. I thought he was exaggerating. Indeed, he was exaggerating. Then the crane extended her hand to me, and I looked her in the eyes just as I would have looked at a man, politely, but with no solidarity. I recalled Paul Newman. Always remember old Paul when you want to set a tone, if you want to be hip, recall old Paul's gaze and think of what he would say:

"Hi."

She stopped and almost suppressed her smile, her eyes lingering on mine, as if it would be easy to chain Paul Newman to herself. Her eyes sparkled with a hint of mauve and shone like a blowtorch trying to melt my steely gaze, and maybe my indifference was able to chip away at her self-confidence. She looked like a little child when she repeated her name to me:

"Angelica . . . and you are?"

"Newman. Paul Newman."

She laughed, and her friend, who meanwhile in the darkness had introduced herself to everybody, laughed, and everyone laughed. The corners of my mouth curled up as I took out a cigarette, lit it, and smiled at her, ironic and wistful. Go away, my girl, just go, let your beauty dazzle whoever is naïve enough to get impaled by it. Just get lost and wipe that pretentious, blinding gleam off your face. What's up with you? Don't you have any problems? Well, sister, I do, and I'm sure that two sets of false eyelashes, two legs, or a row of shark teeth won't be enough to resolve them.

But what problems did I have? None. I was quite content. To me, it seemed that my tough-guy act had hit home. In any case, I had made my audience smile. The truth was that her beauty unsettled me. Any woman's beauty unsettled me, because it was an instrument of power I lacked, whether it be perky tits ensconced in an embroidered bra, or a trace of mascara to enhance her eyes, or the absent-minded loosening of the knot in her hair, or, most of all, a pair of stockings bound in such a tight relationship with her the likes of which I could never achieve. Not that I didn't have my own discrete success with women, but those I successfully seduced, while objectively cute, always seemed inferior to those I couldn't seduce, to those I actually didn't dare even try to seduce on account of their beauty. Too tall. To me, all gorgeous women seemed statuesque, even those who were only five feet, they seemed to tower over me. I hated their arrogant manner of showing off, especially in bars and nightclubs, their perfect bodies, with a derisive smile, as if to say: You'll never have me. I hated the fact that a woman could say *yes*, *no*, *never*, while I would have always said yes. If I had been born a woman, I would have been infamous. In a girl, I always sought imperfection, to the point that only imperfect women—the so-called cute ones—turned me on, in my certainty that the perfect woman was beyond my reach by virtue of some kind of sorcery, by virtue of their daftness, by virtue of the fact that I felt like a superb cyclist who always came in second.

But enough of that. You can't settle for second place. Moral victories are only for losers. I was Paul Newman, right? So, I placed my hand on Rebecca's knee as she was sitting on her stilt-like stool. And she, feeling jealous and left out, put her hand on mine. There wasn't the slightest hint of eroticism in that gesture. It was, rather, an unspoken alliance between a deposed queen who confides in the only subject who has remained faithful to her and a young Casanova who knows that the best weapon to win over a woman is another woman.

Alcapone came back with beers. The atmosphere was that of an absolutely insufferable joy and complicity among the four pool players. Alcapone's playing was legendary. He zeroed in on the balls like a cheetah hiding in the grass zeroes in on its prey, and he put two balls in one pocket like it was nothing at all, like it was just a routine thing. The curly-headed girl praised him, something no other girl had ever done before. So, he arched his right eyebrow and mustered a faint smile, almost as if distracted. However, when it was her turn, he turned into the greatest pool teacher in the universe, didactic, precise, even expounding metaphors. With the ruse of showing her how she should take her shot, he would get behind her and feel her hips up with his clumsy paws. He would whisper in her ear serious suggestions about the geometry of the next shot. The girl, docile and devoted, would bend over the pool table, take the shot, and look at him for approval. In turn, he would nod (paternally), or mumble (messianically): "Don't worry."

We all looked at him flabbergasted. He was living the most beautiful night of his life. In spite of his improbable stories with Filipino or Finnish girls, we knew he had only ever put his lips on sandwiches—even though with the same passion as when placing them on a woman's mouth. He was very fat, and no woman ever gave him a chance. He wore a black felt hat, a velvet vest, very expensive gray pants in the style of the thirties, and dark shiny shoes. Anachronistic but elegant, he looked like Al Capone. Coming from a rich family, he was the only one of us who lived on his own, in an apartment furnished with lavender-colored Scandinavian furniture and a collection of tropical shells, where we spent our time, most nights talking about nothing, wonderfully bored, while decimating his stash of food and wine.

The bond between Niso and the crane was already unbreakable: They were staring into each other's eyes, joking like two high-school kids on vacation. He was obviously handsome and sure of himself, but always in a sufficiently light-hearted way as to not come off as annoying. She was sensual but not aggressive, with a certain charming sweetness. They won two games and lost two, but most importantly they had clearly excluded us from their romantic hijinks. His high point came when she, defending a miscalculated shot, came up with the excuse of jiggling the pool cue too much:

"Forever I bear the punishment of having tried to change my place."

The pretentious nature of that sentence would have nauseated me, had I known that it was in fact a literary quote. But the only one who got it was Niso, who answered nonchalantly:

"Everything is not lost, my dear Charles."

She looked at him, astonished, like someone who finds a brother she didn't know she had, like someone who feels superior but is all alone roaming through a world of dimwits and suddenly, she encounters a kindred spirit, like a woman who, for her entire life, has dreamed in vain of meeting her Prince Charming, and here he is in front of her, with his poorly shaven beard, skillfully holding the pool cue, in his pure white shirt, a killer look in his eyes.

"You know Baudelaire," she murmured.

Oh Niso, awesome Niso! Anyone else would have said yes, I do, cheerful and triumphant, but you didn't even bat an eyelash, you kept on chalking up the cue stick, you looked up as only you could—master of the pause—and just stared at her for three or four unforgettable seconds. Then, in a joking and at the same time serious tone, your unwavering gaze fixed on her eyes, you said:

"*I adore you as much as the nocturnal vault, O vase of sadness, most taciturn one, I love you all the more because you flee from me, And because you appear, ornament of my nights, More ironically to multiply the leagues . . . "*

Here he stopped and even I would have kissed him. Then he sighed, bending pensively over the pool table:

"That separate my arms from . . . " he hit the cue ball, which hit the yellow ball and ended up in the pocket, and he finished with: *"the blue infinite."*

Frustrated and fascinated by a performance that excluded us, Rebecca inadvertently squeezed my hand, and I squeezed her thigh. Our admiration was torturing us. France, who didn't even know how to get envious for the simple reason that he took Niso's superiority for granted, smiled and raised his beer in a toast, the curly-headed girl followed suit, and Alcapone, more dumbfounded by the shot than by Niso's poetic turn, kept repeating, "What a fluke, what a fluke!" And the crane looked at Niso as if hypnotized, I thought she was going to kiss him, but instead she stammered: "No, it's not possible."

That was the first time we saw the look in her eyes, a frightened, terrified look that spooked us all, a scary, ghostly light coming from a London suburb from one hundred years ago, from a deserted graveyard, yet reinforced by the black eyeliner that encircled her eyes (such beautiful eyes, enough said). But in that moment they sent shivers down my spine, and I turned my attention to the pale, curly-headed girl in jeans, then to Rebecca, stone-cold, and then to France, confused, and finally to Alcapone, who hadn't picked up on anything and had continued playing, still cursing and brooding over Niso's last shot.

2. July

The next day, July had already started. An aggressive sun filtered through the curtains and smacked me in the face as if challenging me to a duel. I turned over, then turned again, but there's nothing worse than the sun challenging you to a duel so early in the morning, you run the risk of having a terrible headache throughout the day. Anyway, I was awake now and not happy at all. My mouth was caked with the noxious remnants of the previous evening, all that smoke, and all those beers. Especially the night before. Niso, he was perfect. She, how gorgeous she was! No denying it.

The details bobbled to the surface of my mind randomly, more vivid than I would have liked. Tantalizing thighs, like the flesh of a peach, legs seamlessly slipping into angular ankles, slender, tiny feet slipping into small red shoes, and that look of an Egyptian queen, those impertinent breasts, those lips . . .

I kept my eyes closed to forget, but I was too alert now. The scorching sun was bursting in. Damned sun. Damned summer. Damned Niso. What a shame! He had been, of course, so clever, so very clever! How could I not be envious of him, not feel cheated by God for not being as cool, as elegant, as witty, as cultivated! Oh, God! You teach me that envy is a vice, but the possibility of being envious cannot be taken away from a man. It would be inhuman. I am truly ashamed of my envy and I accept the burden of my shame, but if I did not freely envy Niso—even in the silence and privacy of my small bedroom—believe me, I would be worse, I would be a frog trapped in a frying pan, I would be a shriveled-up moralist with yellow, urine-colored skin, a preacher who represses and accumulates an ominous envy for all those who don't know how to repress their envy like he does.

I would be a hypocrite to reject this envy, because I realize that Niso is better than I am. You need humility and clarity to be truly envious. But I know, I know I could beat him—there is envy, said the poet Cino da Pistoia, only where competition is possible—this is the only reason that France doesn't envy Niso, certainly not because he is better than me!

I realized that even I knew how to quote someone perfectly when I wanted to. Good job, Ema, I said to myself, not everyone can spout a line from Cino da Pistoia, just like that. I got up, reassured, and found a note from my parents. I remembered that they had left at dawn for a vacation and that for a good amount of time I would have the house all to myself, and suddenly a day that had started out badly had immediately turned around.

I made coffee. I went into the bathroom with my coffee and a Donald Duck comic book and got comfortable on the toilet. At last, the world had been left behind, my soul purified. The coffee was strong, and I was consumed by its aroma, it was a morning aroma, an intimate aroma, one of childhood at my grandma's farm. And I also found the smell of my feces comforting, a classically summer smell, as if even my gut was beckoning me back to faraway summers, happy ones, lost ones. The world, inept, stayed outside.

I slowly emptied my bowels, enjoying my coffee and reading my comic book. But I had to stop with the Donald Duck comics if I were to have any chance with Angelica. Hurriedly, I finished my coffee, wiped and cleaned up, looked into the mirror, stroking my two-day-old stubble. Then I threw on a pair of well-worn jeans and a white shirt, like the one Niso had worn the previous day. I liked my looks, even if it was hot outside. I rehearsed a couple of different faces in the mirror, the innocent and sincere look that came instinctively, and a look lit up by an inconceivable irony: I was so handsome. I went out into the streets with the speed of a leopard and hurried off to the library. Immediately I found an old copy of *The Flowers of Evil*. I took it out and the librarian smiled, comforted by the fact that a young person of my age, in a season usually dedicated to leisure, was devoting his time to such serious reading. Being considered serious: Baudelaire would have felt devastated by that.

I ran to the nearest café, and July sunbathed me, splendid and piercing in the blue sky. Even the café smelled like summer: the large windows that looked out onto nature outside, the red leather armchairs, the wooden counter, and the waitress with her little snow-white apron, which, once removed, would have surely uncovered a pair of small, firm boobs, soft supple thighs, and two shapely bare legs. I sat down at a table, and she was already next to me.

"What would you like?" she asked smiling, her mouth shaped like a strawberry, with lively pale blue eyes—she was cute, the kind of girl I liked.

"Mmm . . . I haven't even thought about it yet," and I looked at her with the first look I had worked on in the mirror that morning, the innocent one.

"Do you want to think about it?" She chirped with exquisite courtesy.

I smiled and opened wide my riveting blue eyes, but as if it was nothing at all, almost naively, as if it was only natural.

"No, no. In life you need to make decisions!" I wanted to be witty. Besides, her smile was dazzling. I set the book on the table so she could see the cover and unbuttoned my cuffs so as to roll the sleeves halfway up my forearm. I placed my index finger on my nose like someone who is mulling things over, and, in a carefully considered tone, I offered her the solution:

"Black coffee; a double, please."

Usually I drink my coffee with milk, but that seemed lacking in virility. She nodded, the smile still on her face, and then turned around and waltzed off behind the counter to make my coffee. Her small, exposed calves, colored amber from the sun, were ready to be munched on like you do buttered corn on the cob. I felt I was on the same wavelength with her, with myself, with that bar filled with sunlight, with the universe. I also felt somewhat ridiculous, underneath it all, but she was smiling, and it looked like she was still smiling behind the counter while she fiddled with the coffee machine. After all, I was her only customer. I watched her, wearing my own carefully chosen smile, and began to leaf through the book. I couldn't concentrate, of course, so I didn't absorb a single word; out of the corner of my eye, I was almost sure she was still looking at me. I had to stay on my toes. Here she is. Oh yes, she seems really nice, her eyes sparkling like tiny blue flames.

"Here's your coffee." she said softly.

"Thank you."

We were making progress. Once again, she said:

"I hope I didn't make it too strong."

I didn't answer and continued looking at her, smiling politely, and maybe that was where I screwed up, because she may have thought I was dismissing her. She turned around and went back behind the counter. Damn. I had a knot in my stomach; I needed to remain calm. Maybe she was only being nice because I was the only customer, and anyway she *had to be nice*; that was her job! But she was watching me, I felt she was watching me. Once again, I looked up from my book and once again our looks crossed, embarrassed. Compelled to say something, to explain myself, I rambled on:

"May I have a croissant?"

She lit up, grateful, almost as if I had asked her to marry me:

"Yes, right away, I'll be right back."

"Oh, take your time!"

"No, not at all, here I am. With chocolate or custard?"

"What?"

We both burst out laughing, relaxing a little.

Blessed be that book! Blessed be Baudelaire! He worked miracles. It was an identification sign, a secret symbol of recognition between an idealistic young woman compelled by her job to get dirty surrounded by sad old men and lascivious young ones, and a young artist, so different from the usual patrons, such a rebel—so *unique*. Bringing my hand to my mouth, with a look that would crush ice, I said, in a smoky, fearless voice:

"You pick, I trust your taste."

"I prefer chocolate."

"Chocolate it is."

She smiled again and immediately brought me the croissant, but just then another customer came in, and she turned her back to me before I could say anything else. I didn't appreciate that she also smiled so graciously at the overweight guy who had just come in, but I decided that it was not an authentic smile, but a professional one. I started to leaf through the book again and by chance I found the poem that Niso had recited so well. In that instant, I knew what I had to do. Twenty tense, very long minutes went by. Luckily two or three more customers came in, so that I could fully concentrate on the poem. The croissant was left untouched. I felt my heart fluttering in my chest, madly, it was pulling at my nerves and stretching my muscles, and although it was the first really hot day in July, and the crickets were basking in the sun, I felt cold. Wild eyed, my mouth tense, I kept repeating: *"I adore you as much as the nocturnal vault Oh vase of sadness . . . Ohvaseofsadness . . . ohmosttaciturnone . . . Iadoreyouasmuchasthenocturnalvault . . . Ohvaseofsadness . . . Oh most taciturn one!!!* . . . I know this one . . . *I love you all the more* . . . So, first, I adore you, then I love you, but all the more, all the more! . . . *Beautiful!!!* . . . No, I could say most beautiful . . . *You flee from me.* Period. That's enough. *You flee from me.* Period."

My hands were so sweaty. I stood up gripped by muscular spasms: Give up! But the die has been cast, I can't allow myself to be a coward, I would never forgive myself. I approached the counter, her head was bent over the cash register, she looked up and smiled at me with those joyful and very pale blue eyes, with her mouth, with her whole face, and whispered:

"So, a double espresso and a chocolate croissant . . . "

I waited for her to look at me again, and I said:

"*I adore you as much as the nocturnal vault.*"

"Excuse me?"

"I said . . . I adore you as much as the nocturnal vault . . . o most taciturn one!!! . . . No, wait! O vase of sadness, o most taciturn one! I love you all the more because you flee from me . . . beautiful!!! . . . So very beautiful."

We stood like petrified ice sculptures caught in a terrifying silence. It was painful. I felt I was wheezing like an epileptic and puking my heart out. She was still smiling, but with a lackluster smile, embarrassed for me, the way you smile at crazy people. I turned bright red, twitching, stuttering, sweating and at the lowest of the low: a ridiculous man. I had to say something!

"It's a poem, you see, by Baudelaire . . . as soon as I saw you . . . you reminded me of it . . . hold on a sec. I'll read it to you!!!"

I read it all to her, from beginning to end, it felt like the longest poem ever, and at each verse—emphatic, stupid, mellifluous, and senseless verses!—I sank into the most abysmal shame, feeling the fire of humiliation burning my face and ears. I was soaked with a cold sweat from the tips of my hair to my crotch. She went on smiling through clenched teeth, checking to the left and right that no one was witnessing the pitiful scene—feeling sorry for me and only hoping that I would soon stop that torture. But the only thing more indomitable than shame is the vain and desperate attempt to quash it, such that I didn't budge from there even though I wanted to be nullified, pulverized, dead:

"Well . . . Baudelaire is Baudelaire . . . eh? Do you like it?"

"Umm, I'm not an expert, you know . . . " she said, touchingly sincere, "anyway, thanks . . . "

"Thanks to Baudelaire, eh! This poet who has regaled us with such strong emotions . . . so, you shouldn't be ashamed if you're not familiar with him, you know?"

My God, how dumb! How utterly dumb! She didn't say a word, she just looked at me, making me die on the spot, sinking me into the abyss. Then she said:

"Excuse me, but now I have to take care of the other customers."

"Of course, of course . . . But, what's your name?"

Moving away and looking at me for the last time, she told me her name, but I didn't get it. I was too broken by the humiliation.

I fled like the snake driven out of Eden. I started to run like a madman in the merciless midday sun, insane with fury and shame. I ran like a lunatic with a ferocious rage shrieking inside of me, for me and for God, who had made me so ridiculous. I ploughed through groups of people who surely were happy—I ran home, and after locking the door behind me, at last, I cried.

I spent a hellish half hour, trying to free myself from that horrible feeling, but the pity in her eyes kept flashing in my brain like the high beams of a truck, her face contracted in embarrassment for this imbecile who wanted to act like a stud . . . idiot, imbecile, idiot, huge asshole! But the insults didn't scratch the surface. I took no pity on myself, ridiculous trying to fake it to feel less ridiculous, you're a total jackass, that's what you are, a total jackass! I spent a hellish half hour, going from room to room like a hysterical in a straitjacket, with this pain in my throat—this awareness of being a twenty-year-old idiot, a total jackass, just a jackass!!! Oh, how ridiculous you were with that demeanor of a pensive man, a demeanor shown by all those who have never had any ideas at all, how pathetic you were with those antics of a third-rate poet, like all those who have never written a decent line, how stupid you were, what a jackass you were. Be aware of your limits, rather than try and ape a *poète maudit* or an old American actor or quite simply Niso!

(But just a second. It's actually because I'm aware of my limits that I'm trying to get better, because we are made for great undertakings, because I've been imbued since birth with a hatred for mediocrity, because life seems so silly if you don't attempt to be *great* at least once, running the risk of being ridiculous, running the risk of burying yourself in the mud like a worm, running the risk of derision. Of course, maybe being a cursed poet is not the right path for me, but I cannot accept with impunity, calmly, without reacting, being nothing more than just another man, a mediocre man, another entity that will float over this earth without leaving a mark, proudly comforting himself by saying: I was myself.

I had also stayed true to myself, and to do that I didn't fear appearing ridiculous. Because my true self is above all else what I would like to be, and I would like to be as cunning as Paul Newman and as fascinating as a cursed poet—or is it that "be yourself," a universally shared imperative, hides an enigmatic and threatening invitation not to try, to sit in the corner, to obey, and not to dream? But I do dream, ladies and gentlemen.

It would have been easier had I stayed seated at that table and paid the check without uttering a word: timid and insecure, I would have been the true self that you want. But I had had the courage to be daring. At the expense of unspeakable humiliation, at the risk of feeling broken. I lost, but you, sneering shadows behind the curtains, you didn't even play).

I calmed down. I felt sorry for myself and felt contempt for the world that was laughing behind my back. I stripped down and jumped into the shower. I was dirty and sweaty, and my ribs hurt from crying; I felt empty and lost. Luckily, the water was so cold, it distracted me from my pain. I got out of the shower feeling less awkward, less shattered. The telephone rang and, buck naked and still sopping wet, I went to answer it. It was France.

"So?" (He started just like that, he wasn't one to beat around the bush).

"So what?" (But I knew that I couldn't avoid the topic of the day).

"So what, so what. Two thighs, two rock hard tits. Does that remind you of anything?"

"Listen, don't you think she looks like a crane?"

"A crane???"

"Yes, a crane."

"Or maybe a warthog? Or some promiscuous floozy? Or a sugar beet?"

"Anyway, I bet Niso will take it all."

"The pig!" (But he said it with absolute affection).

"He burned us, huh? He was in rare form . . ."

"Oh well, off-the-cuff, he's invincible. But going the distance, he caves."

"Yes, because he *wants* to cave."

"Same thing."

France was right. Niso was a superb womanizer, refined and lethal. But also exceedingly literary. Women interested him only while unattainable. He dreamed of a woman so perfect that he would be looking for her through all eternity. The previous year we had witnessed an old-style romance: Niso had fallen for a young girl who was with someone else, a girl deaf to the ardent calls of a lovesick swan. Although we thought he was being over the top, Niso moaned, torn apart by her perfume; sometimes he was reduced to tears like some medieval lover. She, who went to the same school as we did, was nice, but resolute. He would look at her the way you look at a statue of the

Virgin Mary. But by fine-tuning his fleeting glances and words, Niso made her feel adored, like the only woman in the world, writing her letters permeated with fire, arsenic, and quotes from plaintive poets, passing them off as his own. Eventually, she started to look troubled—because he was merciless in his own beauty and in the beauty of his words, because she began to resent that her boyfriend didn't speak like that. And she began to suspect that there was another way of being in love, a way that was never pedestrian, but unrealistic, enchanted, unconditional—and she could no longer stay indifferent to Niso's deeply sensual poetry, or to his regal gaze. With each passing day, she shivered more and more at Niso's words, and she longed for his letters as if to quench an unsatiable thirst. From that point on, she could no longer control the passion that consumed her, but, morally incapable of hurting her boyfriend, she avoided Niso. We never understood when his love turned contentious, or if it had always been contentious: Niso alternated between the cruelest invectives, which crucified her and left her desperate, almost begging on her knees (to leave her alone? not to leave her alone?), and the sweetest idyllic moments, when he flattered her with his words or someone else's, and with silky looks.

In the end, baffled by how a poet even nowadays can steal the heart of a young girl better than anyone else, we saw how cruel the poet can be. Amidst tears and regrets, she left her lover, "I am in love with someone else," she told him (why didn't you lie, foolish girl? Maybe because only the truth could exonerate you?), and then in one night of madness, she surrendered to Niso's embrace.

Following that one night, Niso wanted nothing to do with her. Nothing. She begged him through thousands of phone calls, thousands of letters. She sought explanations from us, his friends. But not even we understood, nor—respectful of his continued silence—did we ask him any questions. "I can't do it anymore," he would say. "Besides, it can never be better than this, you must withdraw at the peak, mine is the lover's ultimate gesture: sharing the gift of eternal love. At the cost of my own happiness. Now she will love me forever, and so will I. How many lovers can claim the same privilege?" he would say. Rebecca would take him down, calling him a raving lunatic, telling him to go shut himself in a cave if he was so afraid of things ending—and Niso laughed to himself. As usual, I found a certain chilling wisdom in his words, a certain sincerity, but I didn't know that he was quoting a guy called Kierkegaard, when he said to me one day: *"Once I loved her: but from now on my soul does not belong to her—if I were a God I would do to her what Neptune did to a Nymph: I would turn her into a man."*

"Listen, France . . . "
"You want to know if . . ."
"Exactly."
"Of course."
We loved telling each other our filthiest fantasies. France's imagination ran the wildest:
"So, she is bending over the pool table at a ninety-degree angle to take a shot. I rub up against her ass and she feels my impressive hard-on. Then she turns around and says to me: Excuse me, I'm going to the bathroom."
"She says it just like that???"
"Yeah, but it's code, get it?"
"Sure. But what about everyone else? Me, for instance, what should I do? And has Niso already recited the poem or not?"
"Who cares! These are insignificant details in regard to the erotic tension in the story. What counts is that I got her message."
"Great job."
"But the best part is yet to come."
"The best part! You go to the restroom and you do her, big deal . . . sorry, but I wasn't expecting such a trivial ending from you."
"See, there you are, you're so superficial, with no imagination at all. This is why you steal my copyrighted jerk-off material."
Good old France. He knew how to cheer me up and make me laugh.
"So yes, I go to the restroom, but what do I see? She's completely naked with the pool cue in her hand!"
"Awesome! But she brought the pool cue to the bathroom???"
"Obviously."
"Oh Christ . . . and what did she do with it . . ."

"Nothing. I confess that as soon as I saw her there, naked, posing with the pool stick like Joan of Arc, I went off."

"I understand."

"Oh well," he sighed, satisfied, dreamy, childish, my good old friend France.

"Shall I pick you up tonight?" He asked me.

"Where are we going?"

"To play pool, right?"

"To witness Niso's victory?"

"Who knows? If she shows up . . ."

But if she showed up it would have been uncomfortable, watching them ignore us, and seeing Niso behave in the way I couldn't have that same morning. The wound had been reopened. So, I told France that I wasn't feeling great, not to come by, that I would take my own car, if I felt like it. I knew that if he came over, I couldn't resist going out: but being alone, being alone, I needed to be alone.

It was almost two in the afternoon. The house was so unbearably hot that I took off all my clothes. Even though I felt awful, I was hungry. I made a salami sandwich, and more importantly I drank half a bottle of Tocai wine. I moved from the kitchen to the balcony and then went into the living room. I couldn't stay in one place, but luckily the wine was calming me down. I was sweating Tocai from every pore. Not one fan to be seen; what did my parents have against fans? I went back into the living room and turned on the TV. A former journalist, now on the afternoon show thanks to his impressive tan, was showing off. I turned it off. I felt like July would never end, or at least that afternoon wouldn't. I leaned out the window. The streets were deserted, no shade, the air thick and stagnant, the city was like a pregnant lioness sprawled out on the savanna. An exhausted dog panted as he crossed the street, then he peed on the lowered shutters of the grocery store. Summer, I hate you! You're already so hard to take, and it's only July . . .

But at least the heat eased the pain, dulled it—this pain would have been difficult to swallow in the middle of winter. I thought about what I should do. There was nothing to do. I didn't feel like watching an old Paul Newman movie, I didn't feel up to it, nor did I want to touch myself and spend five interestingly fluid minutes: the image of the waitress would have come back to me, her embarrassed look and her unattainable tits. Christ . . . Christ!

Summer really seemed to hold nothing for me, other than half a Tocai bottle to forget my humiliation. But then the phone rang. I ran to answer it and a voice asked me:

"Paul Newman?"

"Hey, Niso!" I could have hugged him.

"Great joke about Paul Newman, eh! You floored her."

I was touched. On the other hand, we had never skimped on compliments.

"Look who's talking . . . when you caught her off guard with the Baudelaire stuff, it seemed like she would suck you off right then and there! Sorry for being so vulgar, but the image was fitting."

"Really. But I don't know . . . she's a little fake, don't you think?"

I was flattered.

"What woman isn't?"

"I don't deny it. But this one is pushing the limits . . ."

"Even so, you've got her in the palm of your hand."

"Well . . . the way I see it you have more chances than I do. She likes tough guys."

"Shut up, liar! You played a tactically perfect game, covered in midfield, forceful on the offensive. The girl didn't even notice anyone else."

"Well, to tell you the truth I am in shape. You never know what tonight . . ."

"I'm not coming," I interrupted.

He asked me why, but just as a formality. I understood that his head was already wrapped around that night. He thought about it—he thought about it a lot. I knew he wasn't as aloof as he seemed, he was sensitive. I noticed his nervousness, and I found it paradoxical, because I would have never been nervous if I was like him. Or maybe I would.

That afternoon was interminable. It was just five in the evening and the fumes of the wine had already dissipated when Rebecca called. How strange that the whole world was looking for me precisely when I decided to shut it out, at least for a night, to run away, at least once.

Bare naked, I stretched out on the living room's mandarin-colored carpet, like a spoiled lion. The thought occurred to me that she might also be nude.

"Are you naked?"

"No, why?"

"Come on! Why couldn't you say you were?"

"Okay, I'm naked except for a garter belt."

Just hearing her say it I got all cocky, so I slid one hand down to my crotch. I felt emboldened. In any case, there was nothing left to lose.

"I'm naked."

"Damn, you shock me."

Her irony blocked any breath of excitement. I didn't understand women. They retained this magical option of titillating a man with just a whisper, without compromising themselves in the least, and yet nothing. But nothing could stop me now.

"I'm touching myself."

I sensed disgust in her silence, and by changing the conversation she embarrassed me. For an instant, I felt myself plunge back into ridicule. But enough with the humiliation for that day!

"What's going on tonight?" she asked.

"I'm staying in."

"And everyone else?"

"I think they're playing pool."

"Will she be there, that . . . what was her name?"

What a hypocrite! I may be ridiculous, but you're worse than me, my friend!

"Angelica. But I think that I'll call her the crane, because she looks like a crane."

"Please! All you guys were foaming at the mouth!" Then she let out a scornful groan and mumbled *men* . . . trying without success to sound witty. Strange girl. Instead of a down-to-earth guy who would take her out to dinner, who would go crazy from smelling her perfume down the street, who would incessantly mount her on virile and invulnerable nights—a guy with a name, prestige, a family, a hobby, an important job, a moral code, a political stance, a group of collegial and highly personable friends who have known each other since childhood (*think about it, we used to play with toy soldiers together*), and also with a pair of new shoes, a very avant-garde tie, a metallic gray convertible, a collection of beer cans, an uncommonly modern mother and a father who had died of a heart attack (which made the child more mature, more deep, more sensitive than his peers)—well, instead of that down-to-earth guy, instead of that first-rate idiot, she preferred us. Us, her valiant squires. Us pages. Us, in the end, her friends. But not surely as lovers, even though each one of us ardently wished for that. When she wasn't there, we racked our brains over this: while men consume themselves in satisfying their everyday obsessive, urgent lust, women are satisfied with being desired. Actually, even assuming that women's carnal cravings are equal to those of men, and we had doubts about it, intrinsically women will never have the same pathetic, twisted, unquenchable sexual thirst as men—simply because a woman, even an unattractive one, can satisfy this thirst whenever she wants to (while for a man satisfying it is always an arduous achievement). In addition, our good Eve continues to wreak havoc, and women continue to pay for her abysmal reputation. So, even if desire arises, it has to be held in check and, if ever a woman is at the point of fulfilling her passionate impulses, she needs to justify that with sentimentality (Niso proclaimed that ninety percent of intense feelings ended not because, as they say, that's the nature of the beast, but because they were passions evoked purely for sexual reasons, engendered simply to finally have sex. And of course, because loneliness is terrifying when you don't love yourself enough—and women never love themselves enough—and because we all have this insane need to love and to be loved or at least not to have to go alone to a movie theater). Lastly, a female primordial wisdom makes girls realize how male lust makes them the rulers of the world, and so its fulfillment, which would extinguish it, must be prevented. Rebecca could never feel as desired by her hypothetical boyfriend (with whom she would make love) as much as she felt desired by us, who didn't make love to her—but like her hypothetical boyfriend we pandered to her, we courted her, we brought her to the movies or to dinner or to some horrible concert, chasing after the vain hope that sooner or later she would succumb, but also out of simple chivalry, chivalry sprouting from the admiration of feminine beauty, admiration that soon turns into attraction, and we end up back at square one: the man wants to have sex, the woman doesn't.

I said to her: "Look, if I stay home alone tonight it's really because I don't feel like running into a pretentious crane that is convinced she's a swan, and Niso playing the part of the cursed poet all the while staring at her tits. No, believe me, I'm too old for that."

She tried at all costs to mask a certain relief, even going so far as to convince me that she was really cute ("and she is cute, you surely can't deny that!"), but I—determined—kept on ranting over my contemptuous disenchantment for a lowly servant playing the part of a diva ("Look, my dear Rebecca, two thighs cloud the mind of inexperienced guys and prevent them from seeing the gross defects that as a rule a crane has, at least from a sex appeal point of view"). And we went on for quite a while having this absurd conversation between a guy who said and did not believe what the other one wanted to hear and a girl who rejected as unfounded assertions everything that she believed while hoping to be validated.

And finally, it was nighttime, and with the evening came the melancholy. The sun had streaked the endlessly blue sky with traces of red tongues, and the night advanced, peaceful and slow and infinite. I looked out my window, and I was sad. My insignificance troubled me. The dumb morning was coming back like an untamed demon, like an unextinguished remorse: and yet I shoved it aside, I tried to erase it, it was just a mistake from which I would learn. But useful mistakes didn't interest me. Useful pain, the kind you learn from, without which you wouldn't be what you are now. A wreck. I would rather stay ignorant. But the events of that morning had slowly been transformed into a feeling of uncertainty that got wider and engraved itself deep into my young chest: life was a strange contraption. We are forced to justify suffering in some way, to make sense of it all. And so, from childhood we are taught that pain *shapes* us, that the death of this one or that one must help us understand, that Jesus died on the cross for the salvation of Humanity, that pain makes us wiser and stronger.

But I looked out my window and life was passing me by. All the world's sorrow is utterly useless. That morning had been horrible. I, an awkward good-for-nothing drifting off in a desperate attempt to exist. I, a pathetic beggar attempting to be king, at least once, at least for an hour, by God! I don't want to lose. I don't want to cave in to defeat only to tell myself, in the end, how much I've matured, how intelligent I've become in the course of my life, what valuable lessons I have gleaned from my experiences, oh no . . . I want to win.

I knew what I needed on this kind of night, a night as slow as summertime. I took the bottle of Tocai out of the fridge, and then, amongst my father's old records, I found him: good old Frank. While darkness crept into the corners of the living room and outside a warm moon took over the sky, I grabbed the remote like a microphone, and with the Tocai in my other hand—within it all the aching feelings of a life that was slipping away, with its mystery that maybe others could understand better than I—even so, I did sing, *I did it my way* . . .

3. August

And July, which had seemed stuck in time, ended at last. And everything that I thought would happen, in the end, never did, and the crane vanished like a ghost, like an imaginary peril. Almost every night we were back at the Sbruffon Alcapone and Niso probably hoped she would appear together with the curly headed girl in jeans, but nothing. And so, Rebecca was once again the undisputed little princess. We went back to playing soccer on the beach, we reveled in the sun-drenched mornings—slow, azure, perfumed with jasmine—as we happily sprawled out on freshly cut grass, sniffing at it like strays.

    Clearly the crane's presence was still entrenched in France's erotic babblings—titillating France, who got subtle pleasure from recalling those young girl's mare thighs, those warm and pointy breasts under the checkered blouse. Rebecca would get mad, I kept quiet, and so did Niso and Alcapone. But something had changed, yes, something had changed. We should have understood it, but it was summer and everything was saturated with the stagnant heat, and our very senses had become as sluggish as a big fat orange cat in a Ligurian vegetable garden after lunch, napping between a stone fountain and a lemon tree, while his owner sits on a rocking chair and dangles his hand over him, wearing an old straw hat, reading a mystery book, with in front of him a small white table with a carafe of Moscato wine, and this hand pets the big cat's head, gently, ever so gently, and the old man in the straw hat lets his mystery book slip into his lap as he drifts off into sleep (or dies), but in a stubborn gesture of tenderness, he does not want to stop caressing the cat's head—that was summer in a nutshell, a summer still sufficiently long enough to have no regrets yet, dreaming about the frenetic days of college, a iced coffee and a beautiful blonde in love with me, and the relaxing evenings at the Sbruffon.

But then, one night when I was beating the pants off Niso and Alcapone, one night that I felt great, optimistic, invincible, one night spent drinking water and smoking Alcapone's cigars and playing pool like never before—suddenly, I caught a whiff of a smell that was not cigar smoke, and heard a sound that was not the clacking of the pool balls: clickety-clack. Women's high heels, definitely. Deep, enigmatic. High heels recalling rain-drenched nights in New York, long runs to reach a subway train, the smell of nylons, French perfume, and chicken sandwiches. Pool stick in hand, bent over the pool table for my last shot, I didn't even have to raise my eyes from the green felt surface: a roar in my brain, an unequivocal message, an instant, a fragment. (It's interesting how the most feared or wished-for moments in our lives are foretold with malice—almost with sadism—by our heightened nerves. Surely, even death is preannounced a minute before, as if God enjoyed watching the expression on our face.) The moment was so brief, so brutal, that I didn't even have time to get flustered, but with the flawless lucidity that comes to you only in those reckless moments, I looked at her with the eyes of Clark Gable, and I mustered my most devilish grin, something borrowed from Marlene Dietrich in a 1941 flick. Then, without any delay, I looked back down at the pool table, made an incredible shot, and won the game. The crane and her friend cheered and applauded.

The crane kissed a visibly embarrassed Niso on the cheek, and the girl with the curly black hair kissed a visibly overweight Alcapone. Rebecca bit her lower lip, France opened his eyes wide, incredulous. As for me (I was in seventh heaven for what I had managed to pull off), unfazed, I chalked the tip of the cue. Rebecca assumed her look of ice-cold rage, France stared intently at Niso, then at Alcapone, then at us, as if looking for answers or hurling accusations. I scrupulously continued chalking the cue, but I could feel on my skin the tension that saturated the air, and once again I was he, Paul Newman, my hero. "Are you playing with us?" blurted out Niso, trying to affect a relaxed tone. Alcapone slipped his arm around the curly headed girl's waist and started to bleat like a wild sheep in heat:

"Hey, come on, let's make a bet, huh?"

He was too uncouth to realize that his rambling was embarrassing the curly haired girl, who turned her eyes on me—and this time, too, her action seemed purposeful.

"No, we are going to get something cold to drink. Will we see you later?" asked the crane, radiantly.

"Sounds good," said Niso, and this time there weren't any fragments of Baudelaire's verses in his pocket. They walked away pretentious and self-confident, saying goodbye with resounding congeniality, directed especially toward Rebecca—who, truthfully, didn't hide her cold demeanor, her lips barely moving into a forced smile. A few frosty seconds passed. Alcapone started to laugh. He always laughed at the wrong moments.

"You saw each other again!" Declared our ace detective France.

"Your remark is of an obvious nature apparent to each and every one," answered Niso, trying to recapture that sardonic tone that made him handsome.

"Sorry, but . . . why didn't you say anything to us?"

"Well, it's not like we tell each other everything!" interrupted Alcapone with a well-timed remark; he enjoyed too much getting caught up in the details.

But it was true. We had never had a tight-knit friendship: we didn't take vacations together, sing songs by the campfire, share confidences about our love lives, or about sex—except for a couple of times, and those were from our distant past. What bound us together were the mutual experiences we suffered through, such as the two-hour algebra classes on Saturdays. But above all else, we shared that radical contempt, that innate anger for almost everyone else, for guys our age, for television personalities as much as for intellectuals, for journalists as much as for the current comedians, for fanatical idealists as much as for the materialistic ones, for drug addicts as much as for clean-cut types, for bigots as much as for hedonists, for goateed singers who acted like prophets and for prophets who acted like singers, for Italy, for Europe, for the World, for candied fruit.

"To make a long story short," announced Niso, "that night, they asked us to go out with them. Just Alcapone and me. We've already gone out a few times together. We figured that you'd be insulted, so we didn't mention anything."

Niso had regained his composure, he was as cool as a cucumber, and didn't feel as if he must explain himself. But he knew that what he had said made no sense, he *had* to know. And France, who normally wouldn't have even initiated any further discussion, was now unusually obstinate, and, without missing a beat, jumped on it:

"You thought we'd be insulted? What the fuck are you talking about?" And he masked his unexpectedly aggressive tone with derisive laughter.

"We thought you would be offended not because we went out with them, but because they had asked us. I don't know, it seemed a bit awkward. I'm sorry."

"And we kept talking about them, and you kept seeing them . . . great job!" And good old France mimed an applause trying to downplay things, but I knew he was hurt, he felt like they were making fun of him. Then, sitting in judgment atop her high stool, from having observed the situation and sorted the good from the bad, Rebecca said:

"Maybe your two friends don't really like us."

She reasoned just like a woman, there was no denying it. Alcapone, quite pleased with himself, responded:

"Certainly not you!" And he laughed in his usual high-pitched way like a castrato. Rebecca shot him a look that could kill, but fat-ass was very animated, two roosters in the coop, he said, along with some other trite clichés. Then France knew exactly how to end the wrangling and the squabbling:

"So, tell us, did you get laid or not?"

Niso, reclaiming the lost complicity, went into the details. The first time they had gone to see a movie, then stopped for a drink, chatting animatedly about old friends and going their separate ways before dinner after making plans to see each other at the beach the following week. Once there, they had continued chitchatting. The girls had been very friendly and had asked them to rub suntan lotion on their shoulders and thighs—Angelica had an incredible body (Niso added, almost as if he needed to convince us) but Saba's tits are this big (interjected Alcapone)—and what was most impressive was their self-assurance, even the tenderness, with which they pronounced their names: Angelica and Saba. Our lecherous friends concluded the evening in the fat ass's cave, the two girls melting in their hands (a babbling Alcapone maintained) but without getting to do anything erotic with them (Niso pointed out as to avoid any misunderstandings).

The evening ended rather quickly. The two girls returned, and I excused myself. Alcapone didn't pay any attention to me, Niso may have cared some, France—unexpectedly—stayed to watch, and I said to Rebecca (as if she were my girlfriend):

"Shall we go?"

And she, regally, got off her stool, sensually winked at me, smiled slyly, came toward me like a lovesick little girl and slipped her left arm under mine, while waving an affected goodbye with her other hand. I flashed a smile at the two girls and, with all the warmth I could muster, said:

"Bye."

At first, I thought the crane looked flustered, then she seemed to be fuming, defying all logic, triggering in me a triumphant thrill. Obviously, she despises me, I thought. And she despises even more this female on my arm like a sixteenth-century Venetian courtesan. This woman as beautiful as the sun, and mine. It's clear that she despises me because I'm someone who can wrap you around my finger, whose eyes can make you do whatever he wants, someone who is not afraid of you . . .

"Will you stop acting like you're some kind of movie star? You're being ridiculous," Rebecca told me bluntly before we even got in the car. She said it in a way that was meant to be funny, but her voice came out strained and shrill. The most appalling thing about someone telling you how ridiculous you are is that, right at that moment, you do feel ridiculous. I imagine that it has something to do with the fact that being ridiculous is part of being human. Whatever we do, we do it for the first time, even those things that technically we've already done before, falling in love, for example: we are actors with a bad memory who haven't had the chance to rehearse their part. In addition, each of our actions, from the most insignificant to the most awe-inspiring, is thwarted by our own mortality, so that the more important we think we are, and the more seriously we take ourselves and our actions, the more death and the universe snicker behind our backs. And yet, we pretend not to hear the laughter: feeling important and taking ourselves seriously (insisting on being called *sir*, revealing our own shortcomings and virtues, collecting rare books or holy water fonts) is the only way we can be happy. How tragic is the existence of those that don't take anything seriously! I suppose it happens to all of us: those times when all things appear futile and foolish and the whole ephemeral nature of our struggles to keep up with life, juggle our careers, the New Year's Eve dinner, the trip to India to find ourselves, *ourselves*, all of it destined to disappear in a flash. Then! Then is when death and the universe laugh at us! It's horrible.

Yes, you have to take yourself seriously to feel good about yourself, but it's well known that people who take themselves too seriously are annoying. And that's not all: people who take themselves too seriously are dangerous. If only Napoleon had known that what would be left of him was the image of a short, stocky guy with a funny hat and one hand thrust in the vest of his jacket (or just the snide expression "He's a small Napoleon!") maybe he would have stayed in Corsica catching shellfish. In fifty years, when the tragic impact on the present of the deaths of millions during the Second World War will have waned (yes, sadly, even they will become ephemeral!), Hitler will just be a crazy Kraut with a tiny mustache. And, if he had realized it in time, maybe history would have taken a different turn . . .

Taking oneself too seriously is the road to fanaticism, to fundamentalism, to cruelty, but at the same time it means being happy. Besides this funny coincidence (almost as if man in his awareness of the vanity in everything, and thus sympathetic to himself and others, cannot be happy), when someone points out to us how ridiculous we are, the house of cards crumbles. Rebecca kept quiet, and I felt the sting of a slap on the face. I had been backstabbed. I felt ridiculous. I pretended to be flabbergasted:

"What are you talking about?"

"Come on, I was joking. We're a tad touchy, aren't we?"

But she wasn't joking, and she started looking out the window, toward some inscrutable faraway place, as if none of it concerned her. I didn't like her at all. We stayed silent. The night was blue.

"I'll take you home." I said, between being upset and bitter.

"No, let's take a ride," she sighed, but curt.

We drove around. Mestre was empty, deserted, and very beautiful. No one understands that Mestre is beautiful. Considering it ugly is just one of those things that humanity assumes is true; it's like saying that Germans are meticulous or that you need to be yourself. We drove along the corso del Popolo, with its tall dirty buildings. Beneath the arcades, a few scruffy couples were coming out of a movie theater, and a bum was asking for money to buy his last drink of the day, standing in front of the closed shutters of a shop.

The sweet smell of the evening penetrated the car, and Rebecca gnawed on her thumbnail. We went around piazza Barche and through via Colombo, then on via Ca' Rossa, where the houses get smaller, their tiny yards brimming with roses and men in undershirts who lean out of dark windows searching in vain for a puff of cool air. The walls absorbed the humidity of the night, the tree-lined streets were enshrouded in darkness, and Rebecca said in a low voice:

"Who knows if we'll ever manage, one day, to escape from here."

"I will."

"And where will you go?"

At the end of via Ca' Rossa, I turned left and drove down via Garibaldi. The Carpenedo church stood out proudly against the moonless night sky.

"I don't know. But I have to get away from here. Maybe to America."

Then, as she was wont to do when she didn't like the topic or the tenor of the conversation, she changed her tone of voice that became as cheery as a warbling sparrow:

"So, since that little tramp showed up, you've been courteous, you're paying a lot of attention to me, and we leave the café like we are a couple . . . are you falling in love with me?" And with her ironic little index finger, she lightly stroked me close to my lips. Her legs were unforgettable, intertwined like spirals of honey, overlapping each other so tightly that you could almost hear the rustling of the flesh. I placed my hand on her left thigh.

"Stop it, no one is watching us," she whispered. But she didn't remove my hand. If I had been less cowardly I would have insisted. If I had truly been Paul Newman (or maybe just Humphrey Bogart)

I would have said "*You* stop it, dollface!"

Instead, I took my hand away, changed gears, and took her home.

The next day I woke up and realized that summer was walking away without looking back. The sun beat down on the city, polishing the sky a tired blue, like a dishrag washed and left out to dry too many times. I was drenched in sweat, I couldn't breathe, I wanted to move to Alaska. I remembered a story where Donald Duck, to escape the scorching summer heat in Duckville, goes to work in an ice factory (that turns out to be a coal factory instead). I leaned out the window, exhausted. I leaned out on the windowsill and looked down at the sunbaked street: a little old man was shuffling along, stopping at every corner to wipe away the sweat with a handkerchief, and yet he was still wearing his gray suit and vest and his polished black shoes. I found some consolation in watching him. Then a young guy walked by in Bermuda shorts and mirror sunglasses. He looked like a monkey. Water, I need water, I need the Niagara Falls, the snow on Kilimanjaro. Then a girl wearing a purple scarf on her head went by dressed in a small dark flimsy dress, looking untamed like a cat on a dusty street. Naturally, Angelica entered my mind, the crane. My God, what a charming creature! Just running my hand through her hair, hair like a goddess from antiquity, would loosen the knots in my stomach, and my heart would tremble simply squeezing her hips. She had the jade green eyes of a tiger, the proud cheekbones of a Nibelung, poppy-red lips and breasts that I imagined fleshy and white as milk. She seemed to stem from some Indian legend of the jungle or from the foam of the sea.

The night before, she had been wearing a tight black tube top and her delicate green high heels tied around her ankles with a silk ribbon. She was shockingly beautiful. Just the thought of her putting on that tight dress, or taking it off, was killing me. Just the thought of her sitting on the bed untying the silk ribbon and removing her shoes, that alone was a fire in my guts. And yet, even though I thought she was perfect, or maybe just for that reason, I didn't feel romantic at all: my eyes didn't have the same tenderness as France's, or Niso's cultured finesse. She was extremely beautiful, and she was a pain in the ass.

*

Then Alcapone called me.

"Hey, Ema." He didn't say a word, neither did I, until, as if he had been catching his breath, he said: "Listen, next Saturday I want to throw a party here at my place . . . will you come?"

"Even if you don't like it, fat-ass, I'll be there, most definitely. I bet your faithful ones will also be there."

"Right. Listen, can you avoid calling me fat-ass in front of them?"

"How about big belly, would that be better?

"No, not that either, here's . . . "

"Whale?"

He hung up.

I had gone too far. Actually, calling him fat-ass was like diving in his soft layer of fat, nothing cruel or sinful—it was a plunge of affection. In fact, the only things that sometimes triggered some sympathy toward him were the foam on his stomach and his rosy hairless pig legs when he wore cycling shorts. Besides that, I had a hard time putting up with his stupidity and his boorish simplicity. One night, a couple of years before, we were sitting at a table in a bar in town; Alcapone wasn't present that day. Rebecca was saying that Alcapone was nice, had a heart of gold, and we (Niso and I) should stop calling him fat-ass. He's nice, Niso said to her, because he can't be bad. He's not strong enough to be bad. He turns the other cheek because he would rather have friends who call him fat-ass than to be alone. He's not one of the nice ones, goodness is born from strength, he's a coward. Rebecca became indignant with his philosophical musings and counterattacked:

"Is it more cowardly for him to turn the other cheek or for you to keep insulting someone you know will always turns the other cheek?"

"Oh, but I'm the king of all cowards, that's for sure! But talking about present company is not nice, either. And anyway, it's exactly because I'm a coward that I can understand the reasons for Alcapone's pleasant disposition. I call cowardice what you call goodness."

"And instead, I call vileness your cowardice. Whatever the basis of his friendship with you is, he's really fond of you, and you shouldn't call him fat-ass."

"But even this fondness for one another is often a form of cowardice, a necessary pretense for not being lonely. Look at the majority of couples: they're based on the terror of loneliness. If we are ugly or fat or a loser, we convince ourselves we love the only other human being that finds us attractive, who is usually as ugly or fat or as much of a loser as we are."

"You read too much crap by people who have described the world by navel-gazing," hissed Rebecca, and then she smiled scornfully, boy was she beautiful! She took a swig of dark beer and posited:

"The fact that these people, rejected by the world and by people like you because they are ugly or fat or whatever, in the end, they find one another after a lot of soul searching and, no doubt, after a long period of suffering—it's clearly a sign of pure love, predestined and spontaneous."

"Spontaneous!? But love is always a form of imitation! The way we learn to speak to imitate the adults, or we start smoking to imitate James Dean, so we love to imitate Prince Charming and Cinderella. Through our expressions, through our mannerisms, through our feelings, we always imitate an archetypal love story and then we empathize with it to such a degree that we believe that our performance is true love!"

"So, true love, spontaneous love, doesn't exist?" I dared to interrupt him.

"Of course, it exists, but it's as rare as a blue lobster."

"And how do you recognize it, o poet?" asked France impudently.

"By forgetting about yourself. To realize the dream of our loved ones, man or woman must be open to anything. That's the sign of passion, of the only possible love, unwavering: sacrificing yourself without remorse, or boundaries or prudence, mocking your own pride, mocking your own self."

The bar was smoky, rowdy, and hearts and insults had been carved on the small wooden tables. It was a bar masquerading as a Scottish pub: the waiters wore kilts, and you could drink beer from Edinburgh and munch on salmon club sandwiches. Niso had the ferocity of wine and poetry in his eyes; the words he used seemed infused into his very veins, as he led them by the rhythm of his hands, which he shook in midair, moving them sinuously, clenching his fists. He was also imitating someone else, but I had no idea whom.

France's girlfriend, a small pale girl who had been with him for three years, was also there. She was admiring Niso, and I felt sorry for France. Not him, though, he was delighted, happy to have such a scintillating friend. I was amazed that he, always so sharp, could be so dumb. Her eyes were shimmering. Damn it. Niso turned right to her:

"What is your most cherished dream?"

"Well . . ." She blushed, "you see . . ."

Each one of us has some shameless ambition in our heart.

"Come on, come on, don't be shy," the cobra pressed on.

"Well, I act. I would like to make a name for myself as an actress."

Niso, the most sinister of snakes in the world that before killing you will spit a blinding fluid in your eyes, looked at France and said:

"Good, would you be willing to take it up the ass from the most powerful producer in Hollywood, without her knowing about it, to make your lover's most cherished dream a reality?"

Everyone froze. The young girl got all worked up, trying to defend her boyfriend:

"Oh, but I would never want him to do that. I would want to make it on my own, I . . ." But Niso kept on going:

"This detail doesn't figure into our discussion. So, France, what do you have to say?"

"But no, of course! Are you a moron or what?"

By now he was furious, he could have simply said yes and taken it all in stride—of course I'd take it up the ass for her, and I'd enjoy it—but he had an intrinsic honesty (and in this case his macho pride) that always crippled him when he had to simply lie. The cobra doesn't give you any time to think. France said:

"How could I do something that I know she would not want me to do? How could I look her in the eyes, *afterwards*?"

"The nobility of your gesture would skyrocket. Not only an act decidedly against your sexual inclination, but think of the strength you'd need to bear the humiliation, the sense of guilt, the shame—in silence. And all of that just to fulfill your girlfriend's dream, just for her happiness. Congratulations, France!"

"No, no . . . Screw your congratulations! I wouldn't want her to do such a thing for me, so I wouldn't, either."

He was dangerously painting himself in a corner. Then he believed he had found a way out:

"The thing is you think the end justifies the means."

"Oh, that's rich. And you believe that your asshole is more important than your girlfriend's happiness."

Poor France, he was livid (she, on the other hand, had turned a deaf ear). Rebecca kept quiet, and I found her silence sadistic, and Niso drank smugly from his beer mug. But when he stared, almost disappointed, into France's and his girlfriend's eyes, sighing theatrically, "I understand, you're not really in love," I felt that I needed to get involved:

"My dear Niso, egotism, weakness, the fear of being taken from behind—in every way—don't mean you're any less in love. And it's simply not true that you only want the happiness of the one you love: you also want to see her fail, and her unhappiness sometimes, so you can console her. There is a specific resentment, a genuine hatred—I would dare say it is necessary—for the woman we love and for her dreams because we play no role in them, because they're not about us, or they could take her away from us. Therefore, it's not that we don't want to see our loved one reach her happiness, it's simply that we can't, and if we don't want to, it's because we ourselves want to be the sole source of all her happiness—not Hollywood or whatever. And also, this reprehensible narcissism, these unhealthy traits, are the signs of a soul in love: assuming that signs have any meaning outside of astrology and psychology."

I had spoken so eloquently that I was proud of myself, and I looked onto my friends for a sign of admiration: Niso didn't answer me, Rebecca grimaced, while France and his girlfriend smiled gratefully at me. Nevertheless, nothing could stop me from thinking that, when they would stop seeing each other two months later, Niso's venom had played a role. France, of course, didn't harbor any grudges. He's someone who would sooner blame himself for any shortcomings rather than stoke any resentment within himself, and he would rather side with the enemy than acknowledge that he has any. But once in a while, now that so many years have gone by, I sometimes see, once again, that same opaque look in his eyes I saw that night, when, to put the story to rest, Niso exclaimed at the end: "Hey, I feel like I'm in Andreas Capellanus's work *De Amore*."

The party was looming large. It was late on a Saturday in August, all day the sun had been beating down on the deserted city, on the old tiled shingles on the roofs, on the gardens and the peeling paint, and on the tattered posters of no longer relevant old singers who now only performed at country dance halls and asparagus festivals. Now at last the cicadas had stopped their racket, and the nightly news theme echoed from balconies, and I suppose each one of us had only one well-founded concern: what to wear?

    I picture Rebecca, naked on her parents' bed, applying nail polish onto her toenails. She has delicate little feet, like a little girl from a fable, and ankles as white as the petals on a daisy. Niso is already wearing his impeccable, killer shirt. He's handsome with his scraggly three-day beard. He's a poet. France is wearing jeans and a tee shirt and is wondering if one day he'll go bald. Alcapone is at the stove, in his emerald-green vest, which has him sweating like a pig but is also holding in his protruding paunch. He already has his gold pocket watch in the vest pocket, but he still has his slippers on, and he looks like my grandfather. And the two witches? Both will present their most cherished gifts, like the Three Wise Men: the curly headed girl, her firm voluminous tits, ensconced in a plunging neckline to make you forget how bland anything else is; and the crane, two unbeatable thighs, smooth and slick as the summer highways, thus, one hell of a miniskirt. Bah, I'm trying on a pair of blue linen pants, a white shirt with gray stripes, and a toned-down suit jacket: I look like Tony Manero. I also take a stab at that iconic pose before he starts dancing (his right arm straight up in the air, his left arm bent at a ninety-degree angle with his hand on his hip, his right foot bent horizontally at a ninety-degree angle, his left leg stretched straight out on the diagonal), but I'm horrible. Far from me to discredit old Tony, but even he, like the singers on the posters or the nightly news theme song, is a melancholy fossil of summers we never experienced.

*

I ended up getting wasted. Never think about how something will play out while listening to your emotions: the opposite will happen. Envision exactly the opposite of how you would like things to go: it will go badly anyway. It's just that fate can't stand to be predicted, and it knows perfectly well when you're bluffing.

Case in point: after I had finally chosen what to wear that night, a blue plaid shirt, coffee colored American style pants and a pair of trendy moccasins, I shone with hope—I admired myself in the mirror, I was awesome, the jewel in the crown. And I pictured the crane's astonished look. While dancing with Niso, she would not be able to take her eyes off me, as I would blatantly flirt with the beautiful Rebecca, and then Rebecca, she would not be able to sort out the game from the truth, and melted by desire, she would lock her mouth onto mine in the middle of Alcapone's living room, in front of everyone, and, gripped with jealousy, the crane would squeeze her glass so tightly that it would shatter and wound her . . .

The opposite happened. First of all, there were thirty people. Alcapone had invited all the friends from school we hadn't seen since finals, and they stuck with me for the entire evening. In particular, that twat Ledina. She was one of those girls whose favorite pastime is to pour their heart out to the first person they run into, unloading her personal baggage of private emotions studded with pearls of Zen wisdom, not in the least concerned if it's appropriate for the person she's talking to, confident that she will win anyone over with the profundity of her truths. She was so happy to see me again! She was so happy that we kept in touch! She was so convinced that our high school memories were the best of our lives! And she started to recall, shifting between emotional snippets of laughter and affectionate admonishments in the vein of:

"I know that mask of a bastard hides a sweet and insecure young man."

I was too polite to tell her, "Keep your distance, you hag," so I suggested that we get comfortable in an armchair: I sat down and, from the liquor trolley, I grabbed the neck of a bottle of Wild Turkey plus a glass, meanwhile, Ledina, drunk and electrified, perched herself on the arm of the chair and nearly ended up on top of me. The crowd crammed into the living room filled every corner: where the hell is the crane? Where the hell is Rebecca? But I had already given up. So, I started drinking while, willing or unwilling, I listened to Ledina. She said:

"And do you remember when the art professor complained about your long hair? She said it was unaesthetic, that you looked like a girl, and you answered, 'at least *I look like one.*' Wow! She shut the fu . . ."

"Please, stop it with the stereotypical cliches, overused and quite frankly disgusting." Her eyes flashed wanting to be ironic:

"Oh, excuse me, if I knew I was speaking with the Prince of Wales . . ."

"If I had known."

"What?"

"My God! *If I had known that I was speaking.* My God, you even got a high grade on your baccalaureate exam. Ignorant and bad-faith teachers." After an answer like that, I thought at the very least that she would silently get up and leave. Instead, she laughed. There are some people who, in order not to acknowledge they are being scorned, are willing to act dumb, and in order not to be ostracized from society, from a group or from someone, accept being scorned even further. Then finally, Rebecca. She looked at me and promptly picked up on the situation. I knocked back another shot of whiskey and didn't even pay attention to her stark-naked legs. I was that frustrated. She came over to obsequiously acknowledge Ledina, so I took advantage of the momentary distraction to get up and look through the crowd for the cause of the scandal, but as I inched forward, my old school buddies kept stopping me and slapping me on the back as if we were in the living room at Buckingham Palace for the fiftieth anniversary of our graduation. Everyone was so happy to see me again and show the affection usually reserved to welcome home war survivors. The little living room seemed so immense, overflowing with imbeciles and Niso and the crane a couple of needles in a haystack. Finally, I caught sight of France, as white as a ghost, as stiff as a fish stick, with three leeches surrounding him, also bent on giving an inventory of our pointless high school antics. There's nothing more pathetic than this fixation on remembering certain things at any cost, rehashing memories with those who are all too familiar with them and would just rather forget them. At any rate, France's vacant stare did not bode well. I reached the long table laden with flawlessly arranged food, I filled my pockets with saltines, and finally spotted the curly headed girl, in jeans, seated on Alcapone's knee in a wicker chair. She was playing coochie coochie coo with his double chin, poking it with her tiny index finger. Our ecstatic pachyderm, momentarily freed from her spell, noticed me and, perhaps mischievously, asked me:

"Having a good time?" and they kissed each other, not waiting for my answer. If in that moment André Breton had tapped me on the shoulder and read me his manifesto, I wouldn't have found it strange. I stood there, stunned, not believing that the fat-ass was capable of kissing anyone—nor that someone could kiss the fat-ass—and yet, they were sliding their tongues in each other's mouths almost with fury, and the real kicker was that it felt like an ethical slap in the face. I refilled my glass for the fourth or fifth time: I was drunk. I turned my back on them, and people were saying words that weren't registering with me, probably compliments, but why the fuck were they complimenting me? Pardon my French, but only when you're drunk you realize how people say the most nonsensical things. Sober, you're so used to it that you don't even notice, but alcohol gives you back the sense of wonder for stupidity. The people were a vortex, their faces superimposed before me, I saw faces with three noses and four eyes, I saw girls' ankles and I was hard, and I understood—because whiskey bestows analytical skills and a depth of thought that are usually absent—that the French-kissing scene between the fat-ass and the curly headed girl had absurdly aroused me. Ha ha ha, I snickered putting my arm on the shoulder of a former classmate and the other arm on the shoulder of another one: before thinking, before saying anything, get a little whiskey in you! And they all laughed.

Once again, I was on the other side of the living room. Rebecca was Ledina's prisoner. Ledina talked and talked and talked, Rebecca nodded and smiled at her, satisfying her. What a good sport! Then Rebecca looked at me and her eyes gestured toward the hallway: surprised, my glass in one hand and the almost empty bottle in the other, I avoided a couple of nostalgic souls who had already stopped before me eager to bring up my chemistry oral of 1989, I glided through a couple dancing and found myself in the hallway. Nothing. But some light was filtering in from the kitchen. By now I was ready for anything. Silently, hugging the wall, I got closer like the Inspector Clouseau: "Oh, excuse me, I was looking for a glass of water, excuse me," I would say, after catching them red-handed kissing each other—but nothing. Damn, an unsolvable mystery. I sat down in a chair since I could no longer stand up straight. Well, let's finish the bottle! All in all, I was happy. Life isn't bad when drunk. Everything is happiness, everything is good. The red refrigerator is good, the breadcrumbs on the floor, even Alcapone is good and I'm happy for him—finally a girl for the dear old Alcapone, every dog has its day, right? And I'm also happy for Niso, yesyesyes! YESSIREE! In fact, I'd like to make a toast: let's drink to my dear friends and to my defeat!

But when I raised my glass, I heard Niso's voice. Unsteady on my feet, I left the kitchen and found myself in front of the closed door of the bedroom. I'm such an idiot. Where could they have been? Still holding my trusty glass, I bent over at a ninety-degree angle toward the keyhole and tried to sneak a peek: nothing, the key was blocking my view. But Niso's voice came through clearly:

"I love you."

Darn.

"Or maybe I don't love you, no, no . . ."

Make up your mind.

"I kiss the night."

From the ensuing silence, I suppose he was kissing the night. But then he went on:

"Angelica, my exquisite Angelica, how can I tell you what you've meant to me, when I first saw you . . . a bolt of lightning out of the blue, a hot meal for a starving man, a tiger's claw into my heart?"

Make a decision. She laughed, flattered.

"You laugh, I make you laugh? Ah, you little tease . . . Well, just to have you near me, just for the privilege of placing my lips on yours, I'll be your court jester, I'll be your entertaining young boy, your little perfumed clown!"

I had never heard him so cheerful, so happy, so stupid. Then she asked him:

"And what else will you be?"

"I will be everything that you've ever dreamed a man could be, I'll be your torment and your crime, I'll be the thorn in your side and a summer morning, I'll be what you are and don't know you are, I'll be your dust, your ambition, your shame—I'll be your dirty laundry and your nourishment, the air you breathe and the nectar you thirst for, but I'll also be your madness, and a pair of socks to wear, and your loneliness . . ."

"You have such a way with words."

A way with words!? Oh Jesus. Oh Jesus! That's women: you string together a bunch of nonsensical words, and they swallow it all, hook, line, and sinker! What a shame! How disgusting!

But at that exact moment, Ledina again. Hands on her hips, ironic, stern expression, I suddenly found her right next to me.

"What the hell are you doing?"

"Shhh!" And I brought my index finger to my lips, in a hideously slow movement. I was still bent over in front of the keyhole and I hadn't even noticed the excruciating pain in my back: I managed to hear Niso say, "You're killing me" or something like that, then Ledina grabbed me by the arm. What a pain in the ass. I was about to tell her, but I was tongue-tied. She whispered, all happy:

"Really? Do you think that's something you should be doing?"

Then Rebecca showed up too:

"I'm leaving."

From what I could tell, she seemed more bored than beaten. I, on the other hand, was crushed. I didn't think I would take it so badly, or maybe it was the alcohol that made it all worse. Rebecca went through another litany of polite exchanges with Ledina (we absolutely have to call each other, yes, *absolutely*), with maternal affection she advised me to stop drinking, she told me she would call me the following day, and then she finally split. All my grand plans had gone to shit. You couldn't hear anything specific from inside the room, obviously the merry-go-round had already started. I agreed to let the perennially cheerful Ledina drag me away by the arm.

"Wait, not through the crowd, please," I begged her.

And so, we went back into the kitchen. The round clock on the wall showed it was midnight. It was late. I looked in the fridge to see if there was anything to drink. There was a bottle of vodka, Smirnoff white. "No, no, no," intoned Ledina rhythmically, taking the bottle of vodka away from me.

"If you don't give it back to me, I'll break it over your head," and immediately, I flashed her my drunken grin.

"I just don't want you to get sick," she whined. Oh, Christ! All these faces. All these words. Always tossed off to inflate their flaccid egos. But I was a patient drunk:

"Look, Ledina, by now I've had enough to drink to be trashed at least until tomorrow anyway. So, I might as well go the whole way."

I took back the bottle, cracked it open, put an ice cube in a glass, poured the vodka, slipped my hand into my pocket, pulled out a handful of saltines, stuffed them in my mouth. I hoped they would absorb at least a small amount of the devils in the alcohol, so that I could still drink a little more before crashing to the ground. I collapsed onto a hard wooden chair. Ledina remained standing, concerned, talking, saying things that made no sense. She was neither beautiful nor ugly. But she seemed much uglier than she actually was, maybe because of that eternal expression of sacrificial victim, beady eyes, the corners of her mouth turned downward, a thin, curved nose. Her body wasn't all that bad, a close look at her (it was the first time I had done so) revealed bony knees, maybe two tits concealed under a blouse as bland as she was, and a plump ass. But she was so painful. She said:

"Look, I am convinced we should have more of these parties, don't you think?"

Little girl, don't you realize you're talking to someone who doesn't even know his name? But instead, I said:

"Sure."

"You know, we've fought our share of battles together. And that's what lasts. Of course, we haven't always got along, it's not always possible, living side by side for such a long time . . ."

What the hell was she talking about? Had she gotten married, and I didn't know it? And who had taken her? Again, I just said:

"Sure."

"But I'm sure that we love each other. Because we *grew up* together, we *matured* together." That's how it was, she spoke *in italics*. At that moment, the people leaving the party started streaming out. Kisses, hugs, promises to get together at least once a month. Even France, who seemed mummified by boredom or anxiety, passed by. Once again, Ledina and I were alone:

"It was so nice to see France. Really nice. You're going to think I'm an idiot, but this party also did me a lot of good. You know, I was depressed. You know, around this time my parents died, three years ago."

There it was, I knew it. In the end, they always went there. I understand that I may sound cynical, but the tactless way people disclose their personal tragedies always leaves me speechless. Obviously, I lowered my head and said something about how life must go on. About picking up the pieces, about staying strong, about . . . whatever.

Then something strange happened. The door to Alcapone's bedroom opened. Without noticing us, the crane walked by headed to the living room, where, most likely, no one was left except for the fat-ass and the curly headed girl making out. Then Niso came out. I got up, and he noticed me. His expression looked like a heartbreaking cry for help. He tried to smile, and Ledina, who seemed drunker than I, threw her arms around his neck. All six of us ended up in the hallway, I suppose to say our goodbyes. The crane's face emanated an air of despair, or maybe the sex had unsettled her. Niso was embarrassed, Angelica was embarrassed, and I—who was the only one, besides the curly haired girl, that seemed to get it—ended up being more confused than I already was. But something was fishy, something was quite fishy. Ledina, Niso, the crane, and I were on the landing while the curly haired girl lingered a little longer sticking her tongue in Alcapone's mouth. Luckily, Ledina's chattering blanketed the awkward silence. Then Niso left by himself, then the two girls, after lukewarm, disinterested, formal goodbyes. Ledina and I walked toward her house.

"You know that Angelica is the perfect girl for Niso? She's so . . . cheerful! I'm truly happy for him," Ledina said.

"But doesn't she seem a little strange to you?"

"Well, I would be too if," and she snickered.

"You?"

We continued down the alleyway toward her house. The night was extremely hot, a lily with brown petals, it was nearly three o'clock in the morning, and I felt the whiskey weighing me down like concrete, my head felt like a boulder. When we got to her front door, she was about to hug me, and I grabbed her wrists. Like a flash in my brain, and from my brain to my mouth, I heard myself say: "How about a blow job?"

I asked her just like that, as if I were asking her for a smoke. And given that she got wide-eyed but didn't smack me across the face or start smiling with that idiotic laugh, it hit me: she had taken me seriously. She was considering my proposal. I got hard. She stammered:

"But . . . My grandmother's inside . . . "

"Right here then." I grabbed her by the shoulders and pushed her down. She was on her knees. Amongst the stench of urine, the dirt, the dog shit, while the city slept. She grabbed my legs like a child craving affection. I felt her face pressing against my pants. So, I loosened my belt, and as waves of whiskey washed over me, I felt the small pebble of my heart shifting in the filth. In a split second, my pants and boxers were down around my knees, I leaned against the wall, and I shoved it deep down her throat. The dawn was white, humid. I barely felt her saliva on me, I barely felt her tongue twirling around my skin: I was slowly bobbing between her lips, too much booze had sapped my strength, and in the meantime, I lit a cigarette stolen from Alcapone. I ran my hands through her blonde hair, and she grabbed my wrists, so that I wouldn't let go of her head. But I started to feel the effects of the whiskey, and I needed to pee, and so I peed. She stopped for two seconds (two excruciatingly long seconds) then, disgusted, she pushed back, sprang up and backed away from me, with all the pee dribbling from her mouth, incredulous, as if she couldn't understand, she vigorously wiped her mouth with her hand, brought it up to her nose, sniffed it in total disbelief, then, horrified, she stared at me:

"ARE YOU INSANE!?!"

I opened my arms wide to apologize, cigarette butt in my mouth, dimwit smile, while I went on peeing half on my hairy legs and all over my boxers, and half on the dirt in the street. She was spitting out the pee, her eyes bulging out of their sockets, she kept on repeating:

"YOU ARE CRAZY . . . YOU ARE CRAZY . . . AND I'M CRAZIER THAN YOU ARE!!!"

Ashamed, I mumbled something, my pants around my ankles, unsteady.

And then, at last, the last veil was lifted, her eyes filled with hate, and all the Zen wisdom, with which she had tried to mitigate the devastating blows life had dealt her, suddenly disappeared, and her face was full of the ferocious rage of a wounded wild animal, the same rage I would have felt if, after my life had been shattered by tragedy, some drunken douche bag took the liberty to pee in my mouth. She landed a formidable blow to my stomach, which doubled me over, I tripped over my pants and ended up with my face in the dirt, the whiskey crept up, and I started to throw up like a dog, and I retched and I yelped while she insulted me with all the viciousness that had exploded in her chest, with insults that I never imagined she knew. Then, freed at last, she felt sorry for me: she held my forehead with one hand and helped me finish throwing up.

4. September

The next day I woke up with a splitting headache, a sharp disgust for myself (I will never drink again, may God strike me down, I will not drink another drop in my life) and most of all a gnawing sense of shame that perforated my stomach like a dagger. Stretched out, motionless, with a cold facecloth on my forehead (thank God my parents were at the beach), I tried to separate myself from the sense of guilt with endless arguments in my defense: gentlemen of the jury, it's not like I raped her! What happened, happened because of a proposal and an agreement! Sure, sure, the pee. A mistake, a blunder, I agree, a rather excessive erotic game. But the plaintiff nailed me to the wall. The fact that I had treated a woman, with the aggravating circumstance that she was an orphan, as an object. The fact of having taken advantage of her momentary weakness. The fact of the place, which anyone would have considered squalid, dirty, humiliating. Wait a second! I object, gentlemen of the jury! If there is a woman who lets herself be treated like an object, it means that she's a consenting adult. Then the weakness, the weakness. We all have our own tragedies, our own weaknesses: that doesn't mean that we should drop our guard and give ourselves on a silver platter to the predators among us. And finally, the place. But sexuality is all about smut, sweat, saliva, even squalor, it's humanity at its most base animal instincts; there is a much stronger erotic energy in a fetid and filthy alleyway in Mestre than in a pink bridal suite perfumed with almonds!

There was no point. The jury didn't buy it, and—in between running to the toilet to vomit—I spent the whole day asking for forgiveness. I called Ledina five times. I sent her the best bouquet of flowers I could afford (giving away the last bit of change I had left), and I enclosed a letter in which I spoke of myself in such negative terms that I cried the whole time I was composing it. I wanted her to forgive me. Really! Owning up to my sins to reach atonement had disinfected me, but I needed her absolution to purify me. I would think about her parents, whom I had never known, and I would start to cry once again. I was scared they would come into my bed at night and drag me out by my feet. I became Ledina's best friend forever. We went out whenever she wanted, during that summer and even later on—and with the patience of a model prisoner I put up with all her problems, her allegories, and her melancholy. Naturally, with time, absent the sense of shame from that evening, the memory of her mouth overflowing with urine started to provoke unspeakable yearnings, and so I hit on her again, and, naturally, she refused me, sweetly taking my hand and smiling at me: *"Come on, it would be a shame to ruin our friendship."*

August was over, and it was about time. At the Sbruffon, I played the tough guy, as usual. The brief conversations between the crane and me had a cinematic flavor. We looked each other in the eyes like two cowboys before a death-defying duel. As for the rest, the same old stuff: France stood awestruck holding his pool cue, he looked at her while she laughed with Niso, he looked at her while sipping his beer and studying the arrangement of the balls on the felt table, he looked at her, period. Rebecca also looked at her: to size her up. Every once in a while, they spoke to each other, sometimes they even flaunted their female intimacy, they traded a few compliments on mascara or shoes, but as soon as the crane turned her head, there it was, Rebecca's disdainfully curled lip of disdain, that look of the French tailor bending down to assess her rival's ass and legs. The curly headed girl, in the end, was the most friendly one. She was always happy and was blessed with two large, intense breasts, very round thighs, and a small quintessentially Jewish nose. The fact that she was Jewish made Alcapone terribly proud, it aroused him, I suppose his eyes cast her in a sacred light. So, he began to read everything he could find on Judaism, he gave us endless lectures on the Holocaust, and then, deeply moved, he looked her straight in the eyes and hugged her, and it seemed that he was hugging Anne Frank. But what astonished us more than anything else was that she went along with it, she would pull his big cheeks with her tiny hands to plant a kiss on his lips. And Alcapone, the happiest lard-ass in the world, soared, like a hippopotamus in a tutu, and danced—ethereal . . .

Niso had deep, black circles under his eyes. He kept on courting the crane, but he talked, he talked too much. He was gallant, too gallant, and he screwed up his jokes: I had the impression he was starting to lose control, he smiled nervously, he seemed more like me than himself . . .

Something weird had happened in that bedroom.

One night at the end of August, the crane messed up a shot badly and sank the black ball in the pocket, which meant automatic defeat. The lard-ass giggled like an affluent vulture and took advantage of the situation to thrust his tongue into the mouth of the curly headed girl, who by now seemed to accept it without an ounce of shame. The crane threw the pool cue on the felt table in a gesture full of rage, and her eyes—as beautiful as an unruly ocean—filled with tears. I was embarrassed for her. Still, Niso put his arms around her, she covered her eyes, and he tried to caress her. Rebecca and I looked at each other for a second, Saba and Alcapone stared at Niso, France looked at Angelica. Without looking at Niso, Angelica mumbled:

"Leave me alone, you fool, I'm just tired," and, annoyed, she wriggled free from his embrace.

Niso was paralyzed. He turned bright red. His expression ricocheted desperately from Rebecca to me to France, and we all tried to look anywhere else. Angelica raised her head, and stared at us all, without seeing us, then said:

"Please excuse me." And she took off. And Niso—Niso the poet, Niso the invincible, Niso just humiliated in front of his friends—ran after her. Rebecca shook her head with pity, France looked at me with a child's wide eyes, I said: who knows? The other two, as if nothing had happened, carried on molesting each other.

A week later, September arrived with the charm of an immigrant, that gentleman smile full of promises, and so we decided we needed to say goodbye to summer: on a gray Sunday, once again we took the vaporetto, which glides down the Grand Canal and takes you to the Lido, but this time we didn't find any seats astern, so we holed up inside. The Grand Canal was probably just as majestic as it was three months ago, with its ivory and ruby-colored buildings, little gardens, and balconies with young girls and all the rest, but it didn't register at all. Angelica had captivated all my attention, everything was out-of-focus around her mouth, at the bony protrusions of her ankles. And I pretended to be fascinated by something beyond the small window, a contemplative and ruminating demeanor reflecting on the gold and the scarlet hues, a scientific admiration for gondolas and sea gulls. But it felt like I had a third eye on my forehead, and I looked at the lagoon and I saw her, and I watched Venice go by, yes, but I would have sold Saint Mark's Square, the basilica, all of it, just for one of her glances, and I wandered aimlessly in the bowels of the vaporetto hoping for a random chance to meet her eyes.

The sky was a rough dishrag and the sun had already given up. Not that it was a bad thing; the summer had worn me out with its endless, exhausting, relentless days, and the sun had even made me lose weight, left me frazzled, tossed to the ground like a deflated ball—and what did I get in return? Of the thousands of women I had hoped for, not even one. You can still tell yourself that you danced a lot, you rested a lot, you had a great time with your friends, you got drunk like some movie star, you played soccer, and so on. But when you're twenty there's nothing more important than a pair of thighs, the brief jolt elicited by a plunging neckline or a knowing look, the frantic search for a spot to touch one another. When you're twenty, money, a killer car, power still present themselves in all their emptiness: true status is conferred by women, and the actual discrimination is between the guy with a young girl by his side and the guy who is left behind. In fact, I wondered what money, a nice car, and power were any good for other than to get women: working so hard to have a swimming pool, risking my life at a hundred miles an hour, being revered by my subordinates? No, none of this was worth all the worry, the fatigue, the sleep deprivation. All this was only good as a springboard to touch one more woman.

In any event, even though summer was now behind us, saying goodbye to the sun was always a little nostalgic. We got there at lunchtime and walked along the beach. Many others had had the same idea, and like us they retreaded the same footprints that they had left, just ten days before, in the scorching sand. The crane seemed more gloomy than usual, but she was still fantastic. I would have paid good money to find one imperfection in her; I did everything I could to distract myself and not stare at her, but there was something very dignified in her high cheekbones and something deliberately wild in her gorgeous eyes, void of makeup, and something unsettling about her pure, candid skin, and I looked at her with a pang in my heart as she slowly walked against the wind, allowing it to tousle her hair in a kind of frenzy, and to breach her long skirt and expose her perfect legs, *her* legs—never, ever, ever, to be *mine*.

She was so aloof, with her lilting walk like an Arab princess, so brooding in her gaze lost beyond the horizon, so sensual with her nipples protruding into the wind, as if to defy it and in her letting herself be stripped bare by it—that even the figure of Niso, drawn into himself with both arms in his black jacket, walking close to her but slightly behind her, seemed goofy, out of place, ridiculous.

Behind them was Alcapone, stuffed into his Scottish tweed, and Saba, the curly headed girl with the voluptuous breasts, dressed all in denim, who didn't seem to find her doughy beau ridiculous. Rebecca, France, and I trailed them, and we were probably all lost in our own different thoughts. France wanted a woman like Angelica, Rebecca hated a woman like Angelica, and I thought: "But is she sleeping with Niso? And Saba with the fat-ass? And what does it matter to me?"

The water already had dark reflections, as if the black souls of dead fishermen were crisscrossing its depths, and the crests of the waves seemed to foreshadow snowstorms and winter squalls, and on the beach lay the remnants of a now distant summer—plastic tubes, pieces of rubber, squid bones—and all this held a morbid sense of mystery that intrigued and enthralled us. It was sad and beautiful. It was a strange procession against the wind, along the water's edge battered by the high tide, treading on fragments of seashells and crab carcasses, meeting people walking in the opposite direction who didn't look at us, almost as if we were all dead, waiting for a storm. It was just a Sunday in September.

To make sense of a bland day, I suggested we buy a dozen beers, stretch out on the wooden jetty stained by the sea's spittle and thus most desolate, and get drunk in the last sun of the summer. I will always remember the look on Angelica's face. A glimmer of a luxurious childhood tinged it, and even though I found it over the top, it was so beautiful it made me feel like a philanthropist who'd just donated a new toy train to the orphans at Christmas.

"Yes, yes!!!" She shrieked with sudden joy, and the gray sea got lost in her green eyes, and the sound of Latin music caressed my heart. Niso's head was bent down, immersed in who knows what demons. She seemed not to care, at that moment the beers on the pier captivated all her attention, happily ignoring Niso's obvious suffering: the truth is that I would have kissed her, and to hell with everything else, to hell with this trip to the sea and the summer going downhill, I would have kissed her right there in front of everyone. Right then two female arms encircled me from behind and tightened themselves jealously around my waist: Rebecca's body was stuck to mine, I felt her breasts pushing into my back, and she whispered something I didn't understand, and I would swear I saw Angelica's smile transform into a tense grimace, and then I saw her turn toward Niso, a Niso more and more unrecognizable, and take him by the hand, and they walked away together.

I couldn't understand anything anymore. In the brief time it took Saba and Alcapone, holding hands, to come back with a mountain of burgers and beer cans, Rebecca, France and I, dazed, witnessed from afar the typical scene of two unhappy lovers: an intense discussion, she stretches her arms out, he snorts, both of them gesture like neurotic actors in a silent movie, she throws her arms around his neck, he pulls back and grabs her wrists, she tries to move closer, coiling like a cat, and in the end, he relents and hugs her.

We were sitting on the pier watching them (they were about twenty yards away, the sea lapping at their shoes) and I realized I could no longer stand any of them. France looked like Tutankhamun, motionless, wide-eyed. I think he was in love, or maybe he was just depressed. Of course, he couldn't take his eyes off of her, and what I saw as the histrionics of a spoiled child he saw as frailty, which filled him with tenderness. After all, it's only words. But words can change your life; if what they say is true it's hard to fall in love with a hysterical woman, but it's almost a given to fall head over heels for a fragile woman, and even more so with one with a body like Angelica's. And Rebecca? Rebecca had taken out a small old book with a yellow cover, *A House of Pomegranates*, and she had started to read it as a distraction from her dethronement. As for me, I was hungry. The fatty smell of the hamburgers and Angelica's look had whetted my appetite. I know that look. You can't lose your life for a woman. I had my cigarettes for once, so I lit one and smoked.

And here we are, handing out beers and hamburgers to each other, and here we are, on the watery jetty eroded by the salt and the crabs, lying down parallel next to one another: Niso at one end next to the tyrannical crane; then France (whose heart boomed like a lost tom-tom in a virgin jungle, due to his intense proximity to Angelica); then Rebecca, the furious one; then me, the bored one; then Saba with her big boobs; then Alcapone the happy pachyderm to complete the lineup.

The sun strained itself and once again started beating down on our faces like it was wont to not so long ago, so we drank and ate and sweated, stretched out on our backs, our faces to the sun, surrounded by our chattering, mostly the fat-ass's trash talk and his laughs of happiness—maybe he was fondling Saba's huge tits. Meanwhile, you could sense everyone's feelings through the other's silences: a desperate silence, Niso's; an excited silence, France's; a jealous silence, Rebecca's; and so on.

As for me, I had my hands behind my head, a can of beer on my left, close to the hand of Miss Huge Tits. I closed my eyes, leaving only two narrow slits to look through, and I looked at the sky in cinemascope. It was murky and promised no good news. I wanted to register at the university and get to know other people: I was getting tired of my friends, and I felt like an outsider. Everyone seemed preoccupied, for one reason or another, with the integration of the crane and curly big boobs into the group, they all seemed entrenched in our micro reality, but I felt weary. I wanted some fresh air. I sat up, scooched back, and, sitting cross-legged, kept on smoking while I looked at them.

On my left, Saba's eyes are closed, her curls caressing her face, her mouth and chin wet with beer. Her little denim jacket is unbuttoned and so is her pineapple-yellow blouse to the point that I can take a peek at her breasts and at the stylish embroidery of her bra, opalescent like that September sky. Her right hand, the part of her body closest to mine, holds the beer can tightly, decisive but motionless. Her left hand is intertwined with Alcapone's: he, too, has his eyes closed, he chews ample mouthfuls of meat that make his cheeks and face even fatter. His face! It is a spectacle of colors, the final work of an enraged painter: it goes from the pink of his large chin, moist with bitter foam, to a vermillion so violent (from the appetite, the sun, the joy) that it betrays shades of violet on the sides of his nose, an unexpectedly delicate nose, a cyclamen in the mountains, while his forehead is all adorned with minuscule diamonds of sweat. Now his right hand wriggles out of Saba's—I assume it wants to look for food—instead, it rises with an air of sobriety to place itself on Saba's body, in the breasts area, and it moves around. An otherworldly sight. I looked to my right. Rebecca. Head resting on her backpack, she is reading her little book, she is paying no attention to me, she brings the can to her mouth, swallows biting her lips. I wonder if she is doing it on purpose to not even acknowledge my presence with a glance or if she is really so taken with her book, she closes it, puts it on her lap, slips on her dark glasses, places her hands behind her head, and lets herself be kissed by what is left of the sun. Then France: His big head resting on his rolled-up sweatshirt, he is also taking shelter in the cool beer, letting it slide down his throat and closing his eyes as if he wants to chase the world away, to banish any thoughts. And finally, the two lost lovers, here they are: they're having an intense conversation, and it seems like they never understand each other. I've never seen Niso in such a state before.

Then a gust of wind whisked up Angelica's long skirt, exposing her: I saw her suddenly naked thighs, and maybe I, at last, understood Niso. She was so perfectly stunning that it was painful not to have her, to know that she could transcend you, to realize that maybe she already belonged to someone else. Two days later, in a moment of unbridled openness, while France and I were sitting in the car, shocked at how sometimes even a poet needs to vent, Niso told us: "The fact is that I have lost my mind. I know. I monitor every grimace she makes, every change in her expression, in her eyes, like the desperate horse chasing after the carrot attached to the string on the stick that the coachman dangles in front of him. Do you see what I mean?"

"Yes," said France. I didn't, but I got the general idea. I wondered if that desperation wasn't Niso's latest bluff: we had already seen him like this, to be clear. He's someone who needs to play the victim, to feel shattered, even to accentuate his pain so as not to feel bored, just to feel stronger, to enhance the sweet taste of the ensuing victory. No matter how beautiful she was, in fact, I felt that Niso was more beautiful still and that in the end he would be the winner.

France, on the other hand, was just as desperate as Niso. It seemed that Niso's words described his feelings as well, and he realized this for the first time, that he too felt like a horse, chasing after the carrot, and so on. Niso continued: "The thing is that the horse doesn't realize the carrot can't be reached, but I do. I know it perfectly well. I don't understand why love hasn't made me as stupid as everyone else. I should be happy, because she kisses me, because she tells me she loves me. That should be enough. Instead, there is no kiss that satisfies me, there are no words that satisfy me, whenever she stares at something other than me, I'm terrified. I feel I'm being ripped apart. If I think about the mornings when she wakes up without me, in the privacy of her bedroom, with her pictures on the night table, with her clothes in the closet, with everything that is hers, without one single thing that has to do with me, I feel left out, I'm nothing."

It was a night at the beginning of September, it was the three of us, without Alcapone and Rebecca, and we were parked in our usual spot next to a weeping willow in front of the fastened metal shutters of a pharmacy in the Piave neighborhood. This neighborhood, near the train station, is a tangle of tiny streets and alleyways, some of the oldest in Mestre, with small houses and hovels from the forties and fifties and little gardens full of flowers, clay dwarves, and caged canaries, as well as, at night, several whores from wildly different nations in the world. In particular, that was Adele's spot, a prostitute in her sixties, who wore her little sheepskin coat both in summer and in winter. Dear Adele! She was old and ugly, but she still gave the young Lithuanian and Nigerian girls a run for their money. How the hell did she do it? Regular johns, maybe, who evidently were fond of her and couldn't muster the courage to betray her with the newcomers.

The thing is that when we didn't have any more money to seek shelter in the Sbruffon or in any other bar, we liked to park near that corner in old Mestre, with the moon filtering through the willow leaves, a closed pharmacy and an old streetwalker, even though when she showed up we would move away so as not to interfere with her business. In any case, that night she wasn't around so we were quite comfortable, holed up in France's car, but something was different from our usual discussions about love: there were no jokes that lightened the mood and that, for a moment, would interrupt the solemnity of our discussion. No, Niso was in the throes of a genuine desperation that wouldn't allow for any ironic interruption, and this time France—who loved to break up any conversation with a huge laugh—sat there, eyes sparkling, his stare glassy, as if he were listening to the Oracle of Delphi.

As for me, I kept quiet: the serious talk bored me, and I felt a strong desire to say something outrageous and screw everything up— embarrassed by that excess of emotions. Love was an ugly beast, and it was ruining those two. I was alone in the back seat and took out a cigarette and put in my mouth without lighting it. I listened to them, I watched them, and they seemed totally nuts, and I thought: stay far away from this thing, guys, or it'll destroy you. It will turn two tits into two glorious glasses of wine fit for a recovering alcoholic, you will feel all the world's woes weigh heavy on your heart, and you won't be able to laugh anymore. Most of all, you won't be able to laugh anymore.

"I get you . . . " France mumbled, disheartened. His eyes were cast down now, and his voice was trembling. He sounded like a killer that is exhausted from being interrogated and that, in the end, confesses.

Niso understood. "Old friend, you love her too, don't you?" Niso asked emphatically.

France felt liberated. "Yes! But I'm sorry, Niso, I'm sorry . . ." Almost crying.

Niso, compassionate, squeezed his shoulder and spoke in the most kindhearted tone I had ever heard, "For what? What are you sorry for, my friend?! I know, I know, her beauty is a curse! But if she didn't love me, I would want her to love you, I swear!"

I was afraid they would hug. Then France said, "What a fucking story!" to sound more macho, and maybe he felt relieved by my—as usual, down to earth—interruption:

"By the way Niso, did you screw her or not?"

Niso probably despised me, but at least we could breathe again. "No."

A shiver of joy ran through my whole body. France uttered a fake laugh:

"No? But then you've turned into a fucking moron!" Because by this point, he had to imbue the car with insults and swearwords to get rid of the sickening sweetness that had stained him and filled his throat. Niso went on, slowly:

"The night of the fat-ass's party, in his bedroom . . . everything was perfect . . . she was so sweet, I was at the top of my game, technically flawless, strategically perfect . . . but then . . . "

He got quiet, hesitant.

"BUT THEN?" I egged him on.

"Well, I shouldn't say it but . . . we started kissing, I was on top of her, and I can't explain the feeling . . . "

"We can imagine," I said.

"No, no, you can't Ema, it was honey and fire, it was the perfect embodiment of life, and I felt like I was about to explode . . . " He stopped to breathe and then continued: "I wasn't even aware of what I was doing, I was completely hypnotized by pleasure, and I felt like crying in gratitude . . . and then the most blinding lust took over. I lifted up her skirt, and I felt her hot fleshy thighs, and I was in ecstasy, as if it were happening to someone else, my heart was stuck in my throat and my pulse was beating frantically, and it was like a goddess had surrendered herself to me and she . . . "

At that moment, Adele got out of a green Skoda, fixed herself up, and nodded to us. We understood we needed to get out of her workplace, we returned her greeting, and France started the car. But Adele gestured to wait for her. For a second we were puzzled, perturbed; we had never gone beyond some very formal greetings, and for all three of us it was our first contact with the world of prostitution. Niso rolled down the window. Adele came closer, and we could see close up her craggy face and her yellowed eyes.

"Yo, spare a cigarette, boys?"

From the back seat I handed her the pack, and I felt like I needed to say something: "Help yourself, ma'am." She took one and stared at me. Maybe she thought I was making fun of her, I don't know, I was so embarrassed I blushed. She lit the cigarette and said: "But why are you here? Ain't you all got a girl?"

"That's exactly why we're here, ma'am," answered Niso.

She laughed, she laughed loudly, hacking up phlegm, and shook her head with resignation. She could have been our grandmother (who laughs at the prank her grandchildren just confessed to) or the old witch from Snow White. And she was sixty or maybe seventy or two hundred, and for a moment, we watched her in fascination, she laughed, and laughed till she cried, and said, between her tears, "Goodnight boys," and she turned to leave.

Finally, we took off, leaving Adele and her fits of laughter. I picked up the conversation where we had left off and I asked Niso:

"And what about her?"

"She jumped all over me like a lunatic, started to insult me, then she started crying . . ."

"Well, that's old news, she's nuts," I said.

"Come on!" he squawked.

I never heard him like this, irritated and imploring at the same time.

"Hang on a sec, did you say something that set her off, that possibly hurt her?" France inquired, concerned.

"I don't think so . . ."

"Think about it!"

"But I don't know, I must have said something. *You're killing me*, I think."

Yup, I could confirm that. I asked him, "Listen, after that day, did things change?"

"One day she's awesome, she calls me, she spoils me and pretty much gives me the feeling that she loves me. It's a beautiful feeling, I can guarantee it. Another day, she vanishes into thin air, it seems like she never existed, zilch zip nada, and I'm sinking as if shipwrecked with not even a piece of flotsam to grab onto. It's terrible. She's a poisoned sword that pierces me right in the stomach. And yet, there's a certain beauty I can't comprehend in this pain . . ."

He tried to go back to who he was two months before, a week before, five minutes before; he knew he had been an invincible cool guy, an unstoppable seducer, an indifferent brainiac, but he no longer remembered how to do it. You could see him struggle while he sought comfort in a reassuring sentence from a classic, or in a paradox, and maybe he managed to glimpse the mirage of relief. But then, once again, he would drown in the follies of love, in the inability to keep his distance from a woman's tears, in the impossibility of smiling at her cruelty. No, Angelica was captivating, delicate, perfect. Suffering was right.

"Listen, do you think she's keeping some kind of secret?" I asked him earnestly.

"I believe so. She told me there was something I didn't know about her . . . that she would tell me, one day."

I was overjoyed. I lit a cigarette and watched the stars out of the car window. Detective Marlow, the case is yours. Should I blab it all to Rebecca? Nah. And, caught up in the spirit of confidentiality that percolated in us on that night, parked in that surreal place beneath the September moon, should I have told them what had happened two days earlier at the beach?

I was sitting there smoking and, having taken my eyes off the unhappy lovers, I went back to studying the rack of the curly headed girl, now also wearing sunglasses, on my left, softly stretched out on the pier. The fat hand of the fat-ass kept on randomly feeling Saba up until it suddenly slid under her pineapple-colored blouse and her pearl-colored bra, baring her nipples, dark and hard between his chubby fingers. I won't lie, I got excited, then, embarrassed, I tried to look somewhere else. But right at that moment, some cigarette ash fell on the girl's right hand.

"Oh, sorry . . ." I murmured, ashamed, immediately attempting to flick the ashes away with my hand: she squeezed it and smiled. A ray of sunlight lit up distinctly her firm, milk-white, ethereal breasts. And there she lay for at least a minute, letting her tits be touched, squeezed, and crushed by that idiot whale—while she smiled seductively at me and proudly welcomed my gaze.

5. October

My friends were twenty and had big plans: Niso, for example, wanted to become the greatest modern poet. Angelica would think very highly of him, he told me. His idea was something between *The Odyssey* and *The Divine Comedy*: the story of Dante and him wandering from city to city, and from century to century, drinking beer in some tavern in Bavaria with Martin Luther (Dante and Luther would have been great friends, even though they would bicker over the issue of free will) or absinthe in some sordid Parisian brothel at the end of the 1800s, eating fish and chips with Shakespeare through the foggy streets of London, and spring rolls in Beijing. Dante wouldn't have burned any books in the Berlin bonfires, but he would have burned some authors at the stake. He would have madly fallen in love with Marylin Monroe, duked it out with Petrarca, played chess with Joyce, laughed at Montale's poems, and so on. "That Dante! Surly, hunched over, and unfriendly, but a genius, it goes without saying. How wonderful it would be to ask what he thinks of Hitler, Stalin, Fidel Castro . . . and to hear his opinions in verses, a poetic opinion, to draw beauty from these characters," sighed Niso, his eyes sparkling with glory and hendecasyllables.

Rebecca also wanted to write, but not poetry, because the Muses bothered her. She wanted to run off to Scotland or Ireland, rent a castle, and become a millionaire writing tourist guidebooks, sit-coms, or even medieval sagas for children, books devoid of sickness and death, she said, and above all lacking reality. She was not money-hungry, in fact, but she did yearn for enchantment, solitude, and escape. She didn't like her place in time or her country, she didn't like the hysterical horns at traffic lights, the civil service employees, always rude, their leaden faces matching the offices where they were forced to work, she didn't like the conformity of anti-conformity, the demonstrations and the fashion shows, the foulness of language, the pathetic obsession of the zombies in TV shows, and the young go-getters in their fancy little gray suits and rectangular eyeglasses—she didn't like any of it, and she maintained that we all needed to dive into a remote fantasy world, a magical world she would live in and then sell it to millions of readers eager for shelter amongst the mists of medieval secrets: "A beautiful series of gothic novels, the protagonist a young boy with mysterious powers, and monsters, gnomes, magic stones, wizards and princesses," sighed Rebecca, her eyes shimmering with fauns and enchanted forests.

So, as Saba and Angelica began their last year of high school, France and Alcapone enrolled in law school at the University of Padua (but Alcapone would abandon his studies after six months to work in one of his father's restaurants); Niso even set out to pursue two degrees (one in history and one in the classics); Rebecca, foreign languages and literature (she maintained that great novels should be written in English); and for me, it was arts and humanities—the three of us at the University of Ca' Foscari in Venice, which would have allowed us to see one another often and to even take several courses together.

My choice was shrewd: in the arts and humanities courses there were more women than anywhere else. To hell with Dante and little boys with magical powers! The only thing that mattered to me in life seemed to be sex, and I would have even taken a sewing class if it had one additional woman in it. I was on fire, I was young, I was tough: women had started wearing tights again, and it drove me crazy, I pursued their ankles veiled in black through every street, in every bar, I imagined them when they lowered their tights in the university bathrooms, and I felt the blood coursing through my veins like a missile.

And then there was Saba: our complicity and our understanding were by this point a given, although no one had taken notice. I must say, in fact, that I was so smitten with her tacit come-ons, with the way she furtively checked me out, with the dirty way she smiled at me, that, for a while, I forgot about all the rest: the crane and Niso kept on with their antics, France tried, through silence, to confer dignity to his lust, and Rebecca watched it all and no one really knew what her thoughts were.

*

Crimson October, with its colors of blood and grapes, arrived right on time to refresh us. My English-lit lesson had been rather demanding, but it was indeed an orgy of girls, all with their notebooks, warbling in front of a fascinating bearded guy who analyzed fourteenth-century poetry and whose clever witticisms brought the female students to ecstasy. "What imbeciles," whispered Rebecca on my right, "for a good grade they would even sell their mothers." "And you wouldn't?" I asked her. She was wearing a miniskirt that took my breath away, and tights so sleek they tingled my loins. She cast a sidelong glance at me, stopped taking notes, and whispered teasingly: "You know, I wore this skirt just for you."

When she behaved like that, I could have devoured her on the spot, or even married her. Luckily, I was able to distract myself from one fantasy with another: to my left, a robust little blonde with Germanic features was taking notes in a black notebook, resting her bulky breasts on the desk, with two beautiful legs wrapped in a pair of black tights as dark as the Black Forest; in front of me, a delectable little head with long, red hair down to her shoulders that nodded frenetically, making her thin waist quiver, and her behind softly ensconced in her chair, wrapped in a gray skirt with the zipper in the back—all around me, a sea of nylon, of finely embroidered lingerie glued to skin, of shimmering droplets of sweat running from shaved armpits to hips, of perfume sprayed on naked flesh, of tampax, of waxing, of band-aids on blistered heels; each detail, each smell, each flutter of an eyelash morbidly delighted me.

After class, we walked across the street that links San Sebastiano, a former cloister and now the Department of Italian Studies, to Campo San Barnaba, and we stopped in a wine bar located between them. We ordered a carafe of house red and rye bread with cheese and tomatoes, as the sun took over our little table stained with spilled beer, and I was so happy that I told Rebecca what had happened with Saba, the fat-ass's girlfriend.

She looked kind of disappointed.

"It didn't actually cross your mind, right?"

I chomped on the bread.

"No, of course."

I wasn't believable.

"I don't know if you noticed, but Alcapone has never been so happy."

I swallowed a sip of wine.

"Right."

"Look around you, there's plenty of women, why do you have to rain on his parade?"

"You know, she's the one that teases me. Obviously, she realized I'm more handsome than the fat-ass."

"That's not the point, he's totally in the dark, as long as he doesn't know, I don't see why you have to bring up the ugly truth!"

"And why should I sacrifice myself for the fat-ass's happiness?"

"Oh boy, what a huge sacrifice!"

She got pissy and crossed her legs. Beautiful, restless, rebellious . . .

"Listen, since you care so much about the fat-ass's fate, let me make a suggestion: I will preserve the lard-ass's happiness by avoiding any contact with Saba, and you, in return, will give me a wild night of sex."

She looked at me, in the way only she could, slowly bringing the wine glass to her lips, barely raising the corners of her mouth to smile at me—through the wineglass.

"So?" I egged her on, a shiver of lust already running through me.

"I'm sorry, but what has this got to do with me?"

"You see, you women are so great at suggesting sacrifices and good deeds toward others, but you're never willing to help us get things going."

She laughed.

"Does it seem logical to you that I should sleep with you so that you won't sleep with one of your best friend's girlfriend?"

"Why not? It's you who thinks there's something wrong with it, not me."

She shook her head. I had backed her into a corner. I was truly in top form.

We hung out all afternoon. Venice seemed to exist just to goof off. You walk just to be walking, unconcerned with time and life, to slip on the Istrian stones, to get lost in the sky freshly painted by Canaletto, to surrender to the night. We proceeded like vagabonds devoid of memories, in the joyous comings and goings of tourists, students and ancient Venetians, roaming, breathing in the Lagoon's thrilling air of overripe fruit, of melons past their prime, of autumn. We were quiet, we said nothing to each other, and it was a healthy nothing, it made us feel as light as feathers, it made us feel like children—and we knew we were children—and the fresh breath of October, its gentle caress, heralded the coming winter. We crossed the bridge to the train station, where dark Africans sold their wares on large white towels spread on the ground. As I watched them, entranced, I whispered to Rebecca: "I really like Black people. They remind me of the deep dark Africa in *The Jungle Book*."

"By Kipling?"

"No, Walt Disney. The one with Baloo the bear, you know?"

"It's set in India, actually."

"Oh. Well, anyway, there is something that allures me and makes me yearn for Africa."

"But you've never been to Africa!"

"And I would never go, because of the snakes. And yet the blackness of their skin is hypnotizing, and it stirs up something inside me, I don't know. One day as I was passing by a small street market in Marghera, I saw this huge Black woman perched on a minuscule chair reading a detective novel. Her dreadlocks were decorated with multicolored strands, and her nostrils were cavernous, like a slave, and I thought of *Roots*, do you remember *Roots*?"

"The TV show, of course, Kunta Kinte."

"Kunta Kinte, very good!"

"But does the show make you nostalgic for Africa, too? It's not a cheerful story."

"When something is told well, it can become perversely enjoyable even if it deals with slavery. Or maybe I was a child, and I noticed only the colors. Anyway, I stop in front of this huge Black woman reading a detective novel and I can't help staring at her, with her thick fingers, adorned with gold rings, holding the book up, with this orange and blue tunic, with these large violet lips—and then she says to me, with this French accent: "Hey, what are you looking at?"

"And you?"

"Me, nothing, I'm not interested in Black Frenchwomen."

We walked by Santa Lucia, pale and majestic, and then continued along an endless *fondamenta* opposite the Ghetto until we stopped on the Bridge of Three Arches. The sky was clear, and a large green boat, loaded with furniture, passed beneath us:

"Hey, Rebecca; do you know why they call it the Bridge of Sighs?"

"What does that have to do with anything, we're on the Bridge of Three Arches."

"Okay, okay, but do you know why?"

"Everybody knows, because it was the last bridge the prisoners crossed before being led to the Piombi Prison, and glancing at Venice for one last time, they sighed."

"Ah."

"Hey, shall we go see that small church?"

It was San Giobbe. It was dark and beautiful. We were alone except for a sleeping monk, who was sitting in the vestibule at a table with postcards and prayer cards. We passed by silently to look at the paintings and at the altar, and then we sat down. An acrid, humid smell. Centuries and centuries. The mystery of God. Silence. I thought I loved Rebecca, but it was just her tights.

We headed back. It was almost five o'clock, but there was still time to stop at another wine bar near San Sebastiano. I asked for more wine, fried crab claws, a couple of cups of coffee, a few cigarettes. The wine bar was all in wood: wooden chairs, wooden tables, wooden waiters. Inside and out, students were swarming the place, posing as intellectuals. It seemed that to be a student you needed a certain studied grunginess, with flea-infested goatees tied to broad sideburns, or to tiny, needle-like mustaches. Naturally they all looked tired, busy, and overwhelmed; they looked like miners that had just come back from their night shift.

After all, it was a wonderful life, and you had to keep it to yourself: exams would begin only in February, between classes, the day was spent lounging around for four or five hours. Going to class just meant jotting down the few things the professor talked about (a perfectly useless endeavor as the same exact things were printed in *HIS* book, the first item on the list of books to bring to the exam), and the most demanding aspect was showing a passionate interest in the nonsense he was extolling, maybe exhibiting a furrowed brow in the middle of your forehead and the expression of a thunderstruck clown on the way to Damascus. I despised them with mirth. It's not that I didn't feel their same sense of guilt: billions of dollars spent by the parents to do absolutely nothing, ogle the legs of the female students and roam like a drunken boor from one bar to the next . . . Jeez.

But after all, I'm twenty, please forgive me—I'm twenty. Imagine that in four or five years I'll have to look for a job, pay taxes, have a family, *realize my potential*, take vacation time, work overtime to pay the mortgage, and I'll have to sweat like a pig to ensure that my wife and kids will enjoy *a good standard of living*. I mean, you know, right? Reducing life itself to a break from life, waiting for the weekend and for Sunday's agonizing mists, reducing life to an investment for old age, reducing life to the organization of the perfect funeral . . . I got a lump in my throat, and for a minute I forgot all about the fried crab and Rebecca's thighs.

In any case, Niso caught up with us, while outside the day had already turned cold, and darkness crept forward. He had an unkempt five-day beard, his eyes were like slits, he didn't smile.

"Gorgeous legs." That's how he greeted Rebecca.

"Thanks" she smiled, stretching her legs, "but I'm a little drunk."

As if those two things, her legs and her alcoholic impairment, had a common link.

"Did you play pool last night?" I asked nimbly.

"Yup."

He no longer knew how to hide anything. He lowered his eyes to the bottom of his glass as if he wanted to lose himself in it. We understood right away that something had happened. I ordered French fries with a mountain of mayonnaise and stared at Niso:

"So?"

"Well . . ."

Rebecca placed her hand on his knee and encouraged him to unburden himself. He looked at her, like a cat that spots a shadow in an alley.

"Hey Rebecca, am I not handsome?"

"Of course, you are, sweetie."

"And am I not . . . brilliant?"

"The most brilliant," I interrupted, with the empathy wine lent me, "Have some fries."

Niso refused to eat. He was really in love. Rebecca kept her hand on his knee the whole time and she truly seemed saddened. The smell of beer and fried food. For the third time Niso asked:

"And am I not likable?"

"Well, likable, no," I said. "Is Niso likable, Rebecca?"

Rebecca smiled, "No, he's not likable. Handsome, brilliant . . . but not *likable*."

"Mmmh," Niso wondered, "That's most unfortunate, I must admit. However, it can't be the reason for her indifference. I've never seen a woman who doesn't love a man because he's not likable. In fact, I would venture to say the opposite."

I was getting nervous:

"Are you going to tell us what happened or not? We have class in five minutes. Have some fries."

He started to say that he had been with Alcapone, Saba, Angelica, France—in fact, I had had to leave with Ledina, and Rebecca had slipped away to the movies with her girlfriends—yet everything was good. It was all good, and France was sitting on the stool that was usually Rebecca's following the game between the two couples.

"I was in great form, handsome and brilliant like in the old days, although not likable, and she was very beautiful, amazing, a pearl at the bottom of the ocean, and . . . "

"Get to the point, we have no time for metaphors", Rebecca said impatiently.

"It was an analogy," Niso resentfully clarified, and then he told us that he was playing so well that Saba had asked him:

"Who taught you how to play?"

"My father. A good player, or he was until he broke his arm in a car accident."

And out of the blue Angelica turned bright red, burst out crying, and ran off to the ladies' room.

"My God, what a crybaby. She should work in television," Rebecca said, acerbic.

The three of us went to our twentieth-century Italian-lit course. Not a bad class, actually, with a squirrel-eyed brunette in the first row; a blonde amazon with endless legs; a little redhead with freckles, firm breasts, and a perfectly curvy ass, and so on. But the teacher—well, the teacher deserves a chapter of her own. Rumor had it that she was teaching at the university because she had slept with the previous tenured professor, but this was said of all the relatively young teachers, aside from the fact that you'd have had to be a true pessimist to sleep with her. She was short, around forty-five years old, with vacuous eyes like tap water. I will always remember the way she would interpret the novels she threw at us, which broke down in these categories:

Social. The more the author talked about war and disasters, good partisans and bad bourgeois, starving peasants and bored rich people, and so on, the more he showcased his deep civic conscience, the more the book was a strong moral condemnation of the decadence of the times. To speak of war and the wretched poor meant having a moral compass and a sense of commitment; not to write about disemboweled children, desolate mothers, and concentration camps evidently meant being superficial.

Psychoanalytical. If a person said FUCK YOU to another person, it didn't mean *fuck you*; rather he subconsciously wanted the other person to respond in the same way, so as to satisfy his own persecution complex, and, in doing so, exorcize his own sense of guilt for having said FUCK YOU in the first place to finally be able to have a relationship, create a bond with this other character.

Autobiographical. It's impossible to separate the author from his novel, *I am Madame Bovary* and so on, so that if the story shows a man and a woman fighting, you need to bear in mind that, at the time, the author was divorcing his wife; if the protagonist screws a lot of women, you need to keep in mind that the author has always been ashamed of his homosexuality or impotence (as revealed to us in the indisputable biography by his mother-in-law); so, what is written is often hard to comprehend if we don't know the author's life.

Symbolical. This was the apotheosis. Everything was a symbol of everything. A passing train was the symbol of life that goes on, a gray sky the symbol of going gray, the steak on the plate the symbol of the protagonist's petty materialism. A train was never a train, nor was a gray sky a gray sky, a steak a steak. Ah, if only that dwarf had described these books that I hadn't read in simple terms, as they were written! Ah, if only she had put aside all her interpretations based on her sexual frustrations and proof that she didn't know how to enjoy things—be it life or art—and had only spoken about the stories, the smells, the noises in those pages! Ah, if she had kept quiet . . .

Because that class and that woman marked a turning point. In elementary school, Thursday was my favorite day since it was the day we wrote our essays. I had an instinctive passion for words, and grammar was my favorite subject: the subjunctive fascinated me. My beloved teacher, ecstatic, used to call my parents to read them what I wrote, and my father would call his brothers and sisters to tell them what a prodigy I was, and at ten I already knew my fate: to be the editor of the newspaper *The Sport Gazette*. Middle school was a rude awakening. The Italian teacher, a former Communist activist in '68, didn't think so highly of my prose (she said I was rhetorical) and forced me to read books like *My Prisons*, by Silvio Pellico, and then I remember characters like Marcovaldo and Useppe, desperate people who made me detest that anemic style, those dreadful letters typeset on dirty, boring pages of pedantic anthologies, words after words, depressing clumps of useless pages. But the lethal blow was delivered by none other than Alessandro Manzoni. I'd gotten a taste of him in elementary school, I had to swallow him in middle school, I had to gorge myself on him once again in high school. While, like any young boy my age, I was a seething cauldron of hormones, here I was forced to read about Lucia Mondella, the least sexy girl of all time. I started to hate literature, coming to see it as something oppressive, filled with boredom and sadness. In high school, I didn't fare much better. At fifteen, I had to read a book by a certain Alberto Moravia, *Time of Indifference*, when I was anything but indifferent, tormented by love, smoldering with rage, consumed with injustice, whatever love, rage, and injustice might mean for a fifteen-year-old. Then, at sixteen, I was forced to read (during summer vacation!) *A Violent Life*, by Pier Paolo Pasolini, written half in Roman dialect and crammed with dire poverty, and I had the naïve feeling that the more I was horrified, the more that bizarre author reveled in describing such gruesome poverty, including a young boy who in the end drowns to save someone else and so they dedicate the local branch of the Communist party in his memory, the sole outcome being an eternal diffidence for Romans and Communists.

And yet, feeble flashes of light kept me clinging to a certain respect for this thing called literature, thanks in part to Niso's enthusiasm when he used to tell us about this or that book with more passion than any teacher ever did, and partly from certain Latin and Greek translations, in particular that guy Homer, with his epithets and his redundant adjectives, and the dawn with its pinkish fingers that, in itself, delighted me and thrilled me with an unprovoked moment of joy.

But then she arrived, the dwarf with eyes of tap water, the vulgar whore! And that chubby Horace or that implacable Archilochus were no longer there to protect me, and I made up my mind that that's the way it was, that writers were hypocrites who, cozy in their leather armchairs, sipping a steaming cup of tea with anisette by a mahogany desk in front of the fireplace on their country estates, wrote how horrible the world was but praised be the miners! I made up my mind that they were imbeciles who wrote words that didn't mean what they said, that they were boring pedants so pretentious as to pour their own hypertrophic egos onto the page, their family squabbles and various masturbations, eunuchs who wrote because they didn't know how to live. If she had not told me in myriad ways that literature is a serious thing, that a book is "nourishment for the mind" and all this horrible and bitter nonsense—then maybe I would not have turned into such a sad brute thereafter. In fact, that childhood delight in words and for the subjunctive, as I understood much later on, was nothing but my way of perceiving beautiful things, to then translate them, make them mine: the world was revealing itself to me through words. I sensed the beauty of a flower or the sky thanks to the words *flower* and *sky*, and this in turn sparked a desire within me to give form and harmony to my existence, to drink its nectar. When I lost all interest in the beauty of words and subjunctives, I also lost sight of the beauty of life, since I managed to perceive beauty only through language.

And losing sight of beauty means becoming a brute.

Two days later, on an almost chilly afternoon, my florist friend Nicodemo called; he needed some roses delivered. Actually, this was how I earned beer money for my nights at the Sbruffon, delivering flowers. It was an easy job that I really enjoyed: I loved riding around Mestre on my grandfather's old green bike, going into strangers' homes, smelling the spices wafting from the kitchen, seeing faces that lit up for the flowers (for a moment I felt important)—I loved the sultry fragrance of the roses and the way the sun shimmered on the cellophane wrappers, and I loved the tips: at Christmas and from spring to summer, when lovers get married, I managed to put aside a nice nest egg, which I supplemented by handing out flyers for a Turkish guy who smoked like a chimney, and also through the always generous gifts of my grandmothers.

So, I jumped on my bike and rushed to Nicodemo's small store in the Gazzera neighborhood. Nicodemo handed me a beautiful bouquet of yellow roses and a small slip of paper with the address, a tiny street on the other side of the city: strange that the person who had ordered them hadn't chosen a florist shop closer to the recipient's house, but that was something I didn't dwell on. I crossed the city, lighthearted, carrying the roses in the front basket, whistling, already smelling winter in the harsh colors of the sky. I had no problem finding the street, a peaceful alleyway of small silent houses, and I stopped at #36, the number written on the slip of paper, a modest-sized orange home surrounded by a low hedge, with a cheerful garden and a magnificent apple tree, under which a fat gray cat was purring. I rang the doorbell, the small fence opened, I removed the roses from the basket, walked along the stone path leading to a red door (ajar), wiped my feet on the doormat, knocked as good manners had taught me, and called out, "May I come in?" Then I went inside.

Black hair, soaking wet from the shower.

A luminous, sly smile.

A young woman wrapped in a white bathrobe.

It took me a second, I think, to put the pieces of the puzzle together to realize the fourth point, that I knew her, Saba, naked underneath a white robe, leaning against the wall, arms crossed, ten to twelve feet away from me, the shocked man with yellow roses. She was smiling, her black hair was dripping water on her shoulders, on her breasts, and her hair was a wild tangle of black serpents dribbling water, trickling tiny raindrops, they were beautiful.

She came toward me and I didn't know what to say, I couldn't think, and her bare feet left wet footprints on the floor, drops of water falling from inside her robe, there was water everywhere, and here she was, right in front of me, still smiling, looking me in the eyes as I looked her in the eyes, such penetrating eyes, wistful eyes, and my eyes fell to her breast emerging from the bathrobe, and I tried to say something, but she took the yellow roses out of my arms, theatrically burying her face in them, and from there she looked up at me again, dazed man without yellow roses. She sighed:

"What a lovely thought. Do you want coffee?"

She turned around, and I saw her ample ass sway beneath the white terry-cloth robe, I saw her wet ankles, her bare feet nimble on what had become a marsh. I watched her cross the hallway and disappear behind the corner to the right. I followed her, trying to sidestep the pools of water. We met up in the kitchen. I stopped at the threshold and watched her put the yellow roses, cellophane and all, in a large, blue Murano vase in the center of the table, which was covered with a linen tablecloth, while the sun filtered through the French doors, and she seemed so at ease. My heart was stuck in my throat, and I felt as if my brain had been invaded by a thousand different impulses, like an overwhelmed secretary when all five phones on her desk are ringing simultaneously.

I didn't know what to do, I couldn't figure out what she expected me to do, I had been thrust into a scenario that I had experienced a thousand times before in my erotic fantasies, making it even more surreal, and I couldn't control my nerves, embarrassed by my own embarrassment. I saw another drop of water dribble down her ankle, caress her left foot and end up on the floor. To buy some time, I said: "You see that thing you're wearing; it's called a bathrobe: well, you use it to dry yourself off."

She laughed out loud, exaggeratedly. It relaxed me a little. Then she turned toward the pantry and took the coffee out:

"It's just that you caught me as I was taking a shower. I didn't even have time to slip anything on my feet . . . does it bother you?"

Now was the time to compliment her: "Well, actually, a beautiful woman who has just stepped out of the shower, that's a huge disappointment . . ."

I felt foolish, the joke had sounded all wrong. I took two steps forward, moved the chair, and sat down. She put the coffee on the stove and stared at me again with that disarming smile, unambiguously: "Oh, you didn't by any chance think that I did it on purpose to be seen like this, did you?"

"Noooo, nooo . . . no."

God almighty, what a fool! I was stumbling over myself. She had put the ball on a silver platter, and I had kicked it off like a dumb amateur. Now I needed to start from scratch.

I looked at my hands, then looked up, she had sat down next to me, her legs under the table, clutching the lapels of her bathrobe that covered her breast. Maybe it was just chance, maybe it really wasn't a cunning ruse, I thought, but her eyes had fire in them, her hair was wild and cascaded down her shoulders and her face, we sat there as if we were forced to sit through a math class, the yellow roses between us, and then I found the angle: "Who sent you this thoughtful gift? Are they from Alcapone?"

She flushed suddenly from her neck up to her cheeks. I realized that my words could seem to take on a virtuous tone, seemingly reminding her that she had a boyfriend and that this guy was my friend—God, what an imbecile I am!

"Yes . . ."

I flashed a smart-ass smile to let her know that it wasn't a problem for me: "But how . . . ?"

Saba put her head between her hands, which she then ran through her hair. Her breast peeked out at me again between the lapels of the bathrobe. She had goosebumps. She closed her eyes and took a deep breath. She stretched out her hand to rub the petals of a rose, and said: "This morning we walked by a florist's shop, and Al told me you worked there. They had these incredibly beautiful yellow roses I was crazy about, especially because of the golden-red border. See it?"

"It's a first-class border."

"He wanted to give them to me as a gift, no matter the cost, but I didn't want him to spend so much on me, after all, we haven't known each other for very long, and then, I told him, I would rather get flowers at home, maybe with a little card enclosed, as a surprise . . ."

She removed the small envelope stapled to the cellophane, removed the card, read it, and smiled. Her eyes filled up. I felt like I was falling into an abyss. Then she looked at me with her glistening eyes and said: "Well, maybe . . . maybe I made a mistake . . . I'd better go get dressed."

But the coffee was ready right at that moment.

I watched as she poured the coffee into two small orange terracotta cups, and I managed to mentally arrange the following notions: she had always given me sexy looks, she was counting on the fact that I would deliver the roses (after all, I was the only one delivering their flowers), I found her half naked and her glances were getting more flirtatious. Come on! I told myself with increasing certainty, it can't be a coincidence! And I'm not going to be stopped by a stupid card!

I needed to play my role: "It's a shame you want to get dressed . . . "

She turned around and placed the cups on the table, without looking at me, she asked: "Sugar?" I said: "You're so sweet . . . one sugar, thanks," she put in a teaspoon of sugar and became serious, silent, and stirred it in as if she were performing a delicate procedure. "Milk?" she asked, again not looking at me, "You are . . . you are . . . a drop of milk, thanks," I answered, and I watched her, standing there, naked under her bathrobe, I wanted her to smile at me again, I said, "You take my breath away" (our most sincere words always come out sounding so fake).

She moved the chair and sat facing me crossing her legs, she let her robe open up so that her thighs were exposed, beautiful, as smooth as Carrara marble, a large mole on her right knee. She studied me while bringing the cup to her lips. I caved, and I gazed at her small feet with toes painted in silver nail polish, I looked at her sinuous ankles and her strong round calves, and I looked at the joints of her thighs up to where the robe concealed them, I looked at the dark tiny triangle and then I looked up a little more, I looked at the terry cloth belt that kept her robe closed over her hips, soft hips, large hips, and I looked up even more and I stopped at her barely covered large breasts, and I looked up again and we stared at each other, we stared at each other letting go of our alibis, and she placed the cup down on the table, and I sensed an astonishing mix of happiness and fear, and I was ready to grab her, rip off her robe, devour her breasts, to—but lightning flashed through my head: what if all this was just a prank?

I took the orange terracotta cup and brought it to my lips. Damn it, Rebecca had set me up. Now I jump on top of her, and they all pop out from everywhere, Rebecca will point her finger at me saying, "Shame on you!" Alcapone will try to punch me, Angelica will laugh, they will all laugh. I swallowed the scalding coffee, burning the roof of my mouth, and I felt the flames of humiliation scorch my cheeks and forehead. I was sweating. No, come on, I can't do this to Alcapone, Rebecca is right, and then she would fall for me, no no, I have to stay calm, but damn it, why isn't she saying something, she's looking at the yellow roses and the card on the table, she's sipping coffee, surely she's thinking "My God, what a dumbass!"

And she would tell Angelica, and they would both despise me "That prude, that wimp!" Me? A prude!? Me, A wimp!?

Furious, I looked at her, and then the phone rang.

She got up, placed the cup on the table, and said: "Excuse me," and went into the hallway to answer it from the wall phone. I heard her say, a little embarrassed: "Oh, hi. Wait a sec, let me go get the call in my room . . ." I saw her lean into the kitchen, put her finger to her lips signaling me to keep quiet, and she whispered:

"It's Alcapone." She vanished.

I stayed in the kitchen for a little while, took a deep breath, grabbed a tissue from my pocket and wiped the sweat from my forehead. My temples were pounding, my throat was parched. I got up. I tried to pull myself together. On the mantel there was a photo of two newlyweds in a silver frame, I looked at it but didn't see anything, I couldn't see anything, I looked at the yellow roses again, I looked out the French doors, there was a garden but I didn't see it, I couldn't see anything, I tried to tell myself I was calm, but who was I kidding? I turned around suddenly, outside the kitchen, in the hallway, I spotted a large mirror, and I rushed over to it. I put my hands behind my back, and stared at myself right in the eyes, like a sergeant to a private soldier: "And so?" I hissed through my teeth, "are you going to stop acting like an idiot?" I stared into my eyes, and they were very beautiful eyes, sensual, I raised my right eyebrow, I had a penetrating stare, yes, ineffable, I stroked my two-day-old stubble, wet my lips, yes, I was sexy, it's only natural she wants me, she must want me like crazy, there can be no other explanation, I winked at myself: my good looks reassured me to the point that I felt calm and I realized, a bit stunned, that I wasn't turned on.

I wasn't turned on in the least. What the hell? Nothing stirred down there in my boxers, and the only time I had felt the call of the wild was when she was sitting across from me, shamelessly, but that quivering erection wilted immediately, when I was wondering if this was all some kind of damned prank on me. No, I looked into the mirror, smug because of my sense of morality, even though she's naked I don't feel like doing her, I can leave here the same way I came in, kiss her on the hand and not do any damage, refuse with honor her advances and get out of here victorious. "What a man of character!" She would say to Angelica, "I offered myself to him practically nude, and he didn't react, he was incorruptible. He taught me a lot!" And Angelica would answer: "He's probably so used to women falling all over him that it couldn't have been that hard for him." And they would go on talking about me, about my blinding sensuality and my strong character and, satisfied, I smiled back at the mirror, everything was perfect—but then, disappointed, I snapped my fingers: damn it, I always reacted to her intimations, damn it, if I had been so loyal I would have never reciprocated her suggestive glances, damn it, I'm the one who made her think I desired her and wanted the same thing she did, I am her accomplice, damn it! I can't pull back now.

I definitely couldn't pull back. I wouldn't come off as someone strong, but instead as a coward, someone who plays Don Juan and then, when he has the chance to score, he runs away, a worthless playboy. She would tell Angelica, "What an idiot, he acts like a tough guy from the burbs with those looks he gives you and the attitude of a poor man's Rudolph Valentino and when you add it all up: zero, he doesn't even have the courage to look at me. What a fool. You think it was a sudden sense of guilt?"

"What sense of guilt?!" Angelica would react, indignant, "If you have the least bit of moral fiber you don't carry on with those allusions, and if you throw a stone you don't hide your hand. But what can I say, just like all those sex-starved guys who can't get a woman even if they pay her, he's a coward."

Me? I can't get a woman even if I pay her!? Me? A coward!?

Disgusting snake! She had pegged me, of course, but I would make her see the light. I turned to look toward the room with the door closed at the end of the hallway, from whence I could hear Saba's indistinct murmurings. I walked down the hall until I was in front of the door. I heard: "The roses are beautiful, you shouldn't have . . . oh yes, Ema delivered them, he's so funny, he just left."

I put my hand on the door handle. Slowly, carefully, I opened the door.

I walked in with an apt expression, of someone who's opened the wrong door by mistake, oops, sorry I was looking for the bathroom, and instead I ended up standing right in front of her sitting on the bed, the white telephone handset in her hand, nude.

Naked woman on the phone.

Nude. Her robe was on the floor. Nude with her legs crossed. Large, beautiful breasts. Soft bulging stomach. A thick, very black, tuft of hair. Nude . . .

And yet, and yet more than anything else I looked at her small feet, her small feet and those eyes that were now resplendent with an ancient light while they looked at me, she continued whispering,

"Yes, of course, yes" to Alcapone, and in that moment I loved her, in that moment she seemed like the most beautiful thing I had ever seen, I adored her like you revere a holy image – so I dropped to my knees in front of her , I took her feet in my hands and started to kiss them, nearly in desperation, nearly overcome with emotion, with a kind of lustful gratitude, and while I was bathing her feet with my sloppy kisses I felt my heart beating faster, quivering in my throat, and all my muscles swollen with joy, I moved up her body, I moved up with my hungry mouth gnawing at her calves, nibbling on her knees, licking her thighs like a devoted dog, and then, overwhelmed, I looked up, just like a dog who doesn't feel as if his master is paying enough attention to him: Saba continued mumbling a few words into the white handset, her eyes closed and her head slightly tilted backwards, not looking at me, and with her free hand she grabbed my head and pushed me down, uncrossing her legs, urging me to continue doing what I was doing—and I, I was stunned, I dove into her black, sopping wet bush, I dove in all the way into her pink folds, I sank my teeth into her like I was biting into warm wafers.

6. November

The October days overlapped each other like kids playing in the park, fast days, colder and colder, bare as the trees, and then suddenly, November, with its forlorn colors, the black overcoats, the gray fog, the coffee with cinnamon sugar, the felt hats—and I, nude, lying on Saba's bed on a rainy afternoon, my head against the backboard, looking at her: she has her back to me, standing silent in front of the window, wrapped in a blanket. I'm exhausted, I drink mineral water right out of the bottle and I smoke, dropping the ashes into the ashtray wedged between my thighs.

But the room wasn't cold, the radiator was nice and warm, she was leaning her groin against it, and she warmed up to the point that she let her robe fall and stood there naked. I watched her, and with her back to me, I thought she resembled Gala at the window. (Gala was Dalí's wife, Dalí was crazy about Gala, and in a small Venetian inn, next to the church of the Frari, I had seen this reproduction of her looking out the window, the only difference being that in the painting there is a flamboyant sunset over the water, here, none).

I was watching her while the smoke was drying my throat: she had soft black curls cascading down her shoulders, round and solid, her back arched gracefully down to her ass, beautiful, white, lunar, a tender ass to penetrate like butter, a large and cold ass like an uninhabited planet, and then the legs, fleshy, somewhat squat and irregular, not perfect and not long legs, but appetizing.

(Who knows if Dante and Niso would pop in on Gala and Dalí at Port Lligat to briefly say hi to them?)

She wasn't talking. She was immersed in her thoughts beyond the window. I got up and went to the bathroom to pee. I looked at myself in the mirror, earnestly, but I didn't like myself that much.

Barefoot, naked, I skipped out of the bathroom and swooped into the kitchen, the same kitchen that almost a month before had been the source of a thousand embarrassing moments, and I put the coffee pot on the flame. From outside, the feeble light of a winter afternoon infiltrated the room, fading by now, a casualty of the evening shadows: a shiver ran down my spine. On the mantel next to the oven, I saw a framed photo, which I had glimpsed before without really seeing it. I picked it up and studied it. It was a picture taken in the 1970s. Pictures from the '70s always make me sad; the colors are the same ones of a fall Sunday afternoon at five o'clock, when the soccer games are over—those reds and oranges pathetically accentuated like the neon sign on a desolate pizzeria or like the sign above a provincial dance hall. I looked at the photo—Saba's parents as newlyweds in front of their small Jewish specialty store—I looked at the two of them with their eternal smiles, a drop of water trickled unfazed onto the dirty dishes in the sink, from the kitchen tiles gloomy arabesques assailed me, and a thousand horrific drunken gnomes started to skitter in my stomach. I turned on the light, but it was worse. I needed to go back to the bedroom, slip my jeans on, say goodbye to Saba forever, and run, run like a madman through the dark November, run to make my heart burst and to rid itself of the darkness.

Then Saba appeared on the doorway: she had put on the black tights that I had almost ripped off with my teeth just a few moments before, and she was wearing a white woolen sweater. I sensed a jolt of solace in my crotch, I felt better, and I mustered a grateful smile:

"Nothing better than a good cup of coffee, eh?"

She smiled sweetly, even though her eyes were filled with thoughts. After all, since that day in mid-October, it was already the sixth time that we had stolen time and space to let our hands roam over each other's bodies; nothing could stop it, not the chaste faces of her parents in the picture, not the narrow confines of a car, not the unforgiving chill of a street on the outskirts of town, not Alcapone's eternal and trusting smile: it was becoming addictive. I knew I couldn't play dumb, as if it was nothing important, as if I didn't notice the worried look in her eyes, so I asked her, "Is something wrong?"

"No, why?" And she looked at the clock.

"We have time before your parents come home . . . do you need to do something?"

"No . . . listen . . ."

She sat down where I had sat the first time I had been in her house, and this time I was the one who made the coffee, standing, naked. She looked at the clock again, while I took out the small orange cups and put them on the table. I moved closer to her and said: "Would you rather we don't see each other anymore?" but I glanced at her crossed legs and her sweater, and I noticed she hadn't put on any underwear and that her very hairy pubes were clinging to the nylon, so that I immediately regretted my words, The coffee was ready, I turned off the gas and I too sat down, to hide my growing excitement, but she said, "Yes."

She put her elbows on the table and cupped her head in her hands, and she twisted her mouth, thinking things over. She whispered:

"You know, you shouldn't be upset . . ."

"Me, upset? Are you kidding?" I was hard as a rock under the table.

"It was beautiful but . . ."

I was pretty sure she wasn't about to let me leave without a last send-off, so I enjoyed the exhilaration of my erection and graciously said: "Of course, of course, I completely understand, you don't need to justify yourself."

"I'm not justifying myself. It's just that in theory it seemed so wonderful to have two lovers, such an adventurous life, and instead, I don't know, I'm starting to feel bad as soon as you touch me . . ."

Touché. My excitement abated.

"I know, I know, we have a soul, in spite of ourselves."

"Are you okay?"

With both hands she grabbed mine and looked at me the way you look at a lame puppy. That maternal way of hers, certainly learned from some third-rate movie, completely killed my lust. I should have dumped her, dammit! I changed the subject:

"I'm sorry, but could you satisfy my simple curiosity before I get out of your life for good: what do you like in Alcapone?"

"Well . . . first of all, he has a heart of gold."

Here we go again. People tend to confuse obesity with kindness; that's the only possible explanation.

"But he's not helpless, don't think . . ." she went on, noticing my perplexed face, and then, among other things, she said, "You, for example, you're always acting so tough but you're more defenseless than he is, you're shy."

I looked up at the heavens and exhaled resignation, reciting, "I find it utterly despicable this judging of people based on your own fears. If you are afraid that beating in this chest is a piece of limestone from the Carso: *I'm shy*. If you are afraid that I may suddenly turn aggressive and insufferable: *I'm insecure*. If it seems impossible to you that I'm unable to have feelings for someone just because he's a fat-ass, a child, or an old toothless guy: *I'm cynical*. But maybe I had a rough childhood."

She looked at me raising her right eyebrow, she grimaced, then said:

"The way you speak is too fancy, I can't understand you. You and Niso, there . . . you're always having these discussions that only the two of you understand . . . What does Rebecca call you again?"

"Giants with feet of clay," I hissed through clenched teeth.

"Exactly. I'm sorry to have to tell you this, but France and Alcapone are much more spontaneous than you two."

"Well, spontaneity, if it even exists, is not necessarily a virtue, my dear. We do a lot of stupid and cruel things spontaneously."

I was pissed and, in addition, naked. She got up and asked me:

"Do you want a snack?"

That was a great idea, I had to admit. "Well, I *always* want a snack." She smiled at me graciously and her eyes were as calm and as deep as Lake Tiberias, her breasts sand dunes in Palestine. She grabbed a white tray and opened the fridge:

"The olives, where are the olives? You like olives?"

"Obviously."

"Oh, Ema! There's also some green bean salad!"

"This is great news, really."

I was still sitting down, she still had her back to me, and I wondered if I needed to get dressed or if—naked—she would let me steal a lingering kiss on her dark nipples, another caress, another five minutes.

After all, her veiled thighs seemed more enticing to me than ever, now that they were moving away from me, now that she had suddenly been vanquished by regret (but no, no, it had been a slow but inescapable capitulation) and for the first time I admired certain details of her femininity with new intensity, her tempestuous hair, her milky white sweet-scented skin, her childlike voice:

"Hey, I even have some chicken! A quarter chicken, right? We can have my mother's mayo with it, what do you say?"

"It would be a dream come true."

"Stop teasing me. Where are the olives? Maybe under here."

She bent over to look for the olives in the bottom drawer showing me that adorable ass sheathed in nylon, and I sat there—captivated, desperate—hypnotized by that abyssal crack, rendered more remote by the dark color of her tights, a wondrous darkness, a pirate's cave, and I felt something I had never felt before, an inordinate love, a tearing nostalgia, and although I had never said "I love you" and I realized that savvy psychologists would smile and dismiss such a statement, I was staring at her ass and wanted to tell her "I love you!" I was being swallowed by her ass, and I wanted to tell her "I love you!" As a matter of fact, there were no other words to describe all my fanatical devotion, all my phagocytosing love, and I wanted to disappear in that asshole and shout "I love you!"

"You do like olives?"

"Yes!" and I would have pounced onto her ass with a resolute bite between those cheeks, and she would have arched her back while screaming AH! ARE YOU NUTS!? and all the tiny olives on the small plate would have scattered on the floor—Please Saba, don't leave me, I love you!—I would have begged her, hugging her legs, on my knees, and she would have lost her balance and the tray would have fallen to the floor in a whirling feast of olives and leftover chicken and I would have filled her mouth with my whole tongue and I would have sunk my hands into her flesh, into her breasts, into her face, oh how I love you, how I love you my God I'm burning up with passion, and I would have ripped off her tights and I would have sunk myself in her and she would have loved me, oh yes she would have loved me, on a bed of green beans and olives—instead the doorbell rang.

Panic violently replaced desire, and blood drained from every part of my body to rush into my throat: Christ, Saba's parents. I jumped up, my instinct told me to find refuge in her room and hide under the bed. Saba's face swung to the door (with her beautiful tray in her hands), she seemed to think things over for a second, then mumbled:

"Gosh, he's crazy early."

Terrified, I stared at her, whispering, "Who?" (But a horrific premonition chilled me right to the bone).

"Alcapone."

She turned to stare at me with the determination of a secret agent who knows that in ten seconds the bomb will go off. Second bell ring. She brought her finger to her lips and whispered, "Slowly go into my bedroom, get your clothes that I left folded on the chair, and slip into the closet. Don't worry. And take this!"

She gave me the tray full of chicken and mayonnaise, green beans, pickles, and olives. Third bell ring.

I had no idea what was going on anymore, but my heart went into overdrive. A peaceful November afternoon had turned from existential unease to mad lust to pure terror: I felt sick.

Saba's room was clean once again, the bed had been remade, the ashtray emptied, the smell of smoke had vanished in the winter air past the wide-open windows (but I didn't even notice how cold it was). I heard Saba's voice, mellifluous:

"My love . . ."

And then the fat-ass's voice, dumb:

"My love . . ."

My clothes were on the chair next to the window, I put them under my arm, careful not to let even one olive slide off the tray I was holding in the other hand, and with my foot I opened the door of the closet and snuck into it.

I curled up in the darkness of the closet, my head swallowed by Saba's rustling clothes falling off the hangers, caressing my face in a peculiar kind of sensual dance, smelling of lemon soap and lavender (but most of all I smelled Saba's skin) and, as if under a spell, I calmed down, and an ancestral sense of peace and protection enveloped my limbs—the dark, maternal womb, for sure, but also my cell as a novitiate in some Irish monastery in the year one thousand two hundred and three, the pleasure of entering a small deserted church and genuflecting in front of a most tender portrait of the Blessed Virgin—and I suddenly remembered how, as a child, I loved to curl up in my mother's closet, how I would slink away like a cat from light to darkness, and how I got smaller in a corner, almost wishing to disappear, almost wishing to forget myself, almost looking for another dimension, and how I let her perfumed skirts tickle my ears as I relished the darkness . . .

Hunched over in Saba's deep cave, I stood there trying to decipher these images: I'm sure that as a child I was looking for clues about my previous lives, I questioned the darkness about that ermine mantle that I could no longer find, that wine-stained tunic, that green velvet compartment in first class on the train to St. Petersburg . . .

St. Petersburg . . . I must have had important business in St. Petersburg because that name, even later in life, would evoke a desire deep inside of me, a wild thrill of nostalgia, glorious and anxious visions of snow and Cossacks. And such intense pleasures were evoked also by names like *Prague*, *Warsaw*, *Agrigento*, and *Bethlehem*, and I would waste hours in front of the map enjoying the exquisite delights of finding names of cities and countries that would fill my heart—like *Calcutta*, *Corinth*, *China*—while I couldn't care less about others like Brasilia, Los Angeles, and all of Australia.

I also remember that later, when I was about thirteen years old, I had revised my autobiography through the centuries: I had been a Greek philosopher in Magna Graecia, dedicated to the cultivation of dates and olives, then most certainly I was in the Galilee during Jesus's time. I don't want to say that I was actually Him (although back then I considered myself extraordinarily caring and charismatic) because I would have had some kind of remnant knowledge of it, and I was neither that ingratiating effete Saint John, nor that hysterical hypocrite Saint Peter, if anything I was more inclined to think I was Saint Thomas or one of the shepherd boys visiting the cave, or maybe—but only in some moments of humility—the oxen or the donkey. At any rate, whoever I was, I was in the area. After the experience in the Galilee, I was a sorcerer in the Black Forest, a Cistercian monk in northern Europe, and of course the czar of all Russia. In any case, how good

I felt in my mother's closet! As well as in Saba's. But all of a sudden, the bedroom door creaked and I held my breath.

"Come on, come in . . ." Saba's voice.

A turkey's gobble gobble. The fat-ass.

"Mmmh," Saba mumbling again.

The bed springs.

"Hee hee hee," the fat-ass's classic embarrassed laughter.

My heart was racing.

I figured out that Saba had turned the light on, because a soft faint glow was streaming through the small keyhole. At first, I couldn't quite make out her plan, then I remembered how more than once I had shown her some curiosity about the dynamic between the two of them in bed together, and I finally got it. As cautious as a slithering snake in the sand, I tried to move toward the peephole of light, until, accidentally, I rested my left hand on the tray full of food. Luckily, the noise was minimal. I found myself with a couple of green beans stuck to my hand and—what could I do? —I ate them. They were good.

I pressed my eye against the keyhole, and there they were, right in front of me: Alcapone and Saba, sitting on the bed, kissing. God, what a bizarre scene! She was still wearing her sweater and tights, he had his black polished shoes on and his gray suit with tiny yellow pinstripes, his vest and black shirt, a true gangster from the 1920s but with too much whiskey under his belt. They were kissing, and she glanced mischievously toward the closet, what a woman, I thought, and other things not as nice: this was her last gift before leaving, a live-action porn movie framed by a keyhole, a work of art by an eccentric and somewhat baroque artist, Gala and The Fat-Ass, girl with lily-white ass and fat-ass with polished shoes, Medusa with hair of snakes and Idiot with prominent stomach: it wasn't a Champions Cup final, but who was I to complain! I felt the tray with one hand, grabbed a handful of green beans and wolfed them down.

Then, Saba quickly freed herself from her tights and sweater and was once again bare naked, she knelt at the fat-ass's feet and began to remove his shoes, then his socks (gray with little yellow dots), then she unbuckled his belt and with some effort she managed to pull off his pants and his yellow-blue boxers, and Alcapone was left in his jacket, vest, and shirt, and under that, all naked with an erect dick. Saba started to kiss his fat feet.

The whole thing was entertaining, though less arousing than perhaps Saba might have anticipated. As an apostle of Jesus Christ and back there in Siberia I had seen worse. I could see the contour of Saba's magnificent breasts, I saw her naked, filthy, between another man's legs, but in that situation, I dare say, I was more fascinated by him than by her: Alcapone had the same expression on his face as when he was winning at pool, a bright red face, satisfied, but with an air of superiority. One of the most stupid looking faces I had ever seen. That huge white ass, those fat white thighs sank into the bed and strangely reminded me of those of an infant, oh yes, Alcapone *was* a breast-feeding baby, with his jacket and his vest and his hard dick, he was a breast-feeding baby who didn't know a thing about what was happening around him, maybe even taking for granted that a girl with some awesome tits and an enviable ass would bend down between his opulent chubby legs. And maybe he wouldn't have even laughed if he could have seen himself, and I watched him as he leaned back on his elbows and it seemed that the satisfaction was deforming his features, that his sky-blue eyes were exploding into the stratosphere, that the capillaries in his cheeks would burst and bleed, and Saba was now rubbing her tits across his knees (I sank my teeth into a piece of chicken), then she started nibbling the inside of his thighs (Saba's mother's mayo had a certain touch of greatness), his mouth was open like a blowfish's (the only thing I like about chicken is that you eat it with your hands, I would eat everything with my hands because it makes me feel like an ancient Roman in the encampment the night before battle), and then, while I carefully licked my fingers, Saba brought her beautiful face (that, in the past, I hadn't noticed) closer to Alcapone's mad boner, he lightly grazed her black curls with his hands and, as if pervaded by a triple electric shock, I seemed to feel the breath from her nostrils, the tip of her tongue, the moist collar of her lips.

Two days later I woke up around ten. Some days I don't want to wake up any more, I just feel like pulling the covers up to my face and letting the dark wrap itself around me until the evening comes. During that damned November it rarely happened, all things considered, but in the following months it would happen all the time. The cold slid in next to me and ran through my bones, and I, I had a class at noon. I got up, lazy and weary, with sticky eyes. I washed my face with ice-cold water, and I looked horrible. I sniffed my armpits. I stank. No big deal, I sprayed some deodorant on, didn't shower, and dragged my slippers into the kitchen. I missed Saba's kitchen. Even more than her breasts. Just the two of us sitting there, shooting the breeze, leisurely drinking coffee out of her ludicrous terracotta cups, eating leftovers. We had been shielded, for a while, against the outside world. I would ask her about Angelica, "But that Angelica . . ."

"What a pain! You really like her, eh?"

"Me!? Ah!"

"Well, she's very beautiful, I know . . ."

"Very beautiful, don't exaggerate . . . cute, maybe."

"Everyone's crazy about her. You know what they call her?"

"Salome?"

"No, Circe. Because she transforms men into pigs . . ."

"Easy task!"

"No, really, in the sense that she dulls their senses, they lose all their dignity. For example, the last one, before Niso, was a really cool guy, fascinating, even if he was almost twice her age, thirty-five."

"An old guy!"

"Come on! Thirty-five is okay, women mature faster."

"That's true. In fact, they also rot faster."

"Well, anyway, a blond, blue-eyed television screenwriter, a filmmaker."

"Strange. I thought all screenwriters had a goatee and wore black rectangular glasses. I'm taking a film course at university and I can tell you with the utmost certainty: the professor has a goatee and wears black rectangular glasses, and so do all the students, and the girls wear black rectangular glasses without the beard, except a few."

"Okay, nevertheless, he was a cultivated, intelligent person . . ."

"Filmmakers are never intelligent, let alone cultivated. They're intellectuals without intellect. They can't read a book, never mind write one, so they try to convince themselves and everyone around them that movies have some sort of intellectual depth, looking for, behind the images, esoteric sophistry and, of course, symbols, since there's nothing easier than finding symbols. You should see us in this class: we're bored to death watching a nonsensical film, and still, at the end, we're all excited to come up with brilliant metaphors and to discuss historical perspectives and sequence shots and similar crap. What a farce!"

"Okay, anyhow, are you going to let me finish or not?"

"Sure."

"In the beginning, everything was going fine, she was as happy as a lark. With all the guys she had previously been with, as soon as she opened up a little, they, in turn, became morbidly possessive, insecure, and jealous. This guy, instead, given his age, seemed different."

"But?"

"But he ended up being a thousand times worse than the others! He totally lost control. He used to wait for her in front of school, called her twenty times a day, it seems he even lost his job, he went completely off the deep end."

"And she left him."

"She couldn't. She was too caught up in the hope she had finally found someone different, to her it seemed impossible that a man so much older and who seemed so together could act like the twenty-year-olds she had been with until then. And also, she felt a certain uneasiness, again because of his age, since he was almost as old as her father . . ."

"So, what happened?"

"Well, I can't tell you."

"What!?"

"It's something too intimate."

I begged and badgered her to reveal the secret, but she shut up tighter than a clam, determined, and I was determined to drag it out of her, so she bared her breast at me and I said: Okay. You will tell me later.

At three in the afternoon I had my second class, the third one was at six. Then dinner, pool, or a bar: it was always the same old, same old. It was one of those days when life shows us its grim reality, and everything is so gray inside and around us that even if God called us to confirm his existence, we wouldn't get that excited. Not even the aroma of coffee penetrating my nostrils excited me much.

I sat at the table, and I felt I was missing everything, but I didn't know what. I thought I had great parents, that I'd been somewhat lucky with women—certain that one day I'd become very lucky—I believed that my college career would be relatively easy and that, in the meantime, I'd be able to have fun waiting for spring: waiting for spring . . .

That was it; maybe there wasn't much to wait for—that was the problem—there was nothing to wait for except another season, and then another, surely a rather reductive wait for a romantic soul like mine. The coffee was good. Thank God for coffee on rainy days and on snowy days, but I felt a hole inside me. Life was passing me by, and I had nothing important to do. I envied Niso and France who had such big dreams and were passionate. I could imagine how their suffering granted color and dignity to their lives. I imagined their impatient quivering upon seeing her appear around the corner, and I imagined those thorns in their sides when they felt she ignored them.

As for me? She was beautiful and I wanted her, but nothing more. At most, I was interested in learning her secret, but once discovered, I would go back to feeling more bored than before, I was certain. I didn't even have Alcapone's unwavering happiness, immune from evolution, or any sense of guilt or the joyful exuberance of his girlfriend, or maybe Rebecca's competitive nature and determination to get a degree as soon as possible and then take off. I had—in a word—nothing. No feelings, no regrets. Just my coffee. Until a short time before, I had relished these momentary bouts of depression because they made me feel more like an intellectual. Now, instead, I didn't even have that. I was just a twenty-year-old idiot. A twenty-year-old with no balls. A deadbeat stuffed with hormones, salivating over a pair of legs—and that was all.

I got up, washed the cups and plates from the day before, to do something nice—to, at least, make my mom happy when she came home from work; to, at least, make a little sense of my day, so that my life would mean something even if it wasn't interested in taking anything. This led me to meditate on why fat wealthy women would try so hard to organize huge charity events and set up fundraising groups: they must be terribly bored. When life itself has no meaning, the only thing left to do is to become a philanthropist. Probably many had started by having children, to give some meaning to their lives; it had to be this way, and it all seemed very sordid to me. The fact is that this wandering bitterness led me to think about God. I put on a tracksuit, my father's horrible red fleece jacket, and went to church. No one was there. And yet it felt good. The church had been built with dark bricks in the old style, and large frescoes and pseudo-Renaissance paintings gave the impression of a monastic peace. I sat down to observe: God, can You hear me? I had been taught that it didn't matter how long you had stayed away, He would listen to you with even more care—like the Prodigal Son—but I was more modest and conscientious than the Prodigal Son, and I felt that between God and myself there was a lot of unfinished business, and it was difficult to feel carefree while I spoke to Him, as if it was nothing at all. The tiny flames of the candles flickered on the altar. God, if You can, take this concave feeling of life's worthlessness from my stomach, support me, beat me, give me a minimum of substance—God! Life doesn't seem tolerable if I don't give it some importance.

The colors of the saints' eyes were vivid and lustful. Their gestures were resolute, while you could always find a bit of fear in the delicate features of the Madonna, always a slight sense of melancholy. For quite a while I had not resorted to God, now I felt nostalgic. Of course, every night I mechanically recited the *Our Father* for me, for my family, for the world, lumping everything together, but I no longer had that same fervor, that fervor that burned in me during the sincere years of catechism, the ideal of justice and the sweetness of fraternity and the need to be charitable to your fellow man, that overall affinity for Jesus, that total connection with Him—Oh God, great God!

I'm asking for forgiveness.

Hot tears started to flow, hot and comforting: maybe God was truly the essence. I was a little ashamed of crying before Him, I've always hated mystical crises, and since I was young I tried to establish a virile and rational relationship with God, but the sweetness of His presence melted my heart, He was there and He was caressing my head like in the movie *Miracle of Marcelino*.

I cried, I cried recalling myself as a child, I cried because I had lost my courage, I cried because I had a lump in my throat, because it was time to cry. I left the church and life had regained its colors.

Three days later I was sleeping during an archeology class, when Rebecca showed up. She said something had happened. Niso had phoned her and had asked her to come to his house along with France, Alcapone, and me. Why? What had happened? Nobody knew. All we knew was that he sounded heartbroken. That night we were all excited to go to Niso's house, just outside the city. Alcapone didn't come, he was probably too busy making out with Saba, and the frost veiled the countryside like flowering plum clusters. Niso's parents, always extremely nice, were there, and they informed us that their son was waiting for us in his room upstairs.

Niso welcomed us in a bathrobe with a stubble and a glorious smile. I was afraid he wanted to announce his marriage plans. Instead, he told France and me to sit down on his bed and Rebecca to sit on the black armchair at his desk. He filled a couple of glasses with Coke and got to the point: he had broken up with Angelica. That gave me a jolt of happiness. Rebecca didn't bat an eyelash: France downplayed his reaction. "Well, did you ask us to come over so you could tell us your business? We would have gotten the news anyway tomorrow from the tabloids! Have the news agencies already broadcast it?"

So I piled on:

"I will write a very tough, background article in the *Gazette* and I'll call it: 'Why, Niso?'"

Niso forced a smile. Rebecca was dead quiet. Then she whispered:

"Tell us about it."

It wasn't that Niso was crying or seemed inconsolable. Maybe on the inside, he was in shambles. He said he was falling apart, that his heart had been ripped to shreds, but he still had a smirk on his face as if to underline that it wasn't an issue, that it was expected, that he already knew everything. The first thing he said was that he wanted to be alone for a while, and he asked us not to contact him, that he wouldn't be going to the pool hall or to college, that he wanted to stay secluded to recharge his batteries and sharpen his nails. Rebecca seemed convinced of her arguments when she told him that this wasn't the right way to fight, that withdrawing into himself was a sign of weakness and cowardice, that he needed to come face to face with reality. Niso smiled at her but didn't waver: he didn't want to fight *now*, precisely because he was weak and a coward, because he knew he was pathetic and didn't want the world to perceive him as even more pathetic. By world, he meant Angelica, naturally, and he laughed bitterly as he said it, and maybe Rebecca felt stung with jealousy. Then he added that he preferred to confront reality from there, that not being there was the only way to be truly there, that he needed to lick his wounds in order to come back more handsome than before.

"You'll be gorgeous once again!" I said from the heart, urged on by the strange excitement this news instilled in me, and I raised my glass of Coke to make a toast, as I realized that the moment of utmost suffering coincided with the first moment of consolation. Niso's mother came into the room with a tray of cucumber and tuna sandwiches, stroked her son's head in a maternal way, and uttered something about women and love. To be polite, France and I agreed with her, Niso stared at her with affectionate irony, then Niso's mom told Rebecca that she was more beautiful with each passing day:

"My son needs someone like you, rather than that nut case!"

Rebecca blushed slightly and thanked her, Niso asked her to leave, telling her that she didn't understand anything, France smiled, and I, naturally, had my mouth full and was thinking that the folk wisdom of his mother had hit the nail on the head. After his mother left, Niso told us about the last of a series of interminable scenes, at a bar in the center of town in the middle of three thousand people. Angelica had accused him of being a wimp because he had told her that he hated motorcycles and bikers and that they both scared him. And she said:

"Bikers are audacious!" To which Niso replied:

"Poets are audacious, not bikers." Angelica, with increasing resentment, a resentment which seemed inexplicable and uncontrollable to Niso, started raising her voice:

"I want a man with a set of balls, I want a man who is a man, get it?"

"You want me naked horseback riding in Maremma?"

She didn't understand anything. She kept on yelling her ideas and her demands, and Niso just felt embarrassed for the people pretending not to listen while listening.

On the verge of tears, she said: "He must be strong."

"Excuse me, and how would he show this strength? When he gets on the bus, does he validate his ticket with more virility than everyone else?"

But she wasn't smiling.

"No one has ever looked at me with so much hatred, with so much contempt," Niso said, and Rebecca reiterated, "She's just a psycho." Niso answered, "but I love that psycho." Rebecca threw her arms open, almost resigned, and I also didn't understand—those sandwiches were amazing, by the way—how you could have feelings for someone so unstable? Only France seemed to get it. "Her beauty makes me forgive her everything," Niso added, and Rebecca seemed to decide not to dwell on it by throwing in his face that she was not perfect (wasn't she perfect?), but I was inclined to think there was another reason that had chained our Niso to Angelica: he glimpsed through that beauty and that lunacy a pain so human that it deeply upset him and left him hopelessly in love.

And just like that, Niso dropped out of sight. It was strange, it was cold, and we no longer saw him, her, Saba, or the fat-ass at the pool hall. Rebecca spent a lot of her nights studying, so that left France and me to challenge each other to very long and very boring games of pool, drink liters of beer at the usual bar, comment on the waitresses' tits, and go to the movies resting our boots on the back of the seats in front of us, munching on popcorn. Then, even France started thinking about the future and absconded to his house to study: I found myself alone.

I roamed around like a misfit, my hands in the pockets of my long black overcoat, I studied the footprints left by strangers in the snow, I studied the brightly lit shop windows already decorated for Christmas, I roamed around like a dog with no purpose, I looked up at the dark, starry sky and exhaled watching the chilly vapors of my breath evaporate in the air, I roamed around like a bum who hasn't got a penny to his name and who doesn't give a damn, I watched the swarm of Christmas shoppers in the streets, the first few wrapped gifts, and the salespeople in the stores. I lived with a feeling of alienation: in the middle of all these people, of all those things, I was the only one not doing what I should have been doing, the only one in contemplation instead of in action, and yet they were the ones who seemed strange to me. Nonetheless, the earlier contempt I had wallowed in, which made me feel different, wasn't there, and I scrutinized the strangers with a kind of affectionate melancholy, as if I were God. I stopped to sit on a wooden bench, and the women looked at me, perplexed. I felt the winter cold in my hair and in the dry skin of my chapped lips, which I couldn't stop licking, and in my ruby-colored knuckles, but I wasn't miserable. I liked following people, all fired up like in the night before a life-changing event, most of all, I liked being swallowed up by that immense sky, so perfect in its freezing coldness, challenged by the spruces' highest black branches. Then I felt like calling someone. Just like that, to share that feeling of mystery, of the infinite, maybe, of winter. Just like that, to drink a cognac. I felt like calling someone, but I didn't know whom.

"Hi."

She had sat down next to me with the lightness of a feather, I hadn't even realized she was there. Only her voice, reassuring. I turned my face, and we looked at each other as if we were the only ones on Earth. We looked at each other like two pen-pal lovers meeting for the first time, like two lonely souls who have put a marriage announcement in the newspaper. She was so beautiful.

So beautiful.

So beautiful.

I forgot that she was obviously unstable. Her hair jabbed at her face like bursting flames, her high and proud cheekbones gave her a regal self-assuredness, but the eyes—Christ, those eyes! —were permeated by the light of a summer dawn, a celestial splendor, a light-blue divinity, reason enough to say to hell with your businessman's life and become a poet. Only a poet could stand up to her, only a poet could challenge that beauty with the beauty of words, only Niso. I tried to remember that she was just a woman, that she was just plain neurotic, maybe even a witch, who had made my friend suffer—and I tried to not smell her skin or her perfume wafting into my nostrils and over my skin, I tried not to look at the stockinged back of her tiny foot dangling in a high-heeled shoe, I tried to rip my heart out and feed it to the roaches—and it wasn't easy, believe me.

I took out a pack of cigarettes and offered her one. The fact that I was not speaking and that I was only looking at her may have impressed her, but in reality I had to catch my breath and get my thoughts together. She asked me:

"Why all alone?"

"I like solitude."

"Me too."

"But people are not used to being alone, it makes them afraid, so when they see someone on their own, they ask *why all alone*? As if I saw someone surrounded by friends and asked *why all the friends*?"

She laughed. I was very happy. Then she turned serious. I was afraid she would savage me.

"The thing is it takes courage to be alone." She said emphatically.

"Sometimes more than to be with other people. To live among earthworms, vultures, scorpions, you need to be strong, believe me."

I bit my tongue. Holy shit, not that word! Holy shit, now she'll understand that Niso told me everything! Instead, she seemed only intent on continuing our impromptu conversation, "It's true you know! I always knew you had to be very deep."

At that time, the adjective *deep* was all the rage. People, movies, the whole world were judged based on two categories: *deep* and *superficial*. What *deep* and *superficial* meant is hard to say: happiness was superficial, of course, sadness and pessimism were deep, a good talk over world hunger was deep, deep was everything that was not tinged with laughter or jokes. It was a world sick with deepism. I hated the adjective *deep*.

And still, a slight caress strengthened my fatuous ego. I inhaled the cigarette smoke and for the first time in my life I felt deep.

I thought she was asking about Niso, but no, she just seemed interested in me.

"You know, I didn't like you much at the beginning . . ."

"Really?"

"Maybe you didn't like me much either . . ."

It was bizarre the way she spoke in the past tense, as if that unexpected encounter on a freezing-cold winter bench had changed, in a mere thirty seconds, the nature of all our relationships, as if she had erased Niso in the blink of an eye and I had arrived, all of a sudden likable and deep in my solitude. Things were happening way too fast, I realized. I should have told her: "Of course, I didn't like you, *I don't like you*," I should have told her: "You're so beautiful that it's hard not to hate you." But I knew that I had to feign an absolute indifference to her beauty, I mustn't let her perceive how flustered I was, discipline and a heart of ice, a cigarette in my mouth, puffing nonchalantly, she's nothing but a woman, she's nothing but an unstable doll!

"Look dear, it's nothing personal. It's just that I'm a bit disillusioned with other people. Maybe in the past you would have seen me always happy, but then people fuck you over, so you're a bit less happy, or you fake it because your friends, your mom, your dad, everybody wants you to be the way they demand you to be, and they don't know that behind the mask there is someone else, that maybe you don't always feel like laughing . . ." I tossed the cigarette butt in anger and looked at her. She looked at me and I felt like no other woman could ever admire me more, or even love me, like in that moment. I was twenty and a clown. In some part of my brain, I knew it was all a scene from a movie, all make-believe, my words, the cigarette butt, her eyes, mine. Somewhere. But then I started believing it, I started believing I was a solitary hero who found a way into the heart of the most beautiful woman in the world just by raising an eyebrow, and I was so full of myself, full of this intoxicating feeling, that I forgot how beautiful she was so that all the muscles and nerves in my body—shaken by her ferocious beauty up until ten seconds before—calmed down.

It was a miracle. I looked at her, stone cold. I gave her the hint of an ironic smile and patted her cheek. What I was able to do felt incredible. She grabbed my hand with both of hers and squeezed it against her cheek. She looked lovingly at me, in the same way she had looked at Niso five months before when he was reciting Baudelaire: I freed my hand from hers, looked down, a trifle embarrassed, and took out another cigarette. All of a sudden, I thought she wasn't the most beautiful woman in the world, she was as beautiful as many others, and I couldn't devote more than one night to her.

"Listen, Angelica, it's cold and I'd like something to drink. Do you want to keep me company?"

Her smile was radiant. She unwound her stockinged legs and got up. I observed her, as austere as a panther in her long overcoat, but for the first time in my life I didn't start fantasizing dirty scenarios at the first rustling of thighs, because the pleasure of walking arm in arm with her was too exquisite, as were the conspicuous looks from the women who passed us, the vulgar and envious grimaces of the men walking past us—the honor of being the only actor on stage with an ecstatic audience and with her, in the first row, applauding, moved by the monologue of a real man, was too powerful. It seemed impossible, but maybe more intense thrills than sex actually existed.

We went into a yellow and orange bar, with small round polished black marble tables, diffused lighting (even though it was barely seven o'clock), and jazz coming from the speakers. The bartender, a handsome guy with blue eyes and a horrible ponytail, looked at her from behind the bar with a mix of astonishment, regret, and nostalgia. He finished cleaning a glass and smiled his approval at me in some spirit of camaraderie. We sat down. I kept my black coat on because I liked the feeling of the upturned collar on my skin, and because I clearly gave the impression of someone who doesn't just stop anywhere. She, on the other hand, took off her coat, sat there in a garnet-colored little wool dress that warmed her fantastic body, and she crossed her legs sheathed in black tights. The handsome guy with the blue eyes came over right away, beaming like a TV host: he started reeling off everything they offered, I told him we just wanted to have a drink, I whispered Angelica's name almost as if there was a bond of extreme intimacy between us, and asked her what she wanted:

"Some white wine, thanks."

Very refined. Very smiling, sweet, excited. I was immensely gratified. The guys at the other tables looked at us like we were two aliens. The girls with their boyfriends scrutinized me in an unabashed and suggestive way that I had never experienced before. I couldn't figure out whether it was because I was accompanied by such a beautiful woman, or if her beauty in some way had fed my own and I had become irresistible. But I was tough. I let the envy of the posers bounce off me and didn't return a single look in the direction of my groupies. I was a contemptuous runway supermodel, and I said defiantly:

"A Jack Daniel's." The handsome guy didn't bat an eyelash and smiled as if I had complimented him.

Around the round small table, on the half-moon love seat, sat the crane and I. Who would have ever thought? And who would have ever thought that I would have to sit there, with my elbow on the tiny table and with my face resting on my hand, with the expression of a gangster, of someone who has ended up in such a spot by accident—and stay away from me, don't break my balls—while she seems all excited and devoted, intent on believing every increasingly stupid syllable I am inclined to proffer—tell me: who would have ever thought?

I would have. Duh, I knew everything from the beginning. I know women like the back of my hand, and nothing can ruffle my feathers. She seemed to read my mind:

"I think that nothing scares you, not even the devil."

I thought about Circe, and I saw myself groveling in the mud:

"What can the devil do to you that life cannot?"

She stared at me in all her beauty. I had a strong feeling that she was making fun of me and, suddenly, I felt ridiculous. She murmured:

"Listen . . . may I ask you something indiscrete?"

"You can *only* ask indiscrete questions," I whispered.

"Are you afraid of death?"

"I'm afraid of arrogance, violence, injustice, but not of death."

Uh huh! I should go into politics. When I grow up I should be a journalist, an entertainer, or a laundress.

"You see? . . . I couldn't stand this about Niso: he hated any mention of sorrow, of death . . . He used to say: "the less said the better."

The blue-eyed handsome guy came back and served us our whiskey and white wine. He was ruthless in his courtesy. Angelica stared into her wine glass in deep concentration, as if she were watching Niso drowning in it. What the crane obviously didn't know was that Niso had been thirteen when his older brother was killed in a motorcycle accident. We had only learned about it ourselves around six months ago from his mother—she assumed we already knew. Niso had berated her harshly and asked her why we needed to know; it made our blood run cold and that time I didn't even touch the sandwiches on the tray.

I was about to tell her, I wanted to tell her: let her blood run cold, too, and let her go back to Niso on bended knee to ask for his forgiveness, damned idiot of a girl. Instead, I felt sad, I felt a kind of nausea rising in my throat, I downed the whiskey, ravaging the roof of my mouth and my guts, I glanced at her with the first sincere look of the evening—but I didn't say a word. She murmured:

"Listen . . ."

"Mmmh . . ."

"It's a while now that I've been having a crazy idea . . ."

"Only one?"

"Yes, but I don't know if I can share it with you . . . but I'd like to."

She was flushed with excitement or embarrassment, eyes burning, almost drunk. She sipped the wine and licked her lips with her tongue:

"You mustn't think I'm crazy, you mustn't think I'm strange, even if in fact I am . . ." She was quiet for a minute, stared at me, and said:

"Do you feel like spending the night getting drunk in the graveyard?"

I looked at her closely. She had quite beautiful stockings. I would have screwed her on the spot.

7. December

The December sky was white, nothing new. As white as old women's cheeks, as the innocence of children, as the pope's barrage of blessings, white Christmas . . .

As for me, my coffee is on the nightstand, my mother counts the days until the first college exam, outside a deadly cold, and I lie naked under the duvet covering me up to my chin. The radio offers the latest rapper's latest hit, a Christmas song wondering "how can we get stuffed on panettone / when the hungry kids in Somalia, they've got none / how can we feel good / if the black kids ain't got no food"—and so on. My mother finally goes to work, worried because I am not acting like someone who is stressed out about studying. Beyond the window children scream and it smells like pine trees: me, I've already had my fill of melancholy.

Naturally, Angelica. Naturally, I don't remember anything but her velvety tights, and that demented idea of hers. A night in the graveyard. An inky-black night, her deathly pallor, the frightened, crazed look in her eyes. The silent smiling faces of the dead. Of course, I'm scared, death makes my blood run cold, if I scrape my knee I'm already set to write my will, death is *not* something normal. Neither is Angelica, as a matter of fact. Yet, her tight-fitting stockings are a reality, and those pointy titties are asking for satisfaction! But in a graveyard, among the darkness of the cypresses, among the coldness of the marble tombs . . .

"Are you excited?" she asked me.
"About what?"
She was wearing a dumb denim winter outfit, Austrian camper style, with an absurd multicolored heavy fleece jacket, Swiss mountain

climber style. A terribly sad look. I looked at her and started to think that I had no desire to kiss her or do anything else, and the night was freezing cold. I hadn't the slightest interest in slipping through the hole in the barbed-wire fence—that she evidently knew well—to go bust the balls of the dead.

But I couldn't back out. She went through first, crouching down and showing off under the rugged denim a behind drawn by Giotto. I followed her imagining that as soon as I poked my head out, she would decapitate me. But she didn't. She simply wasn't there.

My heart jumped in my throat, in front of a neat row of crypts and flickering flames, two glacial fingers caressed my face. The blood froze in my veins in the millisecond it took me to realize it was her, right beside me. She laughed. I swear I could have put an end to that laugh with a slap to her face. Maybe she picked that up, and she turned frightfully serious.

Slowly and silently, we ventured further into the quiet of the graveyard. Everything told me I should run away: the terribly perfect alignment of graves, one after the other, no deviation, no imprecision, the impenetrable darkness of the rows of cypresses, their deathly smell of dried fruit—not to mention the photographs on the headstones, disconcerting and mute living faces, radiant, naïve. As if they had been caught unawares. As if they hadn't known. As if one day they had gone to have their pictures taken and the one behind the camera had been the undertaker.

"Angelica . . ."

She was walking in front of me, but she didn't turn around.

"Angelica . . ."

Nothing. So, I uttered her name in a loud voice, a splinter in the silence. She stopped on her tracks and her head started to turn around, slowly, slowly, slowly. And then I saw her.

Her face had a deathly pallor. The moon lit it so as to show its deepest contours up to the depth of the icy whiteness of her eyeballs.

I said, "You look great in jeans."

She kept quiet. I thought I had ruined the ambience. I realized that irony was not a welcome guest around there. I thought a shiver traveled up my spine like a frozen worm when she looked at me that way, that maybe she was Death or one of Satan's disciples and that deep in the graveyard they may be getting ready to perform a rite in which I was the sacrificial lamb. She suddenly smiled and said:

"Thanks."

She seemed to know where to go. I just followed her, tightly gripping the neck of the lemon vodka bottle we had brought along, ready to smash it on the spirits' head. I was afraid. The chain of names of the dead on the headstones—date of birth and date of passing—the white crosses, the black alabaster, the gravel that crunched under our feet like the sound of crushing bones, everything made me anxious. But more than any of that, *she* did, the one whose face I couldn't see, only her hair was visible to me, motionless, like funereal spires. Then all of a sudden, she stopped in front of a grave.

"Here we are," she whispered, turning toward me with unusual slowness.

Here where? I asked, but she didn't reply, as if the answer were obvious, and I kept looking at her and wasn't paying any particular attention to the grave—a grave like all the others, I didn't see any difference—and I was looking at her to catch a glimpse of normalcy, a smile, a rational explanation to calm my frayed nerves. But nothing. She looked at me as if I should have understood something, as if I should have understood everything, but I couldn't understand what she wanted me to understand—and the night was black and freezing cold, and the wind howled eerily through the cypresses, and her dilated, dismayed pupils were fixed on me, and I looked down because they scared me, and my eyes fell on the headstone, on the dried flowers, on the inscription:

> HERE LIES NARCISO NARCISELLO
> WHO BELIEV'D HE WOULD LIVE FOREVER
> AND DIED SUDDENLY, THE UNFORTUNATE FELLOW

And I found it so surreal and funny that I became even more afraid because a joke in a graveyard is bloodcurdling, and then I looked up at the photograph, and I felt like an icy hand had touched my heart. Looking at me from the photograph were the smiling, ironic, gentle eyes . . . of Niso.

It wasn't him, of course. Niso was alive, and this was a grave. It was Narciso Narcisello. A handsome man. Someone who resembled Niso, at least in the night shadows, a forty-year-old Niso with a stronger jaw and a less unkempt beard. When I caught my breath once again and realized all of this, I finally calmed down. She sat on the grave, her back to the headstone, and I sat next to her.

"Now do you understand?"

No, but I was happy that her face was no longer possessed but just sad. I popped open the vodka and offered her some. She grabbed the bottle by the neck and brought it to her lips: two full, distinct swigs. Her eyes were about to tear up.

"He was my father."

Narciso Narcisello was her father??? Damn.

"I'm sorry."

"It must have been quite a shock for you, eh?"

And she smiled sweetly. Once again, she seemed beautiful, maybe without knowing it. She dried a tear, and she caressed me. I felt I had to be honest with her.

"Well, he looks a lot like Nino, damn . . ."

"Yeah."

"You must have thought you saw a ghost when you saw Niso . . ."

"A blow to my heart. And . . . my dad used to play pool, he would roll up his sleeves up to his elbows, he loved Baudelaire."

"He loved Baudelaire?"

"Yes . . . and I'm not sure if you remember the first time we met, when Saba and I came to you, but at a certain point Niso recited one of Baudelaire's poems. Do you remember?"

I replied, "*I adore you as much as the nocturnal vault*, of course, from *Fleurs du mal* . . . and to think that I taught him that one . . . if I hadn't, I would have spared you the shock, I'm sorry."

"Oh well, it was just the last straw: my God, I was so frightened that I felt like I was going to pass out when he recited that poem to me."

"That ill-mannered habit of reciting poetry. As if poetry were something to file away to impress the first girl who comes by. Poetry must be forgotten, must be burned, like all pleasure."

I took a sip of vodka, arrogant, steadfast, self-assured. I sensed a look of admiration from her. She stroked my skin again, and shivers ran down my spine. We talked about poetry, quietly whispering in the peaceful graveyard. There we were, sharing a new intimacy, chatting—and the night was splendid.

She told me about her father. He had died two years earlier; she had an immense admiration for him. He was handsome, he was invincible, he was strong, and he feared nothing. I was happy he was dead.

"At first, I was very attracted to Niso, and extremely frightened, like every girl is both attracted to and fearful of her father. Then I managed to separate the two of them—and I don't know if that was good or bad. Because initially I projected onto Niso all the passion I could not develop for my father, and, in doing so, I ascribed all my father's qualities to him. But then, the real Niso unconsciously showed his true colors, in a symbolic competition with my father . . . and he lost."

What an idiot.

Who is the incorrigible imbecile, with his framed degree hanging on his wall and his two-hundred-dollar sessions, that put all those nefarious ideas in your head? What utter trash of a pea brain can make a connection between a dead forty-year-old and a living twenty-year-old just because they have the same eyes and they both play pool? What abysmal ignorance allows you to rationalize and justify any tragic absurdity in life—a father's death, the end of an everlasting love—through a monstrous jungle of symbols, interpretations, and projections?

Pfff.

Instead, I said:

"Sure."

Then, after a couple of cigarettes, the bottle of vodka nearly empty, our asses frozen on the marble grave, and the sky even blacker than before, and the moon fully obscured, and a little drunk, we looked at one another, eyes into eyes, mouths into mouths. Even though she was utterly idiotic and was dressed like an American pioneer, she was still so beautiful, wasn't she? I had a feeling that the morbid atmosphere excited her; I could surely make something out of it, right? Well, let's go.

I got even closer to her, and her breath stank to high heaven. Christ, the same putrid breath of the priests in the confessional when as a kid I used to go tell them about my mischief. Breath like rotten liver, spoiled fish, of someone who is on a strict diet out of poverty or to maintain an enviable figure, and not even the vodka could take the edge off it. I kissed her, my mouth tensed up in disgust, holding my breath. Then I abandoned her closed eyelids and that horrible taste, and eagerly finished the vodka. I was looking at her ankles: she was wearing green woolen socks. My God . . .

"Let's go," I said. She seemed upset but didn't say anything and just kept on smiling, almost on cloud nine, almost happy.

The next day I woke up and knew I had to start studying.

From the day before only that taste of boiled liver lingered in my mouth, nothing more. I needed to reconsider some things. First of all, congrats to me for playing it so cool in the face of such beauty, able to seduce a perfect ten woman without batting an eye or bragging about it. Bravo. Secondly, she's nuts and that's the only reason I managed to seduce her. Yep . . .

Thirdly, the phone rang, and it was Saba.

"You impressed a certain someone, eh?"

I was flattered, and I wanted to feel her up.

"Well, it was a strange escapade . . . "

"I know everything."

"What do you know?"

"That it was a wonderful night, that you turned out to be fearless, that you talked like you had known each other forever, that you know how to be *very deep* when you talk about life and poetry and that, contrary to anyone else, you wanted only one kiss and nothing else. This shocked her and, truth be told, it shocked me too."

You have no idea.

But I was in seventh heaven: I went into the bathroom, stripped naked, and I felt that I was so handsome, courageous, and brilliant to be able to uncover the deepest truths regarding the human soul.

*

Two days after the night in the graveyard, Angelica called me, her voice shaking like a little girl's, but by this point I was tough. I agreed to meet her in the same bar as before, she looked incredible but still had that priest's breath: not to kiss her wasn't a choice, but she didn't know it, and she burned with desire for this incorruptible guy.

I was quite taken with my persona, walking around the city, and I felt like all the girls were watching me, desired me, and wanted to spend an unforgettable half-hour with me. There was just one problem: exams were fast approaching, and I didn't see the sense in studying.

Since the only thing I did at home was pretend, holding a book before my eyes to fool my mother, and spent the rest of my time lazing around the house, watching the Christmas festivities outside my window or myself in front of the mirror—I made the wise decision to go hide in the library.

Mestre's library was filled with dusty books catalogued on shelves and with dusty people catalogued in society. I sat down, with a sense of claustrophobia that choked me out, in front a fat girl wearing small round glasses, to my right a very tall guy with pimples and eyes that bulged out of their sockets, and to my left a laid-back guy, his hair parted on one side, betrayed by his sweat-soaked forehead. What kind of life did these people lead? Ugliness, sadness, and fatigue wrinkled their faces to the point of deforming them. I don't know if what they were studying was so horrible, but it had definitely damaged their skin, leaving them oily and blighted at twenty. They were all bent over their books, all bent over their lives, silently bearing the wait for a degree, a job, a bonus, a promotion, a pension, death: how was it possible that they weren't screaming at the top of their lungs? I felt a moment of desperation, because I didn't know how to escape from it all, so at least I escaped physically: I got up in a hurry without anyone noticing me or showing any sign of life, slipped between two rows of desks filled with people lost in their studies, and suddenly I saw Rebecca and France: their heads bent over their books, silent with their fists on their temples as if to contain their concentration, their mouths sullen and joyless. The relief of finding two partners in crime, two with whom I could share my discomfort, with whom I could have a drink and discuss frivolous things—the relief dissipated right away, and the feeling of being punched in the stomach was complete. Without anyone noticing, I took off.

I spent the following mornings gripped by a demon that crushed my heart. The fact was the others had already gotten on the train and left with the wind in their sails, as if trains were carried by the wind. The vagaries of life didn't seem to affect them. But I didn't want their train, I didn't want that life, so barren, so well planned. What did I want? The singing of the national anthem with me on the podium, the journalists waiting for me at the airport, the young girls tearing their hair out when I pass by. But how? I didn't know how to do anything; I wasn't a good soccer player, nor did I know how to sing or even recite a verse of poetry. And anyway, would it be enough? Satisfy me . . . nothing would ever be enough to satisfy me, thirsty as I was to put my life on par with my audacity, my unbridled ambition, my beauty, my intelligence—to give it a meaning, if it was true that I had a sense of meaning. Damn, I had a sense of meaning more than anyone else.

A few days before Christmas, Angelica called me, and I was astonished at how indifferent I felt, how I wasn't even thinking about the possibility of sleeping with her. The only thing I was interested in, if anything, was to walk around with her to have people take notice. So, I was almost excited to accept her invitation to have dinner with another couple our age.

"You'll like them, they're *special* . . ."

She always used the adjectives that I despised the most.

"What do you mean?"

"Well, her name is Marta, and she heads up a charitable organization, paints, writes poetry, sings in a chorus and is in her first year of Political Science."

"She must consider her life quite bleak to try to plug up all those holes so desperately."

"Nooo, quite the opposite! She's a person who keeps busy, who gets things done, she's someone who cultivates her own interests, she boldly takes a stand on the issues!"

"And him?"

"Ah, him . . . what a guy! His name is Michelangelo, but everyone calls him Micky. He's studying economics, he's in politics since he was thirteen, but he's not after power, he truly believes in the political process, he's an idealist, and I think his motives are admirable, don't you?"

I wondered if Angelica and this guy were romantically involved, there had to be some attraction between imbeciles. The only thing missing was the cherry on top:

"Ah, sorry . . . Would you mind if we went to the macrobiotic restaurant Food&Culture? You know, Marta and Micky are vegetarians."

I was happy, nothing better than spending an evening with three morons to put the oomph back into my life.

An unrelenting cold front loomed over the city, it was the Saturday before Christmas, the electrified crowds quivered through the bejeweled streets, and Angelica was magnificent: ruby lips, a black lace top coddling her delectable breasts, a smoky gray skirt tight at the waist that she tugged up to get into the car, providing me with a fleeting look at the embroidered top of her tights. Something to make you lose control but, instead, nothing: what's wrong? I asked myself perplexed, what's happening to you, you have an intoxicating woman in the throes of a winter chill that strikes her between the legs and makes her nipples as hard as frozen strawberries, a girl that would roll around naked with you in the snow and amongst the glaciers, and you're not turned on at all? For God's sake, you're really a bizarre specimen!

The macrobiotic restaurant was worse than I expected: wicker chairs, large plants in every corner, Zen music from the speakers, a frigid odor hovering between the smell of a gym and that of a hospital. The owner was a scrawny young guy, slightly stooped, with a placid smile and the eyes of a bishop, goateed, with sideburns as skinny as he, a baggy orange shirt with an oriental pendant around his neck, green-and-blue striped pants, and some kind of small Chinese slippers on his feet. Peace reigned in the bar but it reigned despotically. There was, I don't know, such arrogance in the way the menu was written on the blackboard: *soy steaks, fillets of wheat*, stuff like that. A sort of sarcasm I didn't quite get, as I didn't understand that slow and creepy music, that snobbish sense of order and silence, that expression of festive health nuts—not to mention the prices, which would have forced me to do overtime in passing out flyers, together with begging for Christmas donations from aunts and grandparents. But our guests were finally here in the flesh. Michelangelo, the precocious political economist, and Marta the poetic painter philanthropist, among other things, and here is the summary of that sordid evening.

Of course, I had my preconceptions. But then, when you get to know people, those preconceptions become principles: never have dinner with a vegetarian, for example. They were younger than me, but they already carried on them a cumbersome maturity. She was small and round, red-flushed cheeks, sky-blue eyes that measured each and every one of your gestures, and a short, upturned nose filled with freckles that sniffed inside your closets searching for skeletons. He was tall, definitely good-looking, decidedly better-looking than she was, with earnest green eyes and a sincerely fake smile, his hair parted on the side. If there's one thing that makes you shudder, it's when you realize that you've already been labeled, or rather you know that there's no way out, that there will never be anything between you and that it will be the last time you'll see each other—and yet, an atmosphere of friendship takes hold, kindness and celebration, as if that were the first day of a long fellowship.

"So, Ema. Angie told us that you're studying at Ca' Foscari . . ." *Ema*? He sounded just like a father-in-law.

"*Studying* is a big word."

He emitted a piercing laugh, like a squirrel. He stared me right in the eyes, but I think he was focusing on an imaginary dot in the middle of my forehead, like salesmen do when they want to make you feel uncomfortable. He hissed: "Anyway, today a degree is nothing more than a piece of paper, everyone knows, an admission ticket to the world of unemployment. After all, we're in Italy, right?"

"Sure."

"What a shitty country. Sometimes I'm ashamed of being Italian."

He shook his head, I think it was one of his favorite sentences, but evidently people usually supported him. My silence bothered him. Still staring me in the eyes, somewhat annoyed, he asked: "Aren't you?"

"Well, I'm all for the Independent Country of Mestre. A marvelous monarchy, obviously. With balls at the court and parades with elephants and majorettes. For a king, I would pick Ciccio Beon, a dirty, fat guy from my area, perennially drunk as well as a little mischievous. I could see him wearing a crown, it would suit him. I would be his steward."

Michelangelo smiled with a grunt, looked at the empty plate, and then he stared at me again as if to send me muted messages of scorn. Angelica, who seemed to nervously monitor every syllable, every single movement of mine, forced a laugh, but not Marta—she said: "What an oddball!"

The scrawny waiter wearing the Chinese slippers reappeared, Michelangelo took back control of the situation and, polite but cold, ordered green tea for everyone—"Is green tea okay with you, *Ema*?"

"No, I would like some Prosecco, thanks."

I perused the ridiculous menu, while my three fellow diners started to talk about corruption and other things. It was obvious that at that moment they were not saying anything for the sake of argument as much as to display right away their credentials to me, the stranger, so as to show me immediately who they were, what they did, what they were made of. It was interesting to me how they had a visceral need to let me know that they were *intelligent*, even though we had never met before and might never meet again; I had to get the maximum amount of information on their ideas, their thoughts, their activities. I was certain that they did all those things—from politics to charity—not so much out of sincere interest but because they believed that these pursuits cast them as captivating and prestigious in the eyes of any stranger dining with them at a macrobiotic restaurant.

It must be said that during that time in some part of the world another war had broken out. Someone had snatched up a piece of land from someone else, claiming that it was rightly theirs due to some ancient tradition. Another side had said *oh no* and massacred them, and a third party had come to the aid of the first ones and massacred the second ones. The usual things. Naturally, as in every war, media channels and newspapers showed pictures of butchered bodies, screeching mothers racked with pain and children looking for their fathers in the debris. Journalists put on their saddest faces (although the number of readers and viewers had tripled during the conflict), and TV newscasters, before beginning their entertainment programming, confessed to the camera that it wasn't easy to smile and pretend that the war didn't affect them, to stay calm in front of an audience that was, at that very moment, living the tragedy of war—as if every day, every hour, they didn't appear happy or didn't joke before an audience who, taken individually, might have lost a loved one or received the news they had a month left to live or had experienced a personal tragedy more terrible than the tragedy that, however collectively horrifying, was far away and someone else's problem. The fact is that even an immense tragedy like war, when it doesn't affect us directly, is less important than our ingrown toenail, so that it easily becomes a way to incite our vanity. One of those showmen said on stage that "no one wins in a war; everyone loses" and the public applauded him in tears, in an orgasm of noble feelings, and they both felt shivers up and down their spine by sharing so deeply their concerns about the ultimate catastrophe for humanity, and no one dared contest or rationally discuss that sentence, because it would have weakened the emotion, that extraordinary feeling of belonging and fraternity we experience when we are a crowd controlled by an enormous single heart: like going to a rock concert raising your fist in the air mimicking the singer, like laughing at the comedian's subtle joke we don't get, like looking at images of black kids with swollen stomachs crawling with flies, before the commercials start.

Michelangelo said: "We're organizing a concert for peace. We're inviting all the bands in the city, and everyone must come—because we need to raise awareness, we need to stimulate people's consciences."

The sky-blue eyes of the benefactress Marta sparkled, while I pondered that there's no word more racist, despicable, and offensive than *people*.

"We must show our disapproval of the war, we must tell the world that we don't agree, that war is a disgrace! It's the only thing we can do!" The almost furious old Micky pointed out. I had had enough of those two know-it-alls who were convinced they were geniuses because they had intuited that war was bad and that it was necessary to tell it to everyone who hadn't figured it out yet: "Listen, asshole, it's not the only thing to be done, quite the opposite: it's the only thing that shouldn't be done."

There was a glacial moment, the pudgy girl with the sky-blue cat's eyes turned crimson right down to her toes, Angelica lowered her eyes without uttering a word, old Micky's throne had been swiped away from under his ass, and he found himself on the floor babbling: "But . . . but . . . how dare you . . . he's crazy . . . he's a psycho . . ." and laughed hysterically like a drunken whore, looking for support in Marta's and Angelica's eyes.

I guzzled a third glass of wine and said: "Calm down. I didn't want to call you an asshole. But you just are one. Only an asshole could think that some rinky-dink concert featuring provincial rock bands would be useful, except to titillate his own puckered asshole. And this is shameful, because war is death, and you don't play with death, you need to take it down a notch. If war is such an important issue to you, stop broadcasting it from your soapbox in a macrobiotic restaurant with your ass nice and warm and your mouth stuffed with cabbage. Go there as a volunteer nurse and risk your neck to try and save the wounded. Some do, and they do it without fanfare, without parades, processions or demonstrations put in place just to scream NO WAR together so as to ease their conscience." Here I got a little choked up, and I felt like going to the bathroom to cry. But by this point the damage was done, a pernicious and destructive rage was running through my body, and I wanted to unleash it all on this Michelangelo, with his sneers and snickering laugh, shaking his head like a horse, who meant to sound sarcastic and scornful with his comments: "That's it . . . that's how people think . . . it's incredible . . ."

His girlfriend hated me, but she didn't lose her cool, not even for a minute.

I lit a cigarette and kept going:

"Some other possibilities for you: one is to send all of your savings to help those afflicted by the war, and anyway if you are used to spending your money eating this soy slop or organizing concerts with sweaty, pimply twenty-year-olds who strum their guitars, shoot up, and scream that *they* are against all wars, you're truly not losing anything if you break your piggy bank! Then, you can pray. Who knows, maybe God is listening."

The atheist Micky laughed contemptuously.

"If everyone were like you . . ."

"There would be more cowards and less hypocrites."

"Ah, so you know that you are a coward . . ."

He wanted to punch me, he wanted to kill me, he wanted to see me blown up by a land mine. On the other hand, satisfied and freed from any bitterness, I felt like hugging him.

At that point something strange happened. Angelica smiled tenderly at me. Her friends got up in a hurry to show all their contempt for me and to make it obvious that the meal was now over. They blurted out something nasty about my lack of good manners and said goodbye to Angelica, feeling sorry for her, but Angelica barely paid attention to them. We were left alone.

I looked at her, embarrassed, feeling guilty. Sorry, I don't like drama, sorry, I'm going through a stressful time, sorry, I let myself get dragged . . .

But she said nothing, then said:

"You were amazing . . ."

I stood there petrified. She was assessing me, and I felt like a hero.

"You were amazing . . . in less than a minute you showed their true colors . . . how I wish I had your wisdom!"

I looked at her with gratitude. Yes, I was wise. Yes, no one can make a fool out of me: thanks for noticing. I wanted to feel her up between her legs to show her my sympathy, but she wanted to be kissed. Casting aside my scruples, I kissed her and kissed her again.

Christmas Eve night. My parents had gone to celebrate in the mountains, leaving me all alone, but being alone was the only consolation for a future that, more than ever, seemed off. My friends were spending time with their families, some happy, some not so much, nevertheless, they all had the same goal on their minds, the first college exam, an impending target since February was fast approaching: they needed to rev up their engines, and that night was the last chance to relax before the final rush. I wasn't so sure. I turned off all the lights in the house except those in the *presepio* and on my knees on the couch in the living room near the window, I looked outside. The night sky was large, immense, mystical.

Through the glowing windows, I saw cheerful families finishing their dinners in brightly lit houses, probably starting to unwrap the presents under the tree or playing bingo, waiting to go to Mass. The phone rang, my parents wanting to wish me all the best, a little emotional due to the distance between us and feeling bad that I hadn't wanted to go with them. Yes, mom I'm fine, yes mom I'm happy, I reassured her. All in all, it was true, besides I had my glass of Johnny Walker in my hand. I was drinking like a seasoned drinker, and to hell with the future.

Then, around ten o'clock, the phone rang again. It was her. She asked me if I wanted to go out. I asked her if she wanted to come over, since I was alone. She said okay, and I felt something stirring in my crotch. She showed up wearing a long black coat, a long black woolen dress covered in buttons from head to toe, high heels, and stockings with the seam in the back. She wanted to kiss me right away (this insane fixation) and, in spite of myself, I kissed her. When I managed to break away, I couldn't help asking her: "Excuse me, but what diet are you on?"

"Why?" She asked me, alarmed, as I told her to get comfortable in the living room.

"Just because. I know at times you do some modeling, I figured you must be on some kind of diet . . . "

"Mineral water in the morning, a green salad, no dressing, for lunch, and an apple, vegetable soup, or plain rice, and a quarter pound of white meat for dinner."

I looked at her and started to figure out why sometimes she was sad, sometimes hysterical, sometimes depressed.

"Well, I'm warning you that tonight you're off that diet."

"No, come on, I can't . . ."

"For now, just get comfortable on the sofa, take your shoes off, stretch your legs out on the ottoman, take one of those magazines, and be quiet."

She slipped off her shoes, placed her sheathed black feet on the ottoman, and grabbed a fashion magazine from the wicker basket beside the sofa. She looked at me like a happy woman, and I ran away into the kitchen.

I yanked the fridge doors open with renewed pleasure. I grabbed an enormous eggplant, purple, juicy, shaped like the Sultan of Brunei. I sliced it with the precision of a schoolboy into beautiful, round, uniform slices, floured them, sank them into a pair of beaten eggs, dipped them in bread crumbs, and fried them in the olive oil that I had already heated on the first burner; on the second burner, in a pot with two fingers of sesame oil, I emptied half a family-size package of frozen French fries; meanwhile, on the third burner I had toasted a few slices of bread and spread butter and salmon roe on them. I entered the living room with three trays emanating the strongest aromas, contrasting and sacrilegious: she burst out laughing like crazy.

"Sit and eat," I ordered.

"But . . ."

"Eat."

She slid off the couch like a playful pussycat, biting her lip, and grabbed a still-steaming slice of eggplant and popped it in her mouth. It must have felt like heaven to her. Then, she took a roe canapé and let it dissolve on her tongue, slowly biting into it, taking her time, savoring the taste from the tip of her tongue to the back of her throat. I grabbed a handful of crunchy French fries and swallowed them. She imitated me. We looked at each other in silence, our mouths full, our taste buds skittering euphorically. I poured her some red wine. She guzzled it, and from the sides of her mouth Dionysian rivulets ran down to her chin. I took another canapé and brought it to the side of her mouth: she devoured it. Then, the joy of tasting became appetite, then hunger. She started to eat and drink, drink and eat, she wolfed down everything—and there was a lot—meanwhile I had returned to the kitchen where I was heating up the leftovers of a meat pie cooked by none other than my father. I went back to the living room holding the casserole high in front of me like a priest showing a saint's relics to the faithful.

"I can't," she said, tears in her eyes.

"Eat."

She ate. She drank. She ate. She got up to kiss me, she had already undone the last buttons of her long dress and I saw her thighs. I moved her away from me and made her sit down again.

She was drunk, sated, happy.

Back in the kitchen, I looked in the fridge to see what else there was, my mother's meatballs. I fried them, I left half of them plain, the other half I plopped into some tomato sauce. She must have already digested the rest, because she devoured them with the joy of a pregnant lioness and finished off the bottle of wine. I observed her with my elbows on the coffee table and my hands clasped, and finally she seemed like a normal person. She even managed to find space for a slice of chocolate cake and, licking her fingers like a little girl, she said: "This is the best Christmas of my life."

I got up from the table and offered her my hand. She took it, and suddenly she was a little girl, or suddenly I was a man. We went into my bedroom, softly lit by the huge moon just outside the window, and I made her stretch out on the bed. She was long, soft, and relaxed. I knelt down next to the bed close to her face, and although I had no particular desire to, I knew that kissing her was the right thing to do. I kissed her. Finally, she had the taste of a human being, the flavor, with even some tiny spheres of roe lodged in her teeth, but God, it was the mouth of a woman. She locked her arms around my neck and seemed to be burning with passion, her fingernails traced circles through my hair, her tongue appeared desperate, possessed, thick with saliva. I started to undo her dress. She helped me slip it off, as she stared at me, sizzling with fear and desire, or at least that's what it felt like. I peeled off her tights, she arched her whole body back, and I could see up close the wonderful firmness of her skin and muscles: there she was, in black underwear and a lace bra. She remained motionless, a finger in her mouth, her eyes closed, in the penumbra of the bedroom. I wasn't full of passion, at least not like she seemed to be. Maybe I couldn't come to grips with it, I couldn't feel it, it was as if it were a movie that was erotic but also comical, as if that guy wasn't me but my body double. And yet she was breathtaking, I kept on telling myself, and I would have yanked her underwear off, unhooked her bra, and she would have been naked, naked for me, a slut for me. I told myself these things but I just couldn't convince myself.

Then she was naked.

I unbuckled my belt and pushed my jeans down to my knees, but then I thought I had to show her I was the perfect lover, so I started to kiss her ankles with enticing finesse, then her knees, then her inner thighs, and her breathing was heavy in the dark, hence, I thought it was time that I lay myself down on her body and do it. But, while I was trying to free myself as fast as possible of all that surplus, the shirt, the pants, the boxers, the socks, she whispered that she needed to tell me something, I asked her what, she said *something*, okay but what, you didn't get it yet, no, I didn't get it—I'm a virgin.

Mmmh . . .

I got nervous. Also, because I wasn't much of an expert. Also, because I didn't feel like doing it; as a matter of fact, I would have been happy with trying some other things. But I couldn't give up such a prey, just going all the way with her, in my eyes, would have conferred me international prestige. And she wanted it, she expected someone like me to be an insatiable lover. Passionate. Temperamental. And I blindly believed that you can never forget your first love: upon leaving her, she would have cried for me forever, and the idea of her tears excited me, and the thought that the pain she would feel for me would be everlasting filled me with pride. I basked in the vision of her confiding in Saba, and telling her, grief-stricken, what an exceptional lover I was.

"Don't worry . . ." I whispered, with a lump in my throat, laying myself down naked on top of her.

"But . . . you're not using protection . . ."

"Don't worry . . ."

"But are you sure . . ."

The anxiety in her voice was testing my patience even more, I wanted to do it in a hurry but I mustn't do it in a hurry, and meanwhile, with one hand I was trying to caress her face—tense, spasmodically waiting, with her eyes tightly shut—while with the other hand I looked for the right spot. I slammed against a wall. I tried to make my way through with my fingers. But everything was dry and rough, as stiff as a frozen cod waiting for the harpoon, I wriggled out of her arms and slid down to lick her with all the saliva in my mouth. I think she was enjoying it and that it could have been enough for her because she started to arch herself sensually into my mouth, she grabbed my face with both hands and pulled it in as if she wanted to put it inside of her. And I was happy with my face utterly drenched in her juices and a few tiny pubic hairs stuck between my teeth, and down there below I was all self-confidence, which reminded me that my duty was another one—I traveled up her body with my mouth, kissing her stomach, then her breasts, her neck, behind her ears at the hair roots, as my hand searched for that opening—and I went in. A short distinct shriek pierced my eardrums. I stopped for a second, she didn't budge, a frosty silence. Then, I started to penetrate her again, slowly, even though her face was turned to the side and she was clenching her teeth on the pillow while a whiny whisper emerged from her mouth. I thrust all the way in and felt myself swelling inside her, I pulled almost all the way out and entered her again, once more, again and again, as her tense face began to relax and her plaintive moaning transformed itself into a softer and richer sound. And I went in and out staring at her face covered in sweat, her eyes now barely open, her mouth no longer tearing at the pillow but ajar and wet with saliva, she turned and looked at me, she looked at me as if she had seen a ghost, she looked at me terrified and adoring, and screamed oh my love, oh my love! She seemed emphatic even then, as if she was always acting on stage, and I increased my rhythm, more and more frenetic, more and more violent, and I felt I could last forever. I was tired, and I was a barrel of whiskey swaying on the body of a beautiful madwoman, and I had been great, and people would point at me on the street and would call me Latin Lover, but enough of that. I thought about her tights, her underwear, about France's fantasy when he had pictured her naked in the restroom with the pool cue in her hand, I thought about my trusty companion inside of her, and finally I felt a river of incandescent lava build up inside me—I pulled out fast, she whimpered "AH!" as my semen sprayed all over her stomach up to her young breasts.

 Satisfied, I surrendered myself on top of her.

*

Almost two minutes went by, exhausted and limp I was starting to doze off on top of her, when I heard her say "Oh God . . . " She pushed me off her with all her strength, throwing me off the bed, and she rushed into the bathroom like a madwoman holding her mouth with her hands. Slowly, stunned, I followed her. She was on her knees, her hands stretched out onto the toilet seat, gripping it as if trying to keep it from moving, throwing up all she had. A rivulet of blood flowed from her groin, an ivory droplet dripped from one breast, and, kneeling, she vomited. I held her forehead from behind, to help her. I thought she was done, so I flushed the toilet and stroked her hair. She looked up at me, tears welling up in her eyes from the effort, and she smiled. She was gorgeous. She got up, we looked at each other, stark naked in my bathroom on that momentous night, and we heard the church bells ring.

"Merry Christmas" I said. She burst out laughing and hugged me. Then, she rinsed her mouth and squeezed a bit of toothpaste on her finger, and she brushed her teeth. She spread her legs over the bidet and meticulously washed herself. I observed her, sitting on the edge of the bathtub. I asked her:

"Do you have to go home?"

"No, I want to sleep with you . . ." and she turned her face to see my reaction. I was tired and the idea of sleeping with her, maybe wrapped around my neck, didn't excite me. I had never slept through the night with a girl, and, at the time, I thought I would only sleep with the girl I loved. The fact was I couldn't really say no to her. But it couldn't happen in my bed, because Angelica started to throw up again—so we spent the entire night on the little white rug covered by a blanket, she lay with her head in my lap while her long legs hugged the bidet, and I was stretched out perpendicular to her, with my head between the toilet and the bathtub. We spent a whole night chatting about everything and barely sleeping, waking up to help her vomit—and so on, amongst laughs, amusements, and gastric juices in my bathroom, the night of the Holy Christmas.

8. January

A disco. Smoke, psychedelic lights, shouting and yelling. It's almost midnight and soon we'll be celebrating, but where has he gone? Hot as hell, people sweating all over her, but Angelica's eyes search everywhere and don't see him—where is he?

Finally, she notices her rival, Rebecca, sensually swaying on the dance floor with her friend France, so she approaches them and asks if they have seen him. Rebecca shrugs her shoulders, France shrugs his shoulders, she doesn't think it's a good idea to ask Niso, who stands there next to a black rubber rail sipping a drink, melancholic.

Then at last, she sees Alcapone at the bar. She makes a beeline toward him through the crowd (drunk, vulgar, gasping) and joins him. Have you seen him? No. And Saba? I lost her, replies the simpleton. A shard of light pierces her brain, no, it can't be—and if it were? Alcapone obviously doesn't suspect anything, but she knows, Saba has told her everything.

Panic in her eyes. No, what am I thinking, he loves me. Even if he has never said it to me, I still know. I understood it from many little things, from how he made dinner for me on Christmas, from how he took care of me when I was sick, from how he . . .

She moved away from Alcapone, but he followed her. She pushed her way through the crowd, and it was only a minute to midnight, Alcapone followed her like an obese Hindu servant, he followed her, but he didn't understand—but even he figured out that it was almost midnight and his little Saba wasn't there to celebrate with him, where could she have gone?

She went down to the restrooms, shoving aside strangers and hordes of smokers and gin drinkers, ten . . . nine . . . eight, the unsuspecting elephant trailing behind her, followed by Rebecca and

France and Niso, all driven by curiosity, seven . . . six . . . five . . . , the door of one of the stalls was suddenly flung open, and the mask of death appeared on her face.

Alcapone, mouth wide-open, the sound of a broken heart.

Rebecca, mouth wide-open and a twinge of disgust in her eyes.

France, mouth wide-open, and Niso, with a smile.

I was caught with my pants down in front of the whole gang, as I was adjusting my belt with a certain awkwardness, I felt Saba behind me mumble a *no*! desperate, four . . . three . . . two . . . ONE . . . HAPPY NEW YEAR!!!!!!!

The roar of celebration, four mouths with no words, and a smirk that rekindled my affection for Niso; Saba, still half naked, terrorized, staring at Angelica, begging for forgiveness; Alcapone muttering something like *bastard, you're such a bastard*; and me, with my face like an old drunk, what could I say? I said:

"Happy New Year!"

The truth is I didn't care about anything anymore. A half-hour before, suffocated by the insufferable cluster of beasts reveling in their fabricated happiness and flailing around to the rhythm of hideous sounds, embarrassed by Angelica's hugs and kisses right in front of Niso, shocked that those black-clad thighs could only trigger in me a sense of dread, I had searched for solace in the cocktails of a sad and sweaty bartender. But the alcohol had only intensified that grisly, gnawing sensation in my throat, an emptiness that expanded to the point of tearing me apart, the desperation engendered in me by the obscene amassing of drunken bodies venturing awkward dance steps each in their own minuscule space, that desperate attempt at happiness, at being something, the infinite vanity of it all. I saw Saba all by herself, going toward the restrooms, and in a split second I grabbed hold of her and suggested a rendezvous in the bathroom.

"WHAT?" She screamed. Not that she was shocked, she just hadn't heard me.

I took her by the arms and stared at her:

"LET'S FUCK!"

She laughed.

"PLEASE!"

It wasn't passion that drove me, I knew that; if anything quite the opposite, if anything the sudden need to imitate a certain model of perversion or self-destruction, to feel damned, to feel alive among that horrid clot of nobodies (besides the regret of having spent all the Christmas money from grandma just to dive into that sewer), and Saba's face (maybe for similar reasons) lit up, and she led the way, after making sure our friends were distracted. We snuck in, first she then I, into that fetid bathroom stall, without anyone noticing us, not that we cared. I pounced on her like a starving tiger, I grabbed her by the hair, pulling at the roots, "AH!" She shrieked, I bit her cheeks, "You're going to leave marks, please!" She undid my belt and squeezed my cock, I pulled her skirt up, I had a lump in my throat like a soldier coming back from war, I felt like crying, I was full of raging tears, deeply pained, I pulled down her tights together with her underwear, and I sank my fingernails into the flesh of her ass, "AH! Hurry up, please!" I bit her neck, I wanted to taste her blood, she grabbed my cock and tried to put it inside her, but it was quite complicated, my jeans were stuck around my knees, her tights and underwear were barely pulled down past her thighs, some things only happen in American movies. I figured I must take off her tights and everything else, but she also had boots on, dammit, take it all off, I told her, "But we don't have time, we don't have time," "Then, blow me!!!" I implored her, desperate, and so she did get down on her knees, but my passion immediately evaporated and a quiet sadness seized me again, bobbing between my throat and my mouth. Forget it, I said softly, let's get dressed, and right then our jolly gang of friends came in.

Alcapone shoved Angelica out of his way and tried to punch me, but I dodged it, so that he stumbled into the stall and fell on top of Saba, who was crying and trying to calm him down, he trashed around like a plump tarantula. I stared at him, dazed. Then, all of a sudden, they were crying and hugging as they closed the stall door, obviously to patch things up.

"Well, let's hope they can talk it out," I said, to dial down the drama hanging in the air, but no one could hear a word—a party outside and a chill there inside.

Angelica stood there like a corpse, her eyes planted on me, full of disgust, helpless. It was embarrassing. France drifted off. Niso winked at me and turned around. Rebecca stayed behind, she would have killed me:

"My God, you're so pathetic."

Then, unexpectedly, she hugged Angelica, and Angelica buried her head in her chest, exploding into hysterical tears, while Rebecca kept on contorting her mouth to show me all her bilious contempt. They left arm-in-arm.

I looked around. I was the only one left. Everyone was celebrating outside. I put my ear on the door of the stall where the two lovebirds had sought refuge, and I eavesdropped on tears and kisses, sobs and promises: *why did you do it*, I don't know why, *why did you do it*, but I love only you, *why why why*, I felt a little neglected lately, *but if you are my life*, yes but a woman needs to feel it, *oh God, from now on I won't leave you for a minute*, are you sure? *I swear!* You won't think only about pool? *I swear!* And tears and kisses, and sobs and promises. Pfff. I lit a cigarette. Another year down the drain. I studied the smoke rising in the air dissipate among the mirrors of that damned bathroom. I didn't care at all.

The truth is I did feel quite pathetic. But not for the reasons that Rebecca had implied. Not because I had been caught with my pants down on New Year's Eve with Alcapone's girlfriend instead of spending the evening with that idiot Angelica, who had stuck to me like a leech since Christmas, just because I had made her eat and made her vomit.

No, the truth is that I felt pathetic, *like* them.

The only difference is that they didn't know it, seizing in the seriousness and rectitude of their own existence the distance between my sleaziness and their non-sleaziness. All of them were happy to have set a goal for themselves, or in any case, scattered here and there core values that gave meaning to their lives. France, his degree and his sense of honor and friendship; Rebecca, her degree, and a sudden ethical code; Alcapone, his degree and his love for Saba; Saba her diploma and her charity love for Alcapone; Angelica, her diploma, the memory of her father, me. But did it take so much to decipher that what didn't make them as pathetic as me was nothing but ghosts and laughable masks? That if the goal of life is death, in other words nothing, then any goal in life is useless, nonsense, nothing? It doesn't matter, you just have to believe, you just have to delude yourself, you just have to convince yourself that life is a serious, concrete, important thing—and this illusion made them much less pathetic than me. They all had something to live for, except me, and I thought they were so ridiculous! Working so hard to forget that there's no point—I thought they were so pathetic!

Maybe Niso, maybe Niso eluded this impression I had, but I didn't know why yet. Whatever Niso did, he remained detached, calculating, nonchalant. Had a woman thrust a dagger through his heart? Okay, it's alright, no problem. He had yanked it out and tossed it aside. Two days before that New Year's Eve, I had felt compelled to call and tell him about Angelica and me:

"It was just one of those things, old friend . . . she fell in my lap . . . she's nuts."

"But there's a method to her madness," he said, and I had no idea what he was talking about.

"Right . . . anyway, you're not pissed at me?"

"Are you kidding? There is a subtle enjoyment in all of this. Each day I lived to the beat of her batting eyelashes. I followed her like some kind of derelict, I suffered like a pig at the sight of the slaughterhouse, but it allowed me to discover unexpected adjectives, excruciating semicolons."

"Did you write a lot of poems?"

"One. But when I finished it, this happened: deep inside me the old passion faded away, and a new desire hatched, to see her keel over and to dance on her naked body. It's the first time ever in my life that I hate someone, and I hope that this feeling will never abandon me: I could live without love, but hatred adds a sense of competition to my life. The fantasy of getting revenge is intoxicating. And you will be the instrument of that revenge."

"Me?"

"Well, who better than you is capable of humiliating her? She is probably convinced that you're just another fish caught in the net, quivering in agony at her feet . . . because in her arrogance, she is sure that you're no match for her."

Anger grew inside me. I thought about her naked body, about her breasts, about her flashy stockings—angrily. Niso went on:

"The more I think about it the more I'm convinced that you're the only one that can knock her off her pedestal into the dirt. As a matter of fact, I think I'm really going to get a kick out of celebrating New Year's."

On January third (at three o'clock in the afternoon), I was alone on my bed smoking a cigarette while watching my favorite soap opera. The telephone rang. Angelica's voice sounded like it came from the grave. Cold as marble, she asked me if I planned to apologize to her.

"No, *you* should apologize to me for calling at the exact moment that John learns Sheila is his daughter and not Peter's, who is his son instead, so that not only is he not a grandfather, but he's an incestuous pervert—meanwhile, Peter realizes that he's screwed his mother Barbara, as he was in love with his sister whom he thought was his daughter."

"What the hell are you talking about?" And she burst into tears. I felt gratified. These women who cry over me. These women who are consumed with me. Come on, I said, don't be like that, look, this is me, you can't muzzle me, or lasso me . . . I looked at myself in the mirror while her sobs caressed me, and I started flexing. I was really handsome. I was truly a tough guy. No joking: I was Paul Newman.

This was how the days in January went by, so very quickly, between terrifying moments when everything seemed useless, in vain, pathetic, I most of all—and moments when a woman making eye contact or the way I sipped my whiskey sent shivers of excitement through my veins, because the world is a filthy place, I knew that already, life was vacuous but I was still living mine. I am a womanizer with a heart as cold as ice, but in my eyes, the light of genius burns bright, women want me, but I will never stop. Relief can only be found on the run.

I thought I would never see her again, but I was wrong.

"I'm in love with you," she told me. "It's not my fault," I said. There was a deliberate meanness in my words because I knew that whatever I said to her, she would stay there at the table of our usual neon-lit bar looking at me out of her wounded animal eyes. One night, we went to a gospel show led by a Black reverend decked out like a jazzman who bounced between preaching and singing the blues. I had less than a month before my first exam, outside it was cold as hell, and everyone was jumping out of their seats, flapping around, flaunting an irresistible happiness—*Oh Happy Day* . . .

The sweaty, frizzy hair of the preacher shimmered in the spotlight, everyone was clapping along, Angelica beside me in her gray outfit clapping as well. I was also clapping my hands so as not to appear shy, and I felt like an idiot. All that was needed was a sing-along—that's it—and everyone seemed happy. But my world was collapsing onto me. Angelica looked at me and sighed:

"Black people sure have rhythm in their blood!"

"So do the Swiss."

My mother looked at me while putting on a skirt over her pantyhose. I was lying on the bed staring at the ceiling:

"So, are you ready for the exam or not?'

"Mom, exams never end."

"You're only twenty, you smoke, you drink, and you play pool like an old man. Try to give some meaning to your life."

Ah, uncouth mother: you strike where it hurts, and you don't even know it.

"You haven't done a thing since June, you come home at three in the morning and wake up at eleven while your dad and I are killing ourselves with work, I just hoped you had a shred of dignity . . ."

"Mom, college is like this."

"I don't think your friends are living the good life like you, but we're pretty close to the moment of truth, we'll see."

"Mom, you're talking like a mafia boss."

"In any case, if you have so much time on your hands, can't you get a part-time job? Or do you think we're going to support you for the rest of your life?"

"Okay, okay, just don't put a dead horse's head in my bed."

*

We went to the movies, Angelica in a miniskirt, I in the comfort of the room's darkness. Almost as an act of duty, I placed my hand between her thighs, the fingertips dragging on the nylon of her stockings. She whispered:

"Everyone's watching us."

"Let's hope so."

"But I'm ashamed."

"God, you're so boring! You're boring me to death. Like a debate on junkies. Like an art exhibition. You're as boring as a convention, a conference, a rock concert. You're as boring as an Italian movie. You're as boring as a rainy Sunday, tea with sugar, a boat ride . . . "

She was staring at me, appalled. Her eyes, two gelatinous crystals. I was kidding, come on, a little sense of humor, girl, or life will truly turn sour! I stroked her face. She lit up like a little girl taken for a ride on a merry-go-round (as boring as a merry-go-round).

She put her head on my shoulder. Stunned, I stood there. This woman felt for me the same affection I didn't feel for myself. It was weird. Really weird. Her hair smelled of green apples, tickled my neck, but it didn't trigger any fond memories, it no longer brought on those moments of instant happiness that I used to feel sniffing other worlds within a scent. I smelled her hair but felt nothing, it was as if my nares registered that smell and filed it away in a closet for future use. And that trusting gesture—did it move me, did it turn me on? And those hands devoid of rings, white and innocent, that looked for mine, and those thighs so splendidly intertwined? How could I not get any satisfaction, not even the satisfaction of vanity, from the fact that a woman of unmatched beauty loved me? It was as if she loved someone else, someone with my features, of course, but whom I no longer recognized, whom I didn't even know, someone with my name and at this point—probably—even my soul, someone who, in some place in space and time, is as happy as a lark with this cute little head that smells of green apples, with these astonishing legs, with this affection—ah, how I envy you! Wherever you are, in a parallel galaxy, in a fantasy from a few months ago (when just the thought of my fingers grazing her skin electrified my flesh and blood), or simply in the future, when maybe I'll recognize you and make you mine once again, your soul and my name will be reunited, and then I'll finally feel, with sorrow or regret or nostalgia, the sweetness of that cute little head, the springtime freshness of her hair, her life, her love.

When I realized I would never be able to make up for the time lost and thus would not be able to take my first exam, I despaired. The days were crumbling away, and I had no more chances. I found myself alone, at the pool table, at five in the afternoon, at the end of January. The beer foam had left a white mustache above my mouth. I looked at the green felt, and with one hand I threw the cue ball toward the left bank, it rebounded toward the middle bank, bounced off the right bank, and came back to me. Then I started it all over again. A game for the depressed. The beer tasted like failure, the double failure of someone who hadn't even tried.

Then she showed up with her Mohican scout look, with her vampiric high heels. I wanted to be alone, it's not nice to share your personal failures with other people, and yet seeing her comforted me. Maybe I wasn't so bad after all if such a beautiful woman loved me. Okay, she's nuts. Okay, she's an orphan. But still . . .

"How'd you find me?" Not taking my eyes off the pool table.

"You weren't at home, you weren't drinking at the Ravenous Python, you weren't stuffing yourself with sandwiches at the Jealous Locust or eating fried fish at the Snobby Sardine . . ."

"So now you're stalking me?"

"Well . . . let's say I've been observing you." She was smiling, smiling, relaxed, and pure. Lucky you who has goals, a degree to pursue and a reluctant boy to tame! I'd love to have your problems, I'd love to have those scratches you complain about, I'd love to have a rebellious lover who makes me suffer—I'd love to have anything else to do but be at the mercy of myself, counting my chickens before they hatch and crying over spilled milk.

"Mmh . . ." I grumbled.

"What's wrong . . . you're so strange . . ."

"Mmh . . ."

"But you're so very handsome . . ."

"You think so?"

"Definitely . . . You look like Paul Newman."

"Oh, well . . ."

"Tell me what's bothering you."

"Little things, like life. It's inauthentic. It's as if a god was showing me the only possible path while telling me: you mustn't follow that one. I feel like blurting out: Wow, really?!"

She grabbed my shoulders and looked at me the way she must have seen it done in movies:

"But no one can show you the way, not even God! You mustn't think that your destiny is to follow a predestined path just because it's everyone else's destiny! You mustn't be afraid to admit that you're the best and that all the others will always be the ones imitating you, and you will never imitate them!"

At any other moment, I would have blindly embraced those words, they would have corroborated me for days on end, I would have spent many happy mornings admiring my heavenly and prophetic expression in the mirror—but now they just rang hollow and ridiculous, because I had also seen things that way, and I was ridiculous, and she was ridiculous for praising someone like me, she really must be weak and ill—so I grabbed her wrists, pulled her away from me, and said:

"Angelica, Angelica. I'm just a coward. I don't know how to do anything at all, I don't have any talent, I don't know how to make money or kick the perfect assist to our striker, I don't know how to paint or fix a lamp. I know I'm mediocre but I hate mediocrity, and therefore I cannot adapt and, at least, be useful in some way. I'm not even so dumb as to romanticize a glass of liquor, a dangling cigarette, or some faded jeans, or such a miserable fool as to feel wise beyond my years because I come home at four in the morning and hook up with any short skirt in sight, or so sadly stupid as to think I'm special because I studied Bonvesin de la Riva in high school, and sometimes I get the blues. The truth is I don't know how to do anything better than anyone else, and what I do, I do it worse and . . ."

But what was I saying? Astonished, she looks at me, she looks lovingly at me. I'm talking, and I'm enjoying my speech, let's be real, at the very moment I get all those words out with perfect tempo, the sadness is already over, already gone, to hell with sadness! (Let's all kill sadness with rhythm, irony, and the arrogance of kings.)

"Whoa, let's not go overboard. I'm twenty and I am like Gloria Swanson in *Sunset Boulevard*. In fact: from now on, call me Gloria."

Then she asked, sweetly: "Are you coming home with me?"

It was almost six and I had never been to her house.

"You're not going to introduce me to your parents, right?"

I recalled what had happened to her father, I bit my lip, said I was sorry, and she smiled: "My mother comes home once a month. You could say I live alone."

We left the Sbruffon. It was already dark. She asked me:

"Shall we take my car? It's new, I need to break it in. Then I'll bring you back here to get yours."

To me there is nothing less exciting than a car. I can't tell a Ferrari from a tricycle, but her car, which I saw for the first time, left me speechless: it was a metallic green convertible Chrysler, an impressive car, the kind that makes car freaks drool. I slid onto the chair next to hers with that feeling of truce, given to me by nightfall.

Angelica lived on the Riviera del Brenta. The Riviera del Brenta is a strip of land that hugs the Brenta River and connects Venice to Padua. It is dotted with grandiose sixteenth-century riverbank villas built and lived in by Venetian aristocrats to try to evade one of the plagues. I don't know why, but the villas on the Riviera del Brenta make me gloomy: their beauty, immobile and icy, doubled by the narcissistic reflection in the dark water of the river, unsettles me like an eternal autumn. Maybe because all the aristocrats who fled the plague died anyway, maybe because the stone cherubs resemble the ones on a sepulcher, but the truth is I just find myself thinking of a boulevard lined with cypresses that leads to a graveyard.

Of course, her nerves showed in her driving, and she turned on the radio. An inane song blared out. The lights from the oncoming cars hit my eyelids, and I let them numb me. A raw night in January, I told myself dozing off, but maybe, somewhere, it was spring. We turned onto one of those small bridges that cross the river and continued on for a few miles through the cold countryside. All of a sudden, we found ourselves in front of seven-foot-tall walls flanking an enormous black wrought-iron gate, where a conspicuously large sign showcased a red cobra and warned BEWARE OF SNAKES. Suddenly, I woke up from my slumber.

Since childhood I've suffered from certain fears, but always rational fears, related to a concrete chance of encountering the situation in the future: I have always been afraid my parents would die, or even worse that only one of them would die, because, besides my own sorrow, I would have to bear the pain of the surviving parent, a double cross that felt unbearable. Growing up I developed other fears, the one about never being able to kiss a girl, or the one about being called on in math class when I wasn't ready (I never was), and more and more other fears so humiliating that they should never touch a human heart: not finding a decent job after college, not knowing how to make ends meet, feeling—as was the case during that time of my life—useless and petty. These fears come from the mind and can certainly have physical relevance, similar to a prolonged kick to the stomach, a blind vortex in the middle of the sternum. But the other type of fear, irrational and sudden, similar to an icy hand that latches onto your heart, crushes it, and paralyzes your limbs—that I had never experienced: since my childhood I've adored the dark, I've loved horror movies, I didn't give a damn about going to the dentist, I willingly got into fights with guys who were bigger than me, no, I didn't have any phobias at all.

But on one distant July day, in the middle of the golden summer of my childhood, I was heading back home from the reefs where I had fished for the entire morning, carrying my little white rod and reel. I was feeling so blessed, immersed in the jumbled smells of suntan lotion, grilled cevapcici, wild fennel, and crabs cooked on charcoal embers. I proceeded along the red dirt trail that led to our trailer through coastal pines and prickly bushes: by then it was noon, two nice silver fish were agonizing in my basket for my pride, and my mom and dad were expecting me for lunch. Ah, those summers in that little campground on the Croatian coast! I don't think I've ever been as happy. To be fair, I would experience other moments of irresistible joy, a girl's impassioned glance, the first audacious attempt at slipping my hand into a blouse, a day as radiant as a Van Gogh painting, a goal by Van Basten—but never again would I know that heavenly bliss of me as a young boy getting out of my bed at seven in the morning, quietly as not to wake my parents, slowly opening the door of the trailer, and seeing the sublime enchantment, the sea calm like oil, and the sky, clear and immense, stretch out before me. The cloudless sky was as blue as the sea. In the sleepy campground, only the soft sloshing of water against the reefs, everything is light and peace and happiness that doesn't overwhelm me, but is part of me, it's in my bones, it's natural. And I grab my fishing pole leaning against the trailer and the container of worms in salt water (my father and I, our backs scorched by the sun, would hunt for them under the rocks at low tide) and I head off, small and perfect, toward the brilliant blue sea, jump from rock to rock, choosing a suitable spot with the instinct of an old fisherman, baiting the hook with a worm (feeling a thrill of pleasure when the minuscule metal hook pierces the worm's mouth forcing out a tiny bead of blood). I toss out the pole with all the strength in my young muscles and, in the absolute silence of the slumbering campground, barely flecked by the yawn of seagulls—*plop*—the sweetest sound I have ever heard: the sinker touches the water's shining surface and plunges down below.

But on that day in July, a small crowd of people standing in a circle—obviously excited by something at its center—piques my curiosity. I abandon the righteous path and place the rod and the fish next to a tree to thread my way through the adults, to understand what captivates them, and then an icy hand grabs my heart, my limbs become stiff, as if they would snap off my body, a thrill permeates me: an extremely long silver snake lies coiled around itself, horrendous, threatening. I jump backward, bumping into a pair of legs, I feel my pulse beat furiously and the blood, as if taken by madness, flow back into my throat. But I stand there as if hypnotized, and then a girl (in hindsight I would say she was probably fourteen, very pretty, with intense eyes and chestnut brown hair flowing down her shoulders) grabs the snake by its tail (I feel like I am about to faint), and she tugs it, and the snake uncoils itself in all its repulsive length (shining and writhing in the midday sun, people are mumbling admiration, someone laughs), the girl pets its head like one would pet a kitten, and then with both hands she places it around her shoulders (I am dying, my heart is striking its last beats, I feel it sinking into my stomach, goodbye, goodbye mom, goodbye dad!). And now the snake, with horrifying lethargy, slithers on the girl's skin, slithers across her young breasts, slides toward her groin, it is so long, so slow, so silver, it slithers around her hips (while the tail still titillates her neck), and the girl lets herself be wrapped, elated, and the people applaud and I see one last thing that petrifies me: the incessant darting of the snake's tongue over the girl's belly button. And I feel a ferocious rage, a terrified rage, I want to tear the snake and the girl to pieces, I hate them both, then I faint.

There's no need to tell you that on that day my perfectly happy summer days, that perfect harmony between nature and me, came to an end. At every step, I checked around me, afraid the snake would suddenly appear. I still went fishing, but I could no longer stare at the sea, as I had to keep looking over my shoulder. I was terrified it would climb into the trailer, and, despite my father's attempts at reassuring me, it was not possible, I had to thoroughly inspect it every night before going to sleep. That was our last summer in Croatia. After that, the tantrums I threw convinced my father to sell the trailer and rent an apartment in Jesolo, with its colorless and insignificant sea. You couldn't even fish there, but at least it was all sand and no rocks, no unspoiled nature, no sun-parched trees or bushes or fields of stones or red-tinged Istrian soil or yellow flowers, only beaches and swimmers and gelato stands, no path, no poppies, just toilets and changing rooms, we were surrounded by buildings, hotels and guesthouses: there could be no snakes there! Since then, I can't stand seeing snakes even on TV, even a garden hose, with its green, slithering, and long plastic tube, sends shivers down my spine.

"Wh . . . what does *beware of snakes* mean?"

She laughed, and I felt that ancient anger surging in me—which is maybe the same anger that a threatened animal feels toward his predator.

"Are you afraid of snakes?"

"DO YOU HAVE SNAKES IN YOUR YARD?"

And as the automatic gate opened, I was already imagining cobras and anacondas assaulting the car, and my fear was spiraling out of control, my eyes bulging out of their sockets. Take me back home right now, I was ready to tell her, because just seeing something dark slithering in the grass would have killed me.

"Of course not, come on . . ."

My heart rate violently slowed down.

"Are you sure?"

"Of course I'm sure. That sign is just for thieves. You know, as fierce as a dog can be, you can make it fall asleep with a piece of tainted meat, a snake is more difficult. Besides it's scarier. Are you scared, too?"

When I came to, that day in Croatia, the snake was gone, but the girl and the adults had surrounded me. They cared to ask how I was, and then they laughed. I got up, humiliated, and ran away.

"No, quite the opposite, they pique my curiosity."

The house was some kind of enormous Japanese pagoda. The large living room alone could have accommodated my house. It appeared even more gargantuan due to the almost complete lack of furniture: just two long white couches in the middle of the room, placed at right angles, with a low, glass coffee table between them. Three white walls surrounded us. Each one was adorned with a gigantic painting, mostly white, with some black brushstrokes and some red and orange patches here and there. The fourth wall was covered with white drapes. Angelica pushed a small button near the entrance, and the drapes opened up just like a theater curtain, revealing a huge glass window that overlooked the yard. It felt like standing in the center of the room of a gigantic museum in Tokyo, but in the heart of a Venetian night. We sat down, I on one couch, she on the other.

Stunned, I asked: "But you live here alone?"

"Right."

"And . . . your mother?"

"My mother's American. A financial consultant, or something like that. She's a dirty whore. And yours?"

"No, mine no."

"What does she do?"

"She teaches Spanish. A beautiful woman."

"Oh, my mother is very beautiful."

"Well, not like mine, that'd be impossible, hands down, she's a knock-out." She uttered a pitying laugh.

"Ah, these men in love with their mothers . . ."

"As a matter of fact, all my friends fall in love with my mother. It's really annoying." She laughed again. The atmosphere was great. A few hours in Tokyo could only do me some good. She said:

"Listen, I had my Japanese chef prepare some sushi . . ."

"Your Japanese chef?"

"Yeah. You want some?"

She didn't wait for my answer but slipped away into the kitchen. *Her Japanese chef.* She came back, a shimmering smile lit her face, her eyes had a dragon-green sparkle, one hand carried a bottle of white wine while the other held a large tray filled with colorful morsels of food, which she placed on the coffee table. She sat down, clasped her hands like Buddha, and sighed:

"The first time you eat sushi is crucial: either you like it, or you don't."

"Really!? Like pasta and beans, go figure! Or like Brussels sprouts. Or like . . ."

"Come on, you know what I mean."

"Of course. What's that red stuff?"

"Raw tuna."

The color was spectacular, an Asian sunset on the Great Wall. Ah no, that's China, nothing to do with it. Angelica grabbed it with chopsticks and dipped it into a small blue bowl filled with soy sauce and wasabi, that's what she called it, I was clueless. She dropped it in my mouth, I shivered with disgust, then I slowly started to chew. It was good.

"Hey, that's good!"

Angelica lit up like dawn in Osaka, and her smile was so beautiful and appreciative that it moved me, and I wanted to give her more satisfaction:

"It's exquisite, really, great job, Angelica. And these little rice rolls, what are they?"

"They're wrapped in seaweed. These contain avocado and crab. These fish roe, these raw salmon."

"What beautiful colors! Let me try one with salmon."

Angelica was overjoyed, she was a geisha. With the chopsticks she picked up a small rice roll with a dark green wrapper, the bright orange of the raw salmon in its center, and placed it on my tongue.

"Mmmh . . . but," my mouth was full, "why the Japanese motif?"

"My father. He used to say he lived in Japan for three years."

"He used to say it?"

"Well, yes, he also used to say that he first ate sushi at the Emperor's court. He said the Emperor really liked him, but then the Empress fell in love with him, and the Emperor tried to kill him by slipping a royal snake into his bed, and he was bitten. But since childhood, my father had gotten used to injecting himself with daily, increasingly larger doses of snake venom, to become immune, just in view of the eventuality that someone would slip a snake in his bed." I fiddled with the chopsticks trying to pick up another rice roll with pieces of cucumber in the center, it was a hard struggle but worth the effort: it was exquisite. I was chewing blissfully and looked at Angelica, who smiled melancholic at me, as if awaiting my reaction. I said:

"Well, what's wrong? I believe it. It also worked for Mithridates."

"Yes, I believe the idea came from him. But in his stories there was still a kernel of truth: women would fall in love with him. All women."

"Even your mother?"

"My mother was sixteen when they met, during her first visit to Venice. He was a few years older. He told her that he was the exiled son of a sultan from a small independent island in Polynesia, that he was at odds with his father because he had sided with the slaves for the abolition of slavery. And she fell in love with him."

"Americans have a soft spot for human rights, don't they?"

"But then he told her another reason for the clash with his father was his being at the helm of the anti-abortion movement. When my mother became pregnant, she could have entertained having an abortion, but my father was against it, saying that he couldn't betray the ideals of his people—*I didn't go into exile for nothing!*"

"An admirable coherence. Then what happened?"

"The usual things. My mother's parents are very wealthy old farts from South Florida who couldn't believe they could join a royal family, so they made them get married. I spent my childhood in Palm Beach, between governesses and babysitters and those pain in the ass grandparents of mine, who, in the meantime, had realized that their granddaughter wasn't a princess but just the accidental daughter of an Italian son of a bitch. I think they were relieved when my mother, at twenty-one, decided to come here with my father and me."

"And did your mother realize your father would never ascend to the throne?"

"Yes, but she loved him anyway, it was impossible not to love him. I think she kept on loving him until he started traveling around the world again telling his bullshit stories. For five years he had mostly behaved, living the good life in Florida, but once he was back here, he started feeling the old urges."

"And where would he go?"

"Not sure. Uruguay or Malaysia, he would say . . . for business, he would say."

"But how did he make a living? Was he stealing money from your mother?"

"Oh no, he was a prince, he would have never done that. He was a kept man, I suppose. By women. Or men."

"Excuse me?"

"When I was thirteen, he took me on vacation to the best hotel on the Riviera. The last night there, I caught him in bed with the manager."

"Jeez. Was he gay?"

"No, he was a son of a bitch, my grandparents were right."

*

She went on and on, and I ate and ate, and I drank. I was full, drunk, relaxed. Yes, relaxed. Being in Japan listening to Angelica's tales, far away from everything and everyone—I loved it. And Angelica was beautiful that night, and she even seemed normal. She had just turned seventeen when her mother—with whom by now she quarreled every day—accepted a job offer in Stockholm and left her alone in that huge house with her father. But her father was always away. He lived in Milan. He was the managing director of some firm. Angelica couldn't recall its name because her mother had informed her right away that her father actually worked as a waiter in the Navigli district. At that time, Angelica had been seeing a filmmaker, a young guy around thirty-five, who made documentaries. Oh, here we go, I remembered that Saba had mentioned that and had left me wondering about it. This guy had fallen hopelessly in love with Angelica and every night he showed up in front of the pagoda—he begged, he cried, he ranted and raved. And one night worse than any other, he had been screaming obscenities and bellowing inhuman sounds, and he had threatened to kill himself and her. Angelica was terrified. She had thought about calling the police, instead she called her father. Her father couldn't believe he had been given the chance to play the role of the hero, as he had always dreamed, and, in the middle of the night, he raced along the highway, driving at breakneck speed on the motorcycle gifted to him by the Shah of Persia. He crashed at the Venice tollbooth.

"I'm sorry." I felt it appropriate to stop gorging myself—besides the tray was empty. I drained my glass. What a sad story! This was the moment to sit next to her, wrap my arms around her, comfort her with lingering kisses. Her mouth, thank God, tasted like wine, and for a minute the sweetness enveloped us like honey. I put my hand on her breasts and she squeezed it. Then I moved away because a pressing curiosity seized me:

"So, where did the thirty-five-year-old guy end up?"

"He disappeared."

"But he never called you again, to ask for forgiveness."

"I wouldn't forgive him anyway."

I saw a malevolent light come over her eyes, and even though I was drunk, I felt a chill down my spine. She jumped up and held her hand out. I got up. I let her lead me through the enormous living room, then down a narrow hallway, then up a spiral staircase. A door. Angelica let go of my hand, entered the room, and I followed her, staring at her beautiful firm ass. My insidious anxiety was eased by my full stomach, brimming with all that magnificent Japanese stuff and that good wine, but it was still there, hidden in the dark, I sensed it. I wanted to make love to her, to forget, to caress Angelica and kiss her breasts. I felt like doing things the proper way. Angelica turned the lights on, the room was big with a large king-size bed, over which hung a humongous, hideous painting, a hellish explosion of colors, ferocious red and black brushstrokes, the abyss, the bowels of the Earth, Satan's jaws. Christ, I had really drunk too much. Angelica stood about ten feet in front of me, I saw her from behind bent over something I didn't recognize, maybe a glass case. Then she turned around, and I died.

And I died. And died. An electric shock, like a steely claw, scorched my back, pierced my skin, grabbed hold of my heart and crushed it, and I kept on dying and I couldn't stop, death was ripping out my guts, my bones, my brain, an electric shock was killing me, and what was worse was the knowledge of dying, feeling my heart expanding and exploding in my lungs, my blood freezing step by step from the veins to the arteries to every tiny capillary, and the blood rushing to my throat, to my eyes, eyes wide open, and I could see: I could see Angelica grab this huge rattlesnake by the tail, writhing like an epileptic. I saw it open its jaws, furiously snapping at the air. I stared at it, hypnotized, and I was dying, and Angelica smiled like a demon, and her hair turned into more snakes, and I finally felt my heart break, with such vivid pain, and the last thing I saw was Angelica's face get as white as death, I saw her turn around, and then turn around again and then she came over to me, and I felt my frozen mouth, my eyes bulging out, I heard Angelica's voice, I felt her grab me under my arms, and then I saw nothing—dead.

I woke up thirty seconds later, Angelica was slapping my face, behind her legs I saw the snake slither into the glass case, one last shiver paralyzed my limbs—then a furious, tempestuous, blind rage overtook me. I grabbed Angelica's wrists and dragged her down. I suppose my eyes made me look crazed, and I realized I was drenched in sweat. Petrified, she looked at me and said: "I'm sorry." I felt like punching her, but, again, my eyes fell on that repulsive beast in the glass case. I made it to my feet and took off like a bat out of hell to get out of that dreadful room. I went down the spiral staircase, shaken and shivering, barely able to stand on my wobbly legs, a hammer pounding on my temples, retching as I reached the threshold at the front door. Desperate, Angelica chased after me. She didn't even realize I could have killed her. "Please!" she screeched. Her scream shredded my ears, I looked at her: "You're nuts, I never want to see you again . . ."

"Please, forgive me, you told me you were fascinated by snakes . . ."

"That's . . . that's a rattlesnake . . . right?"

"The last gift my father gave me . . ."

"Is it . . . poisonous?"

She looked down at the floor.

I was overcome with fury: I slapped her, hard, in a fit of therapeutic violence—

I saw her lose her balance and fall, I felt better. I grabbed my coat and left, slamming the door. I crossed the yard, punched the gate in a raging fit, tearing my knuckles, screaming at the top of my lungs: "OPEN THIS FUCKING GATE!!!!!" The gate opened, at an exasperating slow pace, and then I ran, I ran as fast as I could, through the foggy night, through the frozen countryside—I ran, as the snake flashed in my head, whipping my whole body—I ran until exhaustion calmed me down, until my temples stopped throbbing, and I started to walk, dripping with sweat in the frozen night, chain-smoking, hysterical, desperate. At the first town, I caught a bus and went back home.

9. February

Angelica was truly contrite, and in the ensuing days she kept calling me to beg for forgiveness, but it wasn't really about that anymore. My anger, little by little, had devolved into a sense of constant boredom. Since that night I had succumbed to ennui, I would wake up with a mass of dread in the pit of my stomach, and my day would drag on afflicted by an endless feeling of futility. No more flashes of happiness or imagination to rescue me—as if the sight of the snake had ripped apart the last veil, forever shutting the door on the tenderness of my childhood or my innocent adolescence, hideously pointing to the nightmarish, desolate land waiting for me. So, I forgave Angelica. I forgave her because nothing mattered to me anymore, not fainting in front of her, not even that she was nuts and the daughter of a nut job. My boredom could withstand it all, my wounded pride, my disgust for her insanity. So, when she invited me to the theater to see *The Importance of Being Earnest*, a comedy by an Irishman, one Oscar Wilde, I accepted.

    I had never been to the theater before, I swear. Well, maybe as a child I had gone to a Sicilian puppet show. Such melancholia. The only amusing thing were the dresses of the old ladies with their faces caked in powder, their pearl necklaces and stretched-out skin, their hair dyed with blue undertones, their old husbands' tuxedoes, and the glamour of the thirty-year-olds with their serious looks, who had to wake up early the next day, and the beauty of forty-year-old mothers who had left their children at home with the babysitter and smoked a cigarette before the start, and the closed curtains, the lights, the velvet theater seats, the clothes in the coat check, and the looks Angelica and I were getting—while searching for our seats.

    We sat down and the play began. I don't know how to describe what happened next. Word after word, witticism after witticism, I smiled with unusual pleasure, I smiled with blossoming happiness, gushing, in ecstasy, like a revelation: the beauty of the words struck me deeply, my muscles twitched, my mind sang, the perfection in the chiseled sentences, their impudent, blasphemous, lighthearted absurdity made me jump out of my seat and shake with pure delight (the delight in human intelligence: the more it's hidden and invisible, the more it bursts out superlative and triumphant). It was an anthem to life for every cell in my body, and every detail infused me with pleasure—the stage's floorboards, the muffled coughs from the audience, the actors' soft and musical voices, their clothes from a dreamlike era, Ernest's yellow tie, Gwendolen's white parasol, the green carnation in Algernon's lapel—oh, this is what I was looking for in the streets and didn't know I had inside me! I craved this, the divine lightness, a fluttering thought, supreme and perfectly useless beauty, because when the futility of life crushes us, beauty's useless nature comforts us, because beauty needs no excuses, needs no goals. Beauty, like God, has its own reasons to exist.

In fact, after each act, I had to rush off to the restroom to cry. I cried, happy, distraught, I thanked God, and I thanked Oscar Wilde. I had no idea what was happening to me, but I knew I was living out the most important moment of my life, I was aware of that, bent over the toilet, laughing and crying. I felt that all of life, with its tortuosity and its bleakness, could suddenly be transformed by words, words could transmute something ugly into something beautiful. Electrical words, exquisite, lethal: happiness was achievable. Was life boring, was life sad, was life over? Yes, but happiness was achievable, and happiness was color (I had discovered colors!) and thought (I had discovered thought!); never had my life seemed so true, delightful, intense as what I had seen on that stage, and I immediately pitied anyone who didn't know Oscar Wilde, who didn't know art and his terrible smile, I felt sorry for all that I had been until that point—and I cried.

I felt like a puny pile of twitching nerves. I applauded the actors like a man possessed, I could have hugged them, I adored and envied them, because they had said what I had heard with so much joy; they were creators, masters, and authors of that happiness and they had to feel that they owned it—although never as much as Oscar Wilde, my benign genius.

"Angelica, but when is Oscar Wilde coming onstage?"

Stunned, she looked at me: "Oscar Wilde died in Paris in 1900."

"Oh . . ."

So, I hugged her. I hugged her with all the emotion I had in my body, I hugged her, kissed her on the mouth, then I nearly screamed, "Thanks, my love, thank you!"

"But . . . but . . . for what?"

"Because I now know what I am, get it? The road, do you remember the road, the one that wasn't there . . . and now, it is! I know my star, my destiny, my life . . . I've understood, I've understood who I am."

"Who . . . who are you?" She stuttered disconcerted.

"I'm the greatest playwright in the world after Oscar Wilde."

That night I couldn't sleep. I was like a man possessed. The most acute obsessions swirled in my mind, a sudden thirst for knowledge, the mad curiosity to read and know everything (from the Bible to the most obscure essay on mineralogy to the recent medical studies on pimples). I anguished over my ignorance. I knew nothing about the world, my life had been barren if everything I had read up to that point consisted only of textbooks, anthologies, and lousy novels about provincial life that the school system had fed me: Why had no one ever told me about Oscar Wilde? And I was certain there were others like him—maybe even in Italy—with such fresh ideas, such breezy words, such trenchant beauty. There had been a conspiracy against my mind, against everyone's mind: they had led us to believe that literature was dullness and dullness over dullness, maybe they feared it like the Church fears sex, maybe literature is too shameless and corrupting a pleasure that it needs to be hidden, otherwise everyone would dedicate themselves to the delight of thought, to the enjoyment of words—and there wouldn't be any more politicians, economists, plumbers, and policemen.

Suddenly life became clear, complicated, fun. I felt that I understood that reading and knowledge were necessary in order to be free, to react to life's aggravations, to always look at the other side of the coin, to never stop, since reading and knowledge were inevitable pleasures if you wanted your life to take shape, get some breathing room, a personality. Gripped by an orgy of nerves, I looked through the books at my house that I had always disregarded, but they all had a scholastic style that made me refuse them: finally I found *The Flowers of Evil* (I had forgotten to return it to the library). I thought of Niso and I envied him; I figured out why he already knew everything and never emanated sadness. I thought of the waitress from the past summer and I felt ashamed, but I grabbed the book, brought it to bed, turned on the light, and started reading.

I rediscovered fragments of the purest light, I didn't get all of it, but the sound of certain sentences was exhilarating, I didn't always love everything, but when I fell asleep at dawn, I felt wiser.

At 7:30 I was already up. I announced to my mother that I had to go to the library because the day of the exam was getting closer; she seemed to breathe a sigh of relief, and I kissed her on the cheek.

Just outside, a sunny, clear morning at the end of January. I studied the sun and thought about it for a few minutes, then it hit me: *o January sun, radiant and innocent, delicate young king, light up the way for me!* I ran along the sidewalk, for which there were three or four interesting adjectives—*uneven, dusty, defiled by dogs*—and I saw the bare trees *like old women*, the girls *like spoiled goddesses*, and finally the library, a dilapidated building *like a withered squash*. I was over the moon because of words, and suddenly I had become good, generous, and kind. I said hello to the old librarian and immediately imagined: she is as reassuring as . . . as . . . I snapped my fingers: *AS A TEAPOT*. I settled in, deeply moved: yes, I was a genius.

Three feverish, turbulent, devastating days went by. I devoured all of Oscar Wilde's works, from the novels to the essays to the comedies, and it tortured my senses, the regret of having spent so much time in vain, the revelation of things that had been inside me and I hadn't known how to express, the joy of verbal jokes, of paradoxes, and bitterness: "The only thing that sustains one through life is the consciousness of the immense inferiority of everybody else." I read his biography, and I became indignant as never before when I learned of how he was treated, and I imagined living in the London of a hundred years ago and showing him all my admiration and support.

Then I dove into Shakespeare. They had mentioned him in school, but just enough to let us think that he was simply a pretentious hack. I read *The Tempest*, *Hamlet*, *Othello,* and *A Midsummer's Night Dream.* I was awestruck, swept away by a rain fluid with colors and sensations. If fourteen-year-old kids knew him, they would fall in love with him and with literature, because Shakespeare encapsulates everything we start to learn about at fourteen: love, hate, envy, jealousy. Instead, at fourteen they killed us with Catholic doctrine and morality-filled tales from insignificant writers who lived in the farthest reaches of the provinces, with tons of poetry (that sounded to us like nursery rhymes) about the pain of living, the futility of life, the tedium of life—while at fourteen life grabs us by the throat, hormones leap like crazed gnomes, we burn from our head to our toes with shame, and we discover fright and exhilaration. Now, ecstatic, I read these men, and for the first time I loved Humanity in general and, in particular, my humanity.

Obviously, going hand in hand with this, my dreams of glory were ablaze. We were at the usual bar, with the blue-eyed bartender and the half-moon love seats, ten in the evening and the cold outside, the look in the eyes of the girls at the other tables, and the look in the eyes of Angelica, a silent look, at my table.

"I was thinking of writing a play," I proudly announced.

"Mmh . . . " She sipped her tomato juice very seriously.

"I want it to be irreverent, intoxicating, polyphonic." I felt the happiness in each adjective, and I was no longer at the table of our hangout but sitting on a stool on a national talk show, explaining the reasons for my incredible success.

"What will your play be about?" she asked, pulling back her hair.

I found Angelica very entrepreneurial, she evaluated my words and listened to me as if I had asked her to direct my masterpiece.

"It's . . . it's a secret."

"But do you know or not?"

"I know it all. Everything is clear in my mind."

"Is it a true story?"

"True, well, true . . . the artist reinterprets."

"My drama teacher has a theater company and even a little theater . . . you know, he's someone who's blown off conventions and compromises . . . he's always saying: 'I would rather have one audience member who, after leaving the theater, looks at himself in the mirror and feels that he has changed, than a flock of sheep who go to the theater as if they were going to the butcher' . . ."

"Sheep that go to the theater? Sheep that go to the butcher? Your friend seems a little confused."

"But it's a metaphor!" she screamed, exasperated.

"Ah."

"A true artist creates just for himself, without considering the public."

"Of course."

"Anyway. François . . ."

"Who???"

"François Guglielminetti, he's half French, half Italian, and a genius . . ."

"Oscar Wilde is a genius. Let's not ascribe that word to the first Italo-French who comes along. Besides, being a genius today is fairly easy. At least in Europe, it's enough to claim you're a genius. And naturally, you do some bizarre things, you are a little bit of a weirdo and say things that no one understands, and it's done: Dalí is a genius, Fellini is a genius. You'd better agree or you seem like a moron, right? This guy gives me the impression of being a proud failure. There's nothing worse than a proud failure, proud of his own flops, happy knowing that future generations will love him. Big deal. Future generations love everyone, and once you're dead, it's easy to be appreciated. You'll always find some future smartass who will recognize your genius when you're dead: but I want the applause of the sheep, you understand, I want flocks of sheep in love with me . . ."

For the first time I sensed a slight shadow of contempt in her eyes, but I didn't pay attention to it. Who knows how many times old Oscar or old Will have been judged contemptuously, scornfully, or indulgently? Yet they both stayed quiet, calm, aware that they had no equals; there are no friends on the cramped paths to glory.

She pondered this, then murmured: "Anyway, François knows how to find the value in young people . . . he knows how to spot talent and he'll thrust you all the way to Olympus . . . I could give him your play and see what he thinks of it . . ."

A burst of happiness resonated in my stomach. Oh God, oh my God, it all makes sense, the old master is dazzled by the greatness of the young playwright and stages his first play, the newspapers report it, people whisper, his striking witticisms travel from mouth to mouth, a female journalist interviews him and falls in love with him, it's a beautiful but conflicted love story, people whisper but he wants to protect his privacy, a powerful entrepreneur buys all the rights to his first play, it's a national success, thank you thank you you're too kind, TV stations wonder about the phenomenon, meanwhile the young playwright buys with his first royalties a cottage by the sea, where he writes his second masterpiece, which becomes a roaring international success, pretty female journalists come from all over the world to his cottage to interview him and fall in love with him—more beautiful but conflicted love stories—Broadway opens all its doors to him, but he's still a modest guy, and he announces his intention to give a million dollars to the war orphans cause, Hollywood takes notice and offers him a deal to write the script for a movie based on his third play, the young playwright snubs Hollywood but then accepts the proposal, he wins an Oscar and, cradling the golden statuette in his hands, he thanks his old master François Guglielminetti who, alas, hasn't had the same good fortune although he certainly deserved it, but then, what is fame in the end? *Right, what is it?* What does all the applause mean? And as the years go by and his successes multiply, and he's considered the most powerful man in the world, the most brilliant man of the century, the author who has upended the arts, eclipsing once and for all Oscar Wilde and William Shakespeare and all the others, feels gradually less excited, increasingly less happy, and each round of applause no longer feels like a tribute to his oeuvre but to his headstone, and he realizes that the audience would applaud for him even if he recited the grocery list, and he hates the audience, and he no longer feels like writing, and he feels petty and mean and close to death, and he looks in the mirror and sees eyes without sparkle and thinning silver hair and flabby neck skin, and his exhausted heart beats under his wrinkled and wretched chest, and he thinks back to his long-gone beauty, to his long-gone insatiable libido, to his long-gone uncorrupted ignorance, and he realizes that art means nothing, fame means nothing—compared to youth.

"Yeah, okay . . ." I told her, overwhelmed by a troubling nostalgia for being twenty.

"When will it be done?" She asked me, like a perfect manager.

"In six days . . . But now, let's go have sex."

My mother was moved by the stack of books on my desk and by my bloodshot eyes staring at my notes. She would bring me coffee and suggest I take a break, and I would feel guilty. Sorry mom, if I'm deceiving you. Sorry mom, but my Muse is calling and I must answer, I'm so sorry mom, maybe someday you will understand.

My head was full of adjectives, full of exciting sentences and enlightening aphorisms—but what was missing was a story. I rummaged through my experiences, through my friends: I recalled Niso's story, his crazy courtship that ended when she left her ex and threw herself at him. Yes, it was a good story to start with, the audience would be amused, critics would uncover a myriad of symbols. To flesh out Niso's character, I based it on Niso, to flesh out the character of the girl, I based it on Angelica—the way she acted toward me, petulant and emphatic—to flesh out the character of the cuckold boyfriend, I based it on Alcapone, just thin.

I imagined the first conversation between the male and the female protagonists set in a school classroom opulently furnished with damask fabric on the walls, a teacher's desk made of inlaid cedar, and small alabaster tables: Oscar's influence was palpable. Nevertheless, I was sure that the critics would grasp the brilliant metaphor of the author who intends to stress the painful divide between what is and what should be. I wrote the first page with frenetic pleasure: I reread it, and it was the most intense moment of happiness in my life.

I threw myself on the bed, exhausted, but ecstatic.

I knew the secret of pure joy.

No paradise could be better.

I reread the page again.

My God.

How can man live without pursuing a dream of beauty?

The chance of achieving something great, aspiring to greatness, all this gave meaning to my life, this was life, this was the soul.

Concepts like soul, God, happiness: in that moment they were so clear, so obvious . . .

Wonder of wonders.

The development of your personality, to create something ineffable, to transform mud into gold, that was the goal, that was the essence, that's it.

My happiness was so excruciating, I couldn't stand it, I had to transform it into serenity to get the chance to contemplate it, so I turned on the TV: here come the celebrities, the rich people that I had always envied. I pitied them. Yes, they were living the good life, but it was not happy, or complete, because they had not written what I had written.

I reread the page: I was overwhelmed. It was so beautiful I felt left out, envying my very self for having written it, and I wondered: damn, I wish I had written it myself!

I thought I should go for a beer, play pool, smoke a cigarette, hang out with vulgar guys my own age—or I would end up entangled in that azure bliss, writing without living, happy to the point of not writing anymore. I reread my piece again and this time I was deeply moved. Christ, I was good. Christ, and you thought you weren't worth a damn, eh? Christ, no one believed in you, boy, how many bitter pills did you have to swallow eh?

It was the time for self-indulgence, for revenge against an ungrateful world.

I ran outside, it was a freezing February full of yellow leaves and bare trees, but my brain was running faster than I could, with sentences and adjectives and amazing stories, and I ran like crazy ducking overcoats and sweaters, but my thoughts raced faster—until I snuck into the first bar I saw, without realizing I had been there before and had sworn never to go back, but the waitress behind the cash register smiled at me. She had recognized me.

"Hi!"

"Oh, hi . . ." I stuttered, confused. I sat down at the bar. I was flushed.

She said, "Do you remember me?"

"Yes, of course . . . Listen . . . I'm sorry about last time . . . last summer . . ."

It seemed like a thousand years ago.

"Sorry for what?"

She was sweet and pretended not to understand.

"Well, I wanted to dedicate a poem to you . . . but it didn't turn out so well . . ."

She looked down, blushed, then said, "Well, no one had ever done anything like that for me before. So, I've been hoping you'd come back."

Oh my God. Life was a beautiful thing.

"Now I'm back. Here I am."

And once again I flashed my knowing smile and my smug look, my heart tenderly in love. Sweet girl, oh sweet girl, forget that talentless jerk who only wanted to get you in bed by reciting awkward poetry; now he's a different man, he's a great playwright, he'll be the man of your dreams and will take you out of this dump, he'll take you away from this mess, he'll write you romantic messages and will dedicate his Nobel to you—oh love, my love, marry me, I beg you . . .

"Oh, let me introduce you to my boyfriend!" She said suddenly.

A lanky guy had sat next to me without me noticing him. He stuck his hand out and smiled. She didn't seem embarrassed, not like I was, and turned toward the gaunt figure saying, "He's a poet, you know . . ."

"Oh!" The string bean exclaimed, pretending to be greatly surprised. "Actually, I'm a playwright."

"Oh, so you write plays," the skinny guy said.

"Right."

She said, "I'm sure you write very well," in a tone of voice that seemed authentic and vibrant to me, but she must have made the skinny guy jealous—because suddenly he became less cordial:

"So, what have you written?"

"Well . . ."

"Come on, come on, tell us!" She chirped, exaggerating.

"Come on, don't be shy," he egged me on, derisively.

They laughed. Were they making fun of me? I wanted to get the hell out of there.

"Let's just say you *want to become* a playwright," said the jealous/smartass/string bean.

"Okay, okay." I pulled out a cigarette, lit it, sized up her friend, looked at her, then took a drag.

"Does *Waiting for Godot* mean anything to you?"

A disconcerting silence.

"That's mine. It's a tale of two men waiting for someone who never shows up. It's pretty dry, nothing happens, I wrote it one morning when I was pretty depressed because I was waiting for the mailman to deliver my military deferment papers, and he was taking forever."

"And did he ever come?"

"Yes, but after the play was over."

"So, Godot is the mailman?" The boyfriend asked.

"That's one interpretation. You could have a future as a theater critic. But remember the postman always rings twice."

I slapped him on the back, I winked at the girl, put my hands in my pockets, and left.

I went home, reread the page and determined that, at last, I had exorcised it. It was beautiful, but I could do better. I was going to write such beautiful things that this page would pale in comparison and one day I'd feel embarrassed by it. No, that would never happen.

The first-born will always be the first-born. But some things should be added: for example, I was fascinated by those two people in the bar. In the play, he became Niso's friend, jealous and cantankerous, and she became the friend of the girl being wooed, sweet and impatient. Then my mother entered the room, and I felt like adding her to the play, so I transformed her into Niso's mother, but then I thought of Niso's real mother and I also put her in the play, but as the boyfriend's mother.

In the end, the play contained three protagonists and twenty-four minor characters: quite a few, but each one brought things that I had either hated or loved, that had struck me in those first twenty years of my life, that I had carried inside, at times unbeknownst to me, and that now were becoming more and more words, thoughts that thrilled me, witty jokes that made me burst out laughing. Sometimes I had to hold my stomach to stop from laughing so hard and to wipe away my tears of gratification. How much fun I was having! The dialogue sprang spontaneously like spring water from virgin rock, pouring out of me from visceral depths, uncharted; then I would go back to it and carve it to achieve the perfect sound, so that the effect would be impeccable, I cut out any gimmicks, searching for the purest clarity, I wanted—as I kept telling myself—the reddish glow of the guillotine at sunset, the cobalt blue back of a whale, the dazzling azure of a Sicilian summer, the gilded yellow of the fields in Tennessee. (Even though, of course, I had never seen neither a guillotine or a whale, or Sicily or Tennessee).

After six days and nights of incessant working, I penned the words "THE END."

My only impression: I had written the greatest masterpiece of all time. Although I knew only a sliver of the totality of literature, I had no doubts that no one had ever written something so intelligent, so brilliant, so engaging. I threw myself on the bed in a sort of ecstasy. I still needed several hours of sleep, it was five in the morning, but a whole world was spinning around inside my head: people's astonishment, tea with the queen of England, the screams of the girls outside the Hilton as I am getting into the limo, charity soccer games, the play staged in stadiums because there wasn't enough room in theaters anymore, a party with Hollywood stars groveling at my feet to write a film for them, and press conferences, and caviar and champagne in the bathtub like Joan Collins in *Dynasty*, and thousands of women begging me to make love to them, and the pope asking me for a private audience.

The next day I gave a copy to Angelica so she could give it to the illustrious Professor Guglielminetti, and one for her, so she could admire me with passion. Then I sent copies to France, Rebecca, and Niso.
 I lived the next four days waiting for a phone call, any phone call.
 I lived suspended between trepidation and triumph.
 I watched TV, stuffed myself with ice cream, pigged out on French fries, stretched out on the bed like a contented cat—I lived, waiting.
 I closed my bedroom door after my mother left; she was so hopeful and so focused on my exam. The world was fantastic in my little alcove, surrounded by books and soap operas, between coffee and the ringing of the phone that startled me each time.

On the day of the exam, I was just as excited as everyone else who was actually going to take it.
 In the waiting room, opposite the professor's closed door, sat about thirty students convulsing from fear and stress. I despised them. Livid, they were getting all worked up about being judged by some crappy professor, while I was waiting to be judged by the whole world.
 At the end of a long gray table (around which everyone was bent over their books in a final attempt to grasp one more kernel of knowledge) sat Rebecca, nervous, pale, but very elegant.
 She looked up from the book she was reviewing, less anxious than the others, and stared at me with icy indifference.
 "Hey . . . " I said, waiting for an answer.
 "Hey. So, did you decide to give it a try after all?"
 "No . . . I've had other stuff to take care of, *as you can imagine*."
 I had a sly smile, of one who knows he is superior without needing to flaunt it.
 "Writing plays?"

She clasped both hands, covering her mouth and nose, but the corners of her mouth turned up and she smiled, looking at me. I felt a thrill of triumph. Your play is a thing of beauty. Your play is extraordinary. I was blown away, you're a genius, I want to make love to you.

"I haven't had the time to read it, but I'm glad you sent it to me."

I felt the blood rush to my head.

You didn't . . . you didn't have the time? I chose to make you part of such a monumental event, and you *didn't have the time*?

"When you find the time, I'll be happy to hear your opinion," I said sharply and spitefully, already picturing the night of the play's premiere, when I would distractedly say hello to her, without stopping even for a minute, racing away through a delirious crowd.

At that moment, France arrived unexpectedly. We greeted each other affectionately, he had a handsome smile that surely implied thousands of compliments, I turned toward Rebecca as if to encourage her to listen to what France was about to say—and he actually said:

"I received your masterpiece!"

I almost peed myself from the excitement, a lump in my throat, I wanted to hug him and cry. Then he added:

"I can't wait to read it!"

"What?"

"It's amazing what you're willing to do to avoid studying! Great job!"

He patted me on the back as he and Rebecca started laughing at me, and maybe their laughter was a sign of affection, and they had no inkling of how humiliated I felt, no idea of the upshot, my veins and my heart slowly turning to ice—they didn't understand how much this meant to me, it wasn't a game, it wasn't a joke. Instead, they were already talking about the Lit exam that Rebecca was about to take and the Law exam that France would be taking the next day, as if my play were just something irrelevant, and they didn't even ask me how or why or if they had been the inspiration for certain characters. Nothing.

Were they maybe envious?

I would have been curious, or in any case I'd have shown a certain amount of interest, out of courtesy, at least . . .

The exam, of course. But a dumb exam wouldn't have prevented me from being curious or polite, at least for five minutes. But I'm an artist, right, I almost forgot. I'm not that mean.

And what if what is so important to me is not that important to anyone else?

I needed proof.

I said my goodbyes and ran to look for a phone booth.

"Hey, Niso . . . "

"My favorite writer! What luck, I actually wanted to call you . . . your last work is pure genius."

"Come on, tell me the truth."

"Eh, *quid est veritas*? . . . It's true, believe me . . . refined, snobby, with such a cruel final scene."

"But . . . and did you see yourself in the main character . . . you know, I had you in mind . . . even if *every protagonist is a projection of the author*."

"What are you talking about?" He laughed, I felt like an asshole, but I needed something else.

"Listen . . . talk to me, tell me more, tell me what you think of . . . "

"What can I say? It's really beautiful, the dialogue is well paced, the characters very paradoxical . . . Some of them are true caricatures . . . "

It was like a thorn piercing my heart.

"Too much?"

"Come on, my friend, it's your first play. The second one will be better and so on. But now you'll have to excuse me, I could talk to you for hours about these sublime topics, but I have this business of an exam to get through. I have to be there in the afternoon. If you come to the pool hall tonight, I'll tell you everything I liked and the stuff I didn't like so much, okay?"

There was something he didn't like much. I took a deep breath, and, devastated, I said, "Yeah, thanks, you know how much your opinion means to me . . . as for everyone else's, well, you know I don't give a fuck . . . but yours will help me get better."

"If so, I won't say anything, my friend, because your play is objectively beautiful and you mustn't pay attention to different sensitivities toward beauty, right?"

"Of course, of course, my friend, but . . . "
"Sorry, but I have to go, and congrats again!"
"Bye Niso!!! . . . And thanks! . . . And . . . "
But he had already hung up.

All of a sudden, I was sad. I was very grateful to Niso, but it seemed that my play had not wowed him the way I wanted it to.

It wasn't hard to put on a face between forlorn and enraged for my mother; I railed against the corrupt and asinine professors who wake up on the wrong side of the bed, but I ensured her that in a month I would show them.

My mother absorbed the shock and caressed me; my dad said, "For now, don't think about it and take a couple of days off to have fun and relax." They were really great people, even if personally I would have preferred that they call me a complete imbecile. Instead, as it was, my throat hurt from my sense of guilt: I promised myself that I would actually take the exam next month.

I locked myself in my room, stretched out on the bed, and I reread the play (titled *The Comedy*) straight through, and I had the feeling that, in fact, there were too many caricatures, empty characters that were too ridiculous.

I regretted it.

On the whole, it was still a great piece of work, and whoever didn't get it was just dumb.

Angelica called. Acting indifferent, I asked her what she thought about it. "It's not bad," she said. I was fuming. IT'S NOT BAD??? I had to restrain the fire in my nostrils. NOT BAD!?! If she'd been right there with me, I would have killed her, that dumb condescending whore, with all her hang-ups . . . NOT BAD!!!! That fucking bitch.

"In any case, François Guglielminetti will let you know in a few days what he thinks. I gave him your number, happy?"

"What the hell do I care what someone with a name like that thinks?"

"Well, come on . . . he can lend a hand, you know."

"I don't want anyone's help. This mindset of helpful acquaintances, pulling strings and bribing people is for lowlifes like you; what I write needs no help, it speaks for itself. Got it, you freaking idiot?"

"But . . . but . . . wh . . . why are you treating me like this?" She sobbed.

"Stop crying, I've had it with your hysterics, you spend more time crying than breathing, what do you think, that you're more sensitive because you cry at the drop of a hat? Or do you have some kind of glitch with your eyes? Besides, when you cry, you're more hideous than usual, you are deformed, you really are a dumbass."

Click. I felt better already.

Three days later, hard to believe, I was studying.

Partly because my friends had passed their exams with flying colors, partly because I owed it to my parents, partly because I wanted to distract myself from my sacred passions.

In any event, I was stretched on the same old bed, wearing a black sweater over my naked chest and my favorite boxers, gnawing on the cuticles of my left hand and underlining a linguistics book with my right hand, when the phone rang:

"Mr. Emanuel Peter Black?" A twinge in my stomach.

"Yes?"

"Dr. Guglielminetti would like to meet you, tomorrow, at three in his office."

I turned a deaf ear to my pounding heart.

I lit a cigarette.

I exhaled a couple of smoke rings, I looked at my grandfather's watch on my wrist, I stroked my three-day-old beard. Triumph was on the horizon, but I was waiting for it, disenchanted.

I headed toward the living room (my parents were working, so I could celebrate by myself), sat in my dad's armchair, and crossed my legs. Then I sprang to my feet, went into the kitchen, took a bottle of red wine out of the fridge, and poured myself two fingers worth.

I tasted it. It was good. It had aged nicely and had a clean, smooth taste.

Yes, I'm someone who prefers concentrating on wine's vintage rather than on the arrival of glory—glory, big deal!

*

Underneath the bell, I read:

> Dr. François Guglielminetti, director-actor-theatrical impresario.

Mmh . . .

The dilapidated building with its windows broken by the rocks of some vandal was in a back alley in the slummiest part of the city. I climbed the spiral staircase and found myself in the reception area of Dr. Guglielminetti's office. It resembled the waiting room of a doctor from the National Health Services, a rusty yellow, the corners of the ceiling eroded from moisture, a ragged green velvet couch on one side and on the other a desk that pretended to be an antique. An emaciated woman with no trace of even the slightest smile, her hair in a bun that made her look twenty years older, was sitting at the desk.

"Mr. Peter Black?"

Emanuel Peter Black, yes, my *nom de plume*. I had spent an entire night coming up with one. Actually the first option I had considered was Ridge Forrester, but it was too haughty and serious a name for my taste, my second choice was Gerd Müller, but its Germanic roots didn't thrill me, so I went looking for a name that would combine nobility and exoticism, character and grit, everything I wanted to have, until at dawn, after a thousand tries, I decided on Black—Emanuel Peter Black.

"Call me Emanuele . . ."

She looked at me with disdain without uttering a word, she resembled Miss Rottenmeier, Heidi's governess.

"I'm young . . . I'm only twenty," I added.

Her nostrils flared.

"Make yourself comfortable on the couch. Dr. Guglielminetti will see you as soon as possible."

A mist of embarrassment pervaded my bones. I was twenty and I wasn't a doctor. I was ashamed. Miss Rottenmeier kept her head down on her papers, I looked around and began to sweat. There was hardly any light, but you could just make out the framed pictures, all black and white, hanging on the wall, all depicting theater scenes. I was struck by one in particular of a man with a wild expression, the eyes a sooty black, but with a pallor to his face and only a few wisps of hair on his head. I got up and approached it to take a peek, but more than anything it was an icebreaker to show Miss Rottenmeier I was alive and curious and smart, even though I didn't have a degree.

I stroked my chin, waiting for her to look at me—it was a very long and painful wait, as if I were invisible—and when at last her stony eyes offered me an inquisitive look, I cracked a complicit smile, pointed at the old guy in the photo, and said: "This guy's pretty old, eh?"

"*That* is Dr. Guglielminetti. He's old because he's wearing makeup, he's wearing makeup because it's the last act of Ionesco's *The Chairs*, just before the suicide."

She turned her attention back to her paperwork, her goddamned paperwork.

Beads of shame dripped from my temples. She seemed to know everything about me, that I was an inexperienced braggart who didn't even know who this Ceausescu guy was. I felt ignorant and boorish, and she hated me. She was right. My presence was an imposition, I had sent my play to a stranger expecting him to read it and open the doors of my success, I had a lot of nerve making fun of someone who had acted on a thousand stages (the photos proved that) without ever stooping to compromise (the shabbiness of the room and the building also proved that).

And yet, I felt it was absolutely necessary to establish a bond with Miss Rottenmeier, to see her smile. I thought that if she smiled at me, if only she were to smile at me, I would have rushed over to kiss her hand in gratitude. I spontaneously plunged into a bathtub of humility.

"He's really kind Mr. . . . Dr. Guglielminetti . . . to see someone like me . . . I mean, I'm twenty, you know . . . it's an age full of limitations . . ."

"Not enough to stop you from writing. In any case, if you want some advice, don't be too modest, Dr. Guglielminetti doesn't like brown-nosers."

A slight comfort caressed my heart.

"Thank you, thank you . . . I'll remember that . . . but I'm not modest, I wouldn't be here . . . nor am I a brown-noser, you know . . . but this is a flaw nowadays, not being one, I mean, it's a flaw I obviously would not give up, but it is a flaw . . . is it a flaw in your opinion?"

The phone rang.

"Sure." Miss Rottenmeier said, almost sighing, as she put down the receiver.

She interlaced her hands in front of her mouth, looked at me for a moment, then said, "Go. Guglielminetti is waiting for you."

"Thank you, ma'am, thank you," I said smiling, and it seemed to me that finally, faintly, she was smiling—with compassion.

I went in. Classical music was playing on a turntable.

His desk was crammed full of papers, manuscripts, and an ancient inkwell, and a nineteenth-century phone; behind him was a display case full of things in no set order (plaques, cups, books). A man, sprawled in a black leather armchair, covered his eyes with his left hand while twirling his right one in the air as if chasing or conducting music.

I didn't know if I should sit on the wooden chair facing the desk or wait until the maestro motioned me to sit. The wisps of white hair looked just like in the picture I had seen, as did the stiff white goatee under a deadpan mouth. He was old. Being so old he couldn't be mean, I thought, my grandparents are the most harmless people I've ever known, old people are patient and wise.

I sat down.

I wondered if I should say good afternoon or good evening, since it was three-thirty in the afternoon. I made up my mind and blurted out, "Hello, Dr. Guglielminetti."

He peeked at me through the index and middle fingers of his left hand, and his sinister eyes stared me down. He stopped conducting the music that seemed to envelop me like a coiling snake, leaving me breathless, as he stared silently at me. I broke out into a cold sweat.

"Thank you for the opportunity . . . that you've given me . . ."

"What opportunity?" He spoke. He had a deep, cavernous voice.

He brought his two fingers together and yawned. (An enormous crude yawn, he was bored to death, bored with me.)

Even before finishing his interminable yawn, my body had turned into a block of ice from fear and humiliation, I tried to say something about being twenty and his magnanimity, that not everyone would agree to see in his office a twenty-year-old, with all his fanciful ambitions, that it was truly an honor. He started yawning again.

The music was strangling me like a noose around my neck, I wanted to bolt, but instead I just tried to say anything to cover his yawns, to reassure him that it didn't matter he was yawning, that I hadn't even noticed, that I understood that he was tired of seeing people like me.

Then he removed his hand from his eyes and started to rummage through the manuscripts on his desk. He pulled out one, mine, and tossed it at me.

"How old are you?"

"Twenty, I was about to say . . . which explains the limitations of my play, that you have certainly found . . . "

"If you were eight years old, the limitations would be justifiable. But twenty . . . at twenty I was in Miller's *The Crucible*, have *you* read it?"

"No . . . "

"And what have you read in your life, tell me, to make you think you were ready to write a play and send it to me, forcing me to read it because my good manners and my erudition—developed over fifty years on the stage—stop me from trashing all the manuscripts that I receive on a daily basis from insipid young guys like you who wake up one day convinced they're geniuses—because you *are* convinced you're a genius and that you've written something brilliant, right?"

I was shattered. I was an ameba. I was done.

"No, Sir . . . it's not like that, one of your students, Angelica Narcisello, urged me to . . . but I didn't want to bother you . . . I'll go now, goodbye . . . "

"Oh no, oh no, that's too easy, *you* sent me *your* play, you forced me to read it, now *you* will stay put, nice and comfy, and you're going to listen carefully to me."

He leapt to his feet (he wore black boots, black velour pants, a white organza shirt with a long black jacket that came down to his knees, and a red ascot), grabbed my manuscript and started to read out the first page:

Why are you looking at me?
I'm not looking at you. I'm studying you.

Oh God, what nonsense had I written?

He uttered the girl's lines in falsetto and the guy's in his deep, cavernous voice. The effect was horribly ridiculous. Without commenting, he evoked the dimness in each sentence, their spineless structure. I felt his sarcasm, his bottomless contempt, my body was a pile of sopping wet bones dripping shame.

He stopped acting, bent over me placing his fists on the armrests, face-to-face, eye to eye.

"Tell me, on whose works did you base your education? I sense some Racine and Corneille here and there, but with Ibsen's pessimism, though the modern structure reminds me of David Mamet, while the deliberately absurd and incongruous dialogues are clearly Pinteresque, early Pinter, at least, while as a whole, the story retraces Laclos's *Les Liaisons Dangereuses* with a touch of Boccaccio . . ."

"Boccaccio, yes!" My body jerked, at last a name I'd heard before. All the others had been one jab to my face after another, I felt crushed by my ignorance, by my arrogant ignorance, and by his level of culture.

But he showed no mercy. He moved away, arms folded, stared at me with steely eyes full of disdain, and smiled.

"Boccaccio, eh?"

I also smiled. Maybe it was over, maybe it was over, I was a puny pile of mud in the world, I was minuscule all curled up into a ball on my chair and didn't dare look him in the eyes.

"You haven't read a single page of any of the authors I mentioned."

In that instant, I woke up, like a dying man raising his head.

"But . . . did you need to say it? But why . . . why are you so mean? . . . It's the nastiness I don't understand . . ."

His eyes lit up in a furious rage. Taking huge strides, he headed toward the door and threw it open for me. Then he crossed the reception area to the other door and threw that one open as well, I followed him like a beaten dog, my head lowered. I slithered out, brushing past Guglielminetti, and a shudder paralyzed my whole body, but I managed to stammer a "Goodbye, Ma'am" to Miss Rottenmeier. "Goodbye," she said sadly, without looking at me, and I had the feeling that she stared at her boss disapprovingly, maybe even with contempt. On the threshold, Guglielminetti tossed my play into the void of the stairwell, pages fluttering in the air, he slammed the door, and I found myself all alone to pick up the sheets of paper scattered all over the steps, and I thought about pounding on the door and screaming something like "You dirty bastard, who the fuck do you think you are???" At least to get some of my dignity back.

But I was nothing, and I was afraid of him, of Miss Rottenmeier, of everything.

10. March

When Angelica called me that same night, the first thing I felt was a deep sense of guilt at the way I had treated her. She had believed in me, and I hadn't treated her any better than Guglielminetti had treated me. It was atrocious. The only way to respond to Guglielminetti's reprehensible reaction would be not to deserve it, but I deserved it all, and this made it all the more unbearable, and in fact I realized that I wasn't at all angry at Guglielminetti—as if he had done right by me.

And so, the first thing to do was ask for her forgiveness, and so as to feel a full sense of penitence, I told her I was ashamed of what I had said to her, that I was a sick person and an idiot with no excuse for my behavior, but she was an awesome, special girl, and I swore to her that from then on she could count on me and I would take care of her.

And the play? And Guglielminetti?

That name was a poison dart to my chest. Forget about Guglielminetti and the play, I told her, right now they're not important, it didn't go as I'd hoped if you really want to know—but that's okay.

But tell me more, tell me more.

I'll tell you, I'll tell you, but now I just want to see you and talk to you, I want to be with you, I think that you and I could be something wonderful together, with no hard feelings and nastiness, don't you think?

You're really strange, she said, let's meet tomorrow at the usual place, okay?

Yeah, the usual place.

The second thing to do was to be brave enough to take the manuscript in my hands, to have enough objectivity to read it from top to bottom and understand.

It was horrible. It was world-class garbage. It was other people's stuff, paraphrased from others, it was the badge of my absolute ignorance that I would never be able to address, of my disgusting presumption as a smart-ass know-it-all, of my limited and provincial mind.

I threw myself on the bed in desperation. I hated myself. And I hated Oscar Wilde, I hated Shakespeare and everyone else I had never heard of, everyone who called himself an artist, what kind of lives did they lead—studying so much, writing so much, maybe more refined rubbish than mine, but still rubbish, random, abstract ideas with no substance.

It suddenly hit me that I should become a businessman, because I was surely a crude and ignorant man, but at least I would make money, I would experience things, I would spend my time and money with whores—rather than being the wan, haggard, destitute artist who never gets laid: go ahead and write pure poetry, artist, I'm getting laid!

But, while eager to get rid of any proof of my shameful, ambitious, and unrealistic artistic past, I didn't have the guts to burn my terrible play. Instead, I dared go into the living room, opened the door, and announced to my parents my intention to quit college and start looking for a job—and that was the third thing I did. It was a shock to my mother, she started going off the deep end and even started crying, my father on the other hand, a discerning strategist, put his hand on my shoulder and asked me:

"What channel is the game on?"

Well done, dad. He'd understood that watching the game together and getting lost in technical debates over the wisdom of removing a defender and adding an attacker without upsetting the balance between the zones was the only thing I needed.

It was cold and rainy. A cold rain and snow, a world mired in mud. I let the rain wash over me. The city seemed to possess an angry soul, oppressive and unsatisfied. Women's mouths were downturned and spiteful, lashed by rain. I was waiting in front of the bar, and it was cold and it was raining, but I didn't care: I hugged myself hunched over in my overcoat, and I was small and despicable, I was what I was. I saw her coming. How she was dressed or what expression her face had, I couldn't tell. The only thing I noticed was the orange umbrella. My heart was full of an unfamiliar feeling: fear of people, of their cruelty. I looked at the men who passed by, and I saw Guglielminetti in each one of them.

"What a bastard . . . I can't believe he was so . . . " she hissed, baring her teeth.

"Yep."

I had told her everything, reliving the merciless scene from the previous day like a form of self-punishment. We were seated at our usual table, it was six o'clock, it was already dark outside. The blue-eyed guy with the ponytail brought us coffee. He flashed his usual smile. I explained to Angelica my intention to put it all behind me, except her of course, and she listened with apparent devotion and suffering, and that suffering, in that moment, united us, two suffering souls and a vicious world.

We ventured out into the melancholic city. I put my arm around her to protect her and keep her warm because I want to start from scratch and be a better person—I would tell myself—I want to be fair and treat her right. Then she said:

"If you want a job, a distant cousin of mine owns a restaurant, soon the season will start up again and he's always looking for waiters."

The seaside city where the Don Arturo Faust restaurant was located was about thirty miles from my house, and yet when I got off the crumbling bus it felt as if I had walked across America or had just come back from spending a season in Siberia. I was alone, without a dime, and had left my pampered life behind; I had lived a sheltered life, spending my parents' money on cigarettes and whiskey, I had hurt everyone I had met along the way; I had betrayed my friends and my girlfriend, I had betrayed God. I had played the villain.

Now I would develop blisters on my feet, my nerves would be shot from exhaustion, I would know the hardships of earning a piece of stale bread.

All of this comforted me.

Don Arturo Faust, the eponymous owner of the restaurant, was wearing a white shirt, green vest, and black pants. He didn't smile but eyed me up and down with his squinty gray eyes. He told me the daily pay rate, an unheard-of pittance (but it was fair, it was fair), and that sometimes you worked more than the required six hours but for tax reasons you weren't paid overtime (it's ok, it doesn't matter, it's only the first step), and that all the potential tips ended up in a common jar and were divvied up among all the employees at the end of the day. He introduced me to the other employees: a fat waitress; a dwarf with a glass eye, who smiled faintly waving hello with her little hand; a lanky thirty-year-old waiter who I guessed was American and said *hi* before turning around; a black Rastafarian with dreadlocks and earphones, who said *yeah* and turned around; and a paper thin, very sad woman (recalling an unwed mother abandoned at the altar), who stood behind the bar, barely raising the corners of her mouth without saying anything; his seventeen-year-old daughter, whom I flashed a sly smile to imply some kind of future complicity (who instead kept on chewing gum and uttered an unsmiling *'ello*); Faust's wife at the cash register, who gave me the most credible smile.

Don Arturo told me to sit, then asked me:

"What did you study?"

"I studied the classics in high school, then I enrolled in college" (I was proud and diligent, and smiled the whole time).

"Ah, that's just peachy." He groaned scornfully.

I felt a shiver of embarrassment run up and down my spine. I was sorry I had tried to show off about my studies. Don Arturo Faust continued to shake his head, perplexed, with a grimace full of contempt that curled his lips. I was seriously afraid he would send me packing—so I tried to convince him otherwise, in an imploring tone:

"Mr. Faust, look . . . I know I have no experience, but give me a shot, studying no longer interests me, and I want to become a great entrepreneur like you."

He laughed, maybe satisfied.

"You need a backbone, you know, you can't make anything up, here we're not like you city slickers, here we work also for them; do you know, do you know when I started working? *When I was six.* At six, your mommy was bringing you coffee while you stayed in bed at six, and she may still do it, but look what I've achieved, eh! Just remember you can't judge, what's the word, intelligence, from books and poetry, what's the use of poetry, eh? Tell me what's the point?"

"There's none."

"Good, none. Poetry couldn't build me no house with a swimming-pool. I wouldn't have no bank account that, that . . . if I studied where do you think I'd be now?!"

His eyes were ablaze. Nonetheless, it seemed as though I had won him over. There was something paternal in his disdain, he wanted to teach me about life, he was gruff but he didn't seem mean. Yeah, not much point in poetry, I agreed, and his hard life, his naïve and grammarless talk touched me to the point that when he told me to shave and cut my hair and have his wife show me my room, overcome by emotion, I wanted to hug him.

My room, on the third floor of a fourth-rate guesthouse, was a hole in the wall with a bed, a sink, and a small mirror. You had to look for the bathroom on the ground floor. Mrs. Faust told me that room and board were included; I was grateful to her as one is to their mother, then she smiled and left after telling me to be ready at six in the morning. Her husband had to have some hidden qualities, because she seemed so nice to me—as for me, for the first time, I felt like a man, alone, far from home with a thousand concerns and not even a toilet to pee in. I looked out the window, some women were walking down the street. I had a smoke. Mmmh. But then I thought of Angelica, and reminded myself that she was the only one who had believed in me, and I mustn't hurt her anymore.

*

The next day, at six, I was in my new uniform: a white shirt with Don Arturo Faust's initials in green on the upper right side and black pants.

"So, try to understand what I am telling you so I don't need to repeat myself" the boss told me, and he began to fill me in on the secrets of the trade as I listened to him almost standing at attention. I was restless, I was enthusiastic, I wanted to be the best waiter in the West, I wanted the boss to wink at me, pat me on the back—instead when I messed up the placement of a napkin, laying it down with its folded corner toward the right side instead of the left, the boss flew into a rage and pointed at me with hatred:

"So, you didn't understand a fucking thing. And you even went to college, shit, I've already told you I don't want to repeat the same thing twice. DO YOU FUCKING GET IT!?!"

He screamed, his face all red. He was barely 5'7", almost fifty, a huge pot belly and his gelled hair pulled back in a vertical comb over to cover his bald spot, with a preposterous ponytail held in place with a red rubber band. He was ugly, but I was afraid of him, he made me uneasy, he crushed me. He followed my every move like a rabid dog, derisively stressing I'd been a student, which made me ashamed. It seemed to me that I was so inept precisely because I had spent my life studying, and, in any case, I believed that his being tough with me was the only way to make me one of them, to get me to understand the job so that at the end of the day don Arturo Faust would put his hand on my shoulder and would tell me:

"I wanted to test you, forgive me, now I know I can count on you."

In fact, don Arturo Faust seemed to be friendly and complicit with the Rasta waiter and the American one (this made me very jealous) and respectful of the dwarf with the glass eye. I figured the sooner I gained his trust, the sooner I would earn his friendship, so I pulled out the sharp knife stuck in my ribcage, and when the first customers arrived, I hurried over to take care of them.

I felt honored to be able to wait on my first customers and go back into the kitchen to announce my orders in a resonant voice, but don Faust stopped my initiative from the get-go.

"Where the fuck are you going?"

The blood froze in my veins.

"I'm going to wait on those customers . . ."

"Where-the-fuck-are-you-going?" and he winked at the Rasta and the American who started laughing (I would have gladly kicked the shit out of them, more so because the latter went to that table and stole my customer).

"But . . . boss . . . I'm going . . ."

"BUT YOU REALLY DON'T UNDERSTAND A FUCKING THING!!! YOU THINK THIS JOB IS A JOKE!!! YOU THINK ANYBODY CAN DO IT!!! *I* TAKE CARE OF THE TABLES!!! *YOUR MORE EXPERIENCED CO-WORKERS* TAKE CARE OF THE TABLES!!! *YOU* BUS THE TABLES AND AT THE MOST BRING THE PLATES TO THE TABLES, DO YOU GET IT OR NOT!?!"

I was mortified.

I was humiliated, I was stripped bare of my presumption that I had understood everything, caught red-handed by my own excessive zeal.

But I was also really pissed. I wanted to be useful, after all, I didn't want to do anything wrong, after all.

The dwarf with the glass eye looked at me. "Try not to get him mad," she said without a trace of hostility, "or it'll be a bad day for all of us." She smiled at me with her rotten, pathetic teeth, and her smile froze as if her mind was on another planet.

I felt sorry for her.

Then I heard a motorcycle roar.

The boss's daughter dismounted from the back seat. She had thin blonde braids and chewing gum in her mouth, and she planted a frosty kiss on the bike rider's mouth—a second rate James Dean, a C-movie James Dean with a slew of pimples, piercings on the nose, and studs everywhere, with such a moronic expression on his face that for a minute, surrounded by such peers as these, I had doubts again about my choices.

"Hey, Anita," I said smiling.

"Mmh?" with a darting glance as if I was scum.

"How's it going?"

"It's going . . . " She chomped, yawning.

"It's going?"

Offended, she stared at me. Then screamed:

"DAAAD!!!"

Her father appeared, hugged his daughter, who half-heartedly hugged him back. They turned their back on me and I stood there, suddenly furious, jealous, and I felt an overwhelming longing for Angelica.

The first day I worked twelve hours, the second thirteen, the third fourteen.

I was exhausted and didn't have an ounce of energy left, in the evenings I couldn't even find the strength to chew—nor, for that matter, was I hungry or did I feel like eating.

I lost ten pounds, at night I dreamed of forks and plates and the famous gnocchi a la don Arturo Faust, and I hated the food in a way I had never hated anything before.

But if only I had gotten a tiny nod of approval, if only I had gotten a little respect, I would have been able to put up with it all: at first, I craved a "Good job!" like a dog lusts after a bone—later on, I just wanted be left alone.

But no such luck.

My fourth day I noticed that the two waiters, the Rasta and the American, one on the boss's right and the other on his left, were snickering at me every time I passed by (I was setting up for dinner while they were sipping beers at the bar).

I had the feeling that even the Madonna was laughing at me at that moment, not to mention those two filthy pigs. So I stopped, my arms loaded with plates, tried to muster my most sinister expression, and asked them point blank:

"What's so funny?"

The American and the Rasta could barely stifle their laughter, and I hated them, I hated them with every fiber of my being, I was a Viet Cong and the Grand Wizard of the Ku Klux Klan.

"But you don't like no women?" The boss taunted me, and tiny tears of laughter appeared at the corners of his eyes.

Ah, if only we had been in a more noble, more refined, more anything of a century! I would have simply slapped him with a white glove and challenged him to a duel—instead, mortally wounded, I answered him:

"Yes, *I* like women."

"Because, you know, you walk a little . . . a little strange . . . "

All three started hooting and hollering, all riled up, their heads thrown back and a tempest of beer swirling in their excited tall glasses, I turned around and continued setting the tables.

"Come on, we're just kidding!" A voice, maybe regretful, screamed at me, behind my back.

"Why am I being smacked around by both the educated and the uneducated?" I told Angelica on the phone as I cried.

I missed her, I missed my friends, I missed Saba, I missed Alcapone (how could I have done all that nasty crap to him?), and I even missed Angelica's friends, the ecologists, because they would have never dared to insult me that way, I missed my mother and her worrying, I missed my dad and our matches together.

I was crying and expecting Angelica to tell me to come home, instead she said:

"Come on, hang in there, *you* can do it."

I couldn't disappoint her and I hung in there. I sucked it up and put my nose to the grindstone. I tried not to make any mistakes, not even one, and I didn't look anyone in the eyes, I ignored the boss and my coworkers and that slut of the boss's daughter, until one day Mrs. Faust put her hand on my shoulder and told me:

"Great job . . . you know, my husband thought you were too intelligent for a job like this . . . "

"Does that mean I'm stupid enough?"

"No, no . . . I'm sorry, I didn't mean it that way . . . I meant that you showed determination . . . even though someone like you could do so many greater things."

She was a good woman, and for a minute she dulled my hatred. How could she have married a petty merchant like her husband? I didn't get it. On the other hand, you could see them at four in the morning, after working twenty hours at an unfathomable rhythm, with bags under their eyes and on edge from frayed nerves—you could see them count and recount the day's take, the mystical light of greed in their eyes—and it didn't matter if, in fact, it was a dog's life, due to both the quality and hardship of the work, because counting their proceeds excited and moved them just like the first time, because they counted and they were happy.

My seventh night I brought a Brazilian salad rather than a Greek one. Don Arturo Faust got furious, in front of all the customers sitting at the tables:

"YOU'RE AN IDIOT!!! YOU ARE A DUMBASS!!! DON'T YOU KNOW THERE'S OLIVES IN A GREEK SALAD, FUCK, AND THERE'S CORN IN THE BRAZILIAN ONE, FUCK!?! . . . AND YOU EVEN WENT TO COLLEGE!!!"

The restaurant customers laughed at me, hiding their amusement behind their hands. The women seemed to revel in the spectacle of public lambasting, while the men arched their eyebrows as if proud of having brought them to such a great event. The Rasta and the American smiled cruelly: proud of their professionalism, they thought it appropriate that anyone who didn't know the difference between olives and corn would be deemed unworthy of their title and should be stoned.

Assailed in that manner, I went back to the kitchen reeling. I could have killed them all, only their slow deaths would placate me, would heal my soul mangled by the humiliation, by the meanness, by the laughter of the women—by the total absurdity of those words, of those screams.

Like for Christ at Calvary, Veronica's kerchief was soothing, as was the affectionate tone of the bartender-single mother:

"Come on, don't let it get to you . . ."

And I: "But . . . It was just a mix-up with a salad . . . I could have just brought it back . . . It's not like I dropped it on someone's head."

She went on: "Oh no, the boss is right: if we all brought Brazilian salads instead of Greek ones, we'd be screwed! But he's like that, it'll blow over and he won't even remember."

It was a circus. It couldn't be any other way. People are completely crazy. They're evil. They're all clowns. And if there's one thing I've hated since I was a child, it's the circus, and the clowns have never made me laugh. Astonishment replaced pain. Knowing the difference between corn and olives was essential for these people, and humiliating and denigrating those who didn't know the difference was natural. The more people perform an insignificant activity, the more energetically they defend its dignity: for a waiter it was a badge of honor knowing the difference between a Greek salad and a Brazilian one. No joke, it was a circus.

"Good evening, Professor, the usual?"

The boss was more obsequious than with any of the other client: besides, the Professor came for dinner every night around eleven when the place was half empty.

As the boss's wife had explained to me, he was a retired, childless, English literature professor. Once upon a time he used to come in fairly often with his wife, then his wife had died and he'd lost some marbles: in fact, he always ordered for two, always the gnocchi a la don Arturo Faust, as if there were someone eating with him, presumably his wife.

He ate his meal in silence, not touching the other plate, he poured wine into both glasses and drank only his, then he would politely say good night and leave.

The boss put his hand on my shoulder and whispered in a fatherly tone:

"Why don't you go talk to him for a little bit, eh? He's someone who has studied a lot you know, and you're the only one here with whom he can talk . . . "

I was flabbergasted. The same wretched Roman soldier who had dipped the sponge in vinegar and stuck it in my mouth now seemed meek and impressed.

People, Christ, people are strange.

And I, too, who twenty minutes earlier would have strangled him with my bare hands stood there as if paralyzed by his kindness, and his heavy hand on my shoulder felt like a balm—I was honored to be granted the exclusivity of welcoming this guest.

And so, I approached the table, I, the ambassador of the owner's pride and esteem, nervously said:

"Good evening, Professor . . ."

"Good evening."

"You know, they told me that you are a distinguished expert in English literature . . . so I wanted to tell you that I love Oscar Wilde . . . and I would love to hear your thoughts on this great Irish author who . . ."

I realized I was talking like a literary textbook, and I blushed. Yet, he smiled graciously and invited me to take a chair. I was about to say that I still had to work, but at that moment don Arturo came to the table, showcasing his best smile, and he once again put his hand on my shoulder to instruct me that I should remain seated, then he turned to the Professor and said:

"It's my pleasure you're getting acquainted with this young man, Professor, he is working as a waiter now, but someday he will become a professor even superior to you!"

I was shocked. The most incredible part was that he seemed absolutely sincere.

The professor nodded indulgently, then once we were alone, he invited me to eat. I had some scruples about eating his late companion's dinner, but he reassured me:

"I order for two, otherwise they will think I'm crazy to eat alone."

"What?"

"I was joking. A joke a la Oscar Wilde, right?"

Right. And I have to admit that don Faust's gnocchi were pretty good, and the wine wasn't bad either. Once again, he asked me about my passion for Oscar, and I decided to dispense with doctrine, and I spoke to him unafraid my ignorance would show, I explained what I had felt and he listened, he told me that what delighted him about Oscar was that even his darkest stories exuded happiness, and joy for life, yes, I felt the same way! And then we went on to talk about

Shakespeare, and he told me about a couple of tragedies, which I hadn't read yet, that sounded fantastic, we drank and smoked and ate, then he asked me if I wrote and, blushing, I answered that, yes, I had written a play—and I told him about the appalling business with Guglielminetti (the fact that he'd never heard of him gave me a massive boost of confidence), and he told me that he would love to read something of mine, and my ambitions and my passionate pride began to take root once again, growing stronger. Feeling squeamish, I said, "I don't know," and I explained that my disappointment had been so devastating that I had chosen to simply exist.

"But where is the pleasure in existing if you don't write about it?" he asked me.

Exactly.

"Thank you, professor, would you allow me to pay for dinner?" So I went to the boss and straight out told him I was quitting, I asked him to give me what I was owed minus the cost of the professor's meal, he was no longer smiling and, after paying me, he turned his back on me.

I felt I should be mean to him, but it was a rational need, I didn't care about anything anymore. I looked at the bartender (who stared sadly at me), at the boss's slut daughter (who ignored me), at the Rasta and the American (officious and dripping with sweat, true professionals), at the waitress with the glass eye and at Faust's wife, who both smiled at me—and then I said:

"Goodbye."

11. April

And now? Even my sparkling optimism had been tarnished after those two months. I was rocking back and forth at the back of the bus taking me back to Mestre on one of those amazingly comfortable red velvet seats, and I sank deeply into the seat and into my own commiseration, I had to press my fingers on my eyes to hold back the tears, even though the bus was half-empty and there was no one around me.

But I had never before perceived my soul's presence to this degree. It was laid out bare on my chest, from the root of my neck to my mouth to my stomach, ravaged like a Roman fort trampled by the wrath of the Carthaginians at Cannae, tears and blood over the scorched soil of Apulia, even though Quintus Fabius Maximus had attempted to stall, earning himself the nickname *cunctator*, the delayer, exactly like me—because in high school I was great at stalling during my physics oral exams. The memory made me smile. And I don't know about Quintus Fabius Maximus, but as for me, from that razed battlefield rose a glimmer, like a reflection on armor, the shimmer of a broken sword, or maybe it was just the ancient farms of a fascinating era lining the countryside kissed by the sun; the fact is that, mixed with the compassion for myself, a kernel of light was germinating within me, a sense of peace, the impression that every crucifixion heralds a resurrection, the resolute belief that someday all the pain would be useful, delicate on my pages, and the days of glory and revenge would come, the days of Scipio the African, and I would nail don Faust, Guglielminetti, and all of Carthage.

I had returned home with a cardboard suitcase and my unrealized dreams, feeling like the prodigal son: everyone hugged me, everyone kissed me. My mother was in seventh heaven when I announced my plans to go back to college and that in May I would take the exam. At the pool hall, France couldn't stop teasing me:

"Excuse me, you who have experience, can you serve us some beers?"

I smiled, more or less.

Coldly, Rebecca asked me:

"So, have you given up writing?"

I had the impression that Rebecca had genuine contempt for my behavior toward Alcapone and Angelica, for my artistic ambitions, for my failure even as a waiter, or quite simply, I attributed to her what I, in fact, felt about myself, nevertheless fully aware that Rebecca's contempt was not softened by the excuses I gave myself in front of the mirror and didn't feel like sharing with her: come on! It had all been a set of circumstances and situations! And Hannibal's army was stronger – let's admit it!

And if I didn't feel like mitigating the contempt I'm sure Rebecca felt by explaining my weaknesses to her, it wasn't just because I was tired and because I found her contempt and her cold-hearted attitude annoying, but because her contempt came in handy: it increased the pity I had for myself, the desire to forgive me; it restored a degree of faith in myself.

I don't know if it was contempt, but I soon realized that even Niso had changed. He always tried to be nice, of course, but it was as if he had put up an iron curtain of courtesy between us. It shocked me to understand—and understand only now! —that Niso was not that supernatural being with the gift of divine indifference, the supreme intellectual I had always considered him to be, but rather, he was a man in love, damn! And his love for Angelica was terribly worldly, dammit! And his best friend had slept with the girl he was in love with, and there was no way that all this would not have engendered a crevice between us, not made him twice as jealous, mortally wounded!

I pondered over our phone conversation just before New Year's Eve, when I filled him in on my involvement with Angelica (but obviously he already knew about it), I remembered his affable demeanor when he reassured me about any possible hostility toward me and told me how his love had turned to hate. He had been meticulous and convincing in warning me about Angelica, and I had been moved by his loyalty in shielding me from her, in alerting me about her and her poison arrows, in flattering me by telling me I was the only one who could triumph over her, and in doing so, avenge him—and, honored by his friendship, I had no other wish than to avenge him and wash away the shame.

Yes, Niso had put me in the right state of mind to not care about Angelica in the least and to kill her instead, if possible, so that even though he might not have methodically planned the bathroom scene with Saba—he had certainly allowed it to happen. But what I hadn't understood at all is that Niso, with his persuasive and hypnotic phone call, had also in parallel laid the groundwork for his revenge against me. I don't know to what extent Niso had imagined how things would progress from there, in a series of interconnected events only superficially linked that had led to my humiliation at the hands of Guglielminetti and don Faust, but he had probably envisaged my public mockery (his calculated courtesy, Rebecca's contempt, Alcapone's and Saba's immediate exit from any bar I showed up to), and he certainly understood eons before what would soon happen, something that—again!—I hadn't understood yet.

I didn't begrudge him getting his revenge. I wasn't even that convinced of it, the only thing I knew for sure was he hid his hostility behind his graciousness, that he considered it necessary to hide behind the mask of the aristocrat to conceal any plebeian emotion like jealousy. From my point of view, I was too drained to discuss it with him and maybe ask for his forgiveness, and I couldn't even feel bitter for our floundering friendship, and besides I felt that his own revenge, which had ruined me and led Angelica to feel the same pain she had caused him, seemed suddenly useless and petty to him. The taste for revenge is lost as soon as we act on it.

And yet, there was still Angelica. She showed up at my house riding her new motorbike, an appalling canary yellow and tempest purple jaguar, wearing camouflage pants, shiny boots to her knees, and a man's shirt. I hugged her, kissed her, and shared my misadventures and my pain. But then I felt an emptiness, as if telling her all this stuff had humiliated me once again, I felt like a sissy, a little four-year-old girl all naked except for a diaper. It was time to get sex back, to reestablish my virility. But she looked at me tenderly and compassionately.

"What's wrong, are you sad?" I asked her.

"No . . ."

"You shouldn't feel sad for me."

"Actually, it's not for you."

"Ah."

"Today is the anniversary of my father's death."

"I get it." We were sitting on the living room sofa. I wanted to undress her, make love to her, maybe drink coffee and laugh. Again, with her father. Damn that crazy Narciso Narcisello and damn his decision to die, veiling forever Angelica's eyes with sadness. Damn these dead fathers who spring to life at the most inopportune moments. Damn me for not finding a comforting word, I couldn't feel sorry, I just wanted to get into those hideous pants.

I crept closer, I brushed aside her hair, I started to kiss her on the neck, she put a hand on my chest, she looked at me with her forceful stare, "Why don't you tell me about *your* father?" She asked me.

Pfff. What was I supposed to tell her? I didn't have any captivating stories, stories about *adversarial relationships*, we had TV programs and movies chock full of that crap to make you believe that something similar also existed in reality, but that wasn't my case, and I no longer had arrows in my quiver to concoct any tall tales.

"My father has blue eyes. He comes from the sea, just like in the song. When he was eight, his father fell overboard and died. It's pretty weird because his father, my grandfather, built sailboats, model sailboats, and the only memory my father has of his father is that he had promised they would build a sailboat together, and then he died. Falling overboard. Come on now, if you start crying, I won't tell you anything else."

"No, please, keep going!"

"My father, at eight years old, was at his father's funeral and felt like having sweet pears. A bizarre idea that has been etched in my mind. I went to see my grandfather's grave in Istria, in a minuscule graveyard on a steep cliff overlooking the sea, always drenched in sunlight, with an intense aroma of salt and Scottish broom. A beautiful place. My grandfather had the same eyes and the same facial expressions as my father, it's incredible, and therefore the same eyes as me. My grandfather's best friend, a Communist professor with a marvelous beard, a member of the Resistance, is buried next to him. My grandfather was not a Communist, he was a sailor."

Angelica was crying. I thought about my father at eight wanting to eat sweet pears at his father's funeral, I thought about his father's eyes, kind, deep, I thought about the beard of his best friend, who was his friend even though he was a professor and a Communist, and I thought about the sailboat my young father would never have—and I got all choked up. I started crying, too, and for the first time in twenty years I felt all the pain, loneliness, and poetry of my father without his sailboat. I cried for him, for my grandfather, for the Communist professor in the Resistance, for myself, and I cried for the beauty and fragility of the world, and crying, I said to Angelica "I'm sorry, I'm sorry about your father," and I meant it.

And so, crying, we got undressed and, crying, we made love. A strange, ridiculous, and sad thing. Still naked, she stayed on the couch.

I slipped my boxers on and shook that uncomfortable feeling hanging over me.

"I'm making coffee, want some?"

"Yeah," and she smiled faintly.

I fled into the kitchen. An enormous feeling of stupidity weighed heavily on me and gave me a headache. My eyes ached, so did my chest. She often laughed with me, she always laughed, even at the most inopportune moments, but not that morning. In that moment, I really missed that laughter.

I came back with two steaming cups of coffee.

She had gotten dressed, except for her boots, and was sitting with her elbows on her knees, her head between her legs, smoking, lost in thought.

"Coffee's ready."

She looked up at me and, oh man, please, come on! Don't be so sad. I sat down next to her, and we silently drank our coffee. I played with her hair. Come on, life goes on. Struggling to control her emotions, she looked at me again. I put on some happy music and improvised a funny dance. Usually, my funny dances made her laugh like crazy. Not this time. There was something serious and at the same time desperate in her amazing eyes. Damn, they were truly amazing. Moist, fragile, dazzling, and for a minute I was engrossed in them, since the first time I'd seen her—almost a year ago! —I hadn't seen them look this beautiful, I had almost forgotten. I stopped dancing. I felt powerless in the face of such sadness, and at that point I hoped she would leave and never come back, because it was springtime and I couldn't do anything about it, because her father was dead and I couldn't bring him back, because the coffee was good and that night there would be a Paul Newman movie on TV and the following day I would start studying again, and I needed peace of mind, clarity and sincerity to think about myself, to feel happy and . . .

"Do you love me?"

That's how she asked me, out of the blue.

I almost choked on the coffee. She stared at me and there was no way out. She stared at me, and I had to answer her. She stared at me, and we were just done making love, and her father was dead, and she was suffering, I could have proffered a treatise on the meaning of the verb or taken refuge behind an idiotic smile, but I couldn't make her suffer anymore, I couldn't play with her feelings, I couldn't tell her lies (why not, why not, why not?)—and so, exhausted and naked, my back to the wall, I said:

"No."

Suddenly she got up, and I felt devastated, please forgive me but I couldn't lie to you, please, now I'm not ready but give me time to learn, but she was already on the doorstep, she turned around, and said sweetly:

"No need to justify yourself. You said it, it's not your fault."

"No, Angelica, I don't even know why I said it . . ." I listened to my plaintive voice, the voice of a fighter up against the ropes.

"Because it's true."

"No, Angelica, it's just that, I don't know . . ." Please, ref, ring that bell!

She put her hand over my mouth to silence me. Then she spoke: "I'm going away. For a week. I'm meeting my mother in Stockholm. Thursday, I'll be back."

I was wiped out, weary to my bones, knocked out on the mat.

"I'm going to miss you so much, Angelica."

She smiled, staring at me, boring a hole in me but without a single tear, she laid her lips lightly on mine—and she was gone.

I discovered it was true that I would miss her. I eagerly studied the fourteenth-century poets, sipped a Coke, and waited. I would watch the game with my dad, play pool by myself, and wait.

At the end of every day, I felt a slight excitement because I was one day closer to Angelica's return. I pictured her arrival, after not seeing each other for a long seven days, she would look at me the way you look at a god, and I would give her a red rose. Yes, red, Angelica. Do you know the language of flowers? Yes, it means *love*, Angelica. I wanted to do so many things for her, invite her to my house for dinner, introduce her to my parents, and surprise her with a stuffed animal. Imagining her eyes full of joy for my thoughtful gestures, my heart swelled with tenderness.

Making her happy seemed like a divine calling, and since I didn't feel what she felt for me, I was under the impression that my way of loving her was more noble than the common one: I only wanted the best for her, her happiness, not mine. And then who knows, maybe I would be able to truly love her, I wanted to with every bone in my body—maybe I would never be able to stay faithful to her—but maybe love her one day, yes.

My mother was watering the fleshy geraniums, and I woke up blooming.

Finally, Thursday.

I made coffee, took out my books, and waited for the phone to ring, waited to hear her voice tell me "My love, I'm back." I sat down to study, galvanized, fresh, handsome.

I had bought two theater tickets for some Shakespeare play, and I couldn't wait to tell her—but the morning had gone by, and she hadn't called.

Never mind, I enjoyed studying the fourteenth-century poets in that anxiety-ridden and tense atmosphere, but at three o'clock she still hadn't called, nor at six, night fell and still no call.

It was bizarre.

Actually, it was bizarre that she had never called during the whole week. I got nervous, I had spent a shitload of money on Shakespeare, and even though she was the one that should have called me, I ended up calling her:

"Oh, hi . . . " she said drowsily.

"*Oh, hi?*"

"How are you?"

"Good, thanks. Did you just get back?"

"I got back two days ago."

Mortified and outraged, I swallowed a mouthful of saliva.

"Sorry, but couldn't you have called me?"

She said nothing. It sounded like I was whining, I knew it, so I tried to tie my disappointment to the money I'd wasted on Shakespeare.

"I'll reimburse you," she grumbled, half asleep, sounding annoyed, as if she just wanted to end the unpleasant conversation and go back to bed (maybe with another guy? *Maybe with another guy?* Was that even possible?). She wasn't even the least bit grateful I had called her, or that I had planned a romantic evening for two—and I felt humiliated and hurt. Then she said:

"Listen, we can see each other tomorrow, okay?"

"I'm not sure if I'll be around."

"Well, if you are, call me."

The next day, I didn't call her and neither did she. I was up to my eyeballs studying and a subtle sense of anguish radiated through me. Her indifference tore me apart like a machine gun. She's crazy about me, at least she was until a week ago, nothing that strong can simply change, not in a week, surely it's a well contrived tactic, believing she could trick me with her indifference, but she is actually consumed with love for me and waits for me to call her, I can see her: she is telling herself not to call me, she is telling herself not to even think about me, when I call her she does somersaults of joy, but she doesn't change her ways and keeps pretending indifference (silly girl! Do you really think you can fool me?), but my presence, my voice, and my jokes are poisoning her mind, and she roams around her room like a caged tigress hugging her pillow against her chest and madly biting into it.

I can see her, right, and meanwhile I'm roaming around my room like a caged tiger hugging my pillow against my chest and madly biting into it. I stop in front of the mirror, I see my sunken eyes and I laugh: oh, my old friend, this is how you are, you're really like this, women only interest you when they don't give themselves to you!

Pleased with my Casanova's personality, I went back to studying.

One day went by, then another.

I studied and she was right in front of my eyes, I sipped my coffee and the rumble of a motorbike startled me, my heart bounded in my chest when the phone rang—but nothing.

And what if she was really fleeing from me? What if she had realized that I would have caused her too much suffering, that I would have always cheated on her (it was true, it was true), what if she would rather not see me anymore instead of submitting to the daily torture of watching me act so unobtainable and handsome? What if she was just afraid of me, afraid of loving me too much, afraid I would squash her tender little heart like a gnat?

I was touched, and I called her.

She wasn't there. (Where was she?)

I called her again the following day, she wasn't there. (Where is she? Where is she? Who is she with?)

I called her a thousand times, I needed to tell her she could trust me, but where was she, where had she fled to forget me—or maybe, you coward, you're at home and you're not answering the phone?

I went downstairs, got in the car, and drove to her house. I rang the bell, gripped by a sudden apprehension. She really wasn't there.

I decided to wait for her in the car stationed at the curb a few yards from the gate with the snake emblem and bide my time like a bird of prey lies in wait for the sparrow.

An hour went by. That's it, I'm leaving. Maybe five more minutes, then I'll go. Two hours went by. A woman appeared, my heart tumbled into my throat, I crouched beneath the steering wheel: but it wasn't her. Three hours went by. I smoked. Dusk was falling, better this way, I could conceal myself more effectively—but what am I saying? Another five minutes and then I'll head home, enough playing the private eye!

I had been there for six hours, I had imagined at least twelve hundred times the scene of how I would get out of the car, she would look at me, I would say, "Hey babe, where are you running to? You can't run away from yourself," she would cry and hug me. When she finally arrived, I felt ashamed of my endless stakeout and I hid behind the dashboard. I peeked out to spy on her. She looked for her keys in her backpack, beautiful, she found them, she was relaxed, she was calm, she was tanned, she buried her face in the wisteria growing on the gate, she was beautiful, she was relaxed, she pressed a button on the keychain and the gate opened. She went inside and closed the door and left the world outside, me outside.

I drove, and I was a mess. Another cigarette, another look in the rearview mirror, music on the radio. An uninspired deejay was talking over the songs, miserable Australopithecus. I turned it off, a thousand questions pounded away at my brain.

Why?

Why was she doing this?

Is it possible that, contrary to my every previously held belief, love can end?

What is it that I don't get?

Why?

Days went by, and April's cruel sun singed my wounds. On exam day I showed up well dressed and tense, I knew that if I didn't pass, I wouldn't have the strength to get back up, I wouldn't have the strength to win back Angelica.

I sat down on the wooden chair and the teacher was a nice woman: she asked me a question I didn't understand, she repeated it but I still didn't get it, then I mumbled something—I realized that I was half dead, that I wasn't really ready to go through an oral exam—I was about to throw in the towel, when out of the corner of my eye I saw her, she was standing at the classroom door watching me take the exam.

I took off like a rocket, fantastic dialectics, razzle-dazzle, and other magic tricks: congratulations, the professor said, I feigned modesty but thanked her. Then, I was right next to her.

"Great job."

She said it just like that, miming an applause, impaling me with her gorgeous eyes. Was she serious? Was she being ironic?

"How come you're here?" I asked her quietly, sharply.

"I thought you wanted to see me."

"Me?"

"Well, if you don't want to, I'll leave . . . " and she turned her back on me.

I felt myself sinking back into the depths of despair. I grabbed her arm:

"Wait. Let's go for a drink."

At the bar, filled with noisy and useless people, neither one of us ordered anything, as if our stomachs had closed up from anger or despondency, as if a foreboding sky were hanging over us.

"Did you miss me?" She asked me, broodingly.

"What kind of a question is that?"

"So?"

Her insistence invigorated me. I knew I was weak, but I had to show that I could be strong. I asked Oscar Wilde for help:

"Angelica, a man who is master of himself can end sorrow as easily as he can invent pleasure."

"Did you even think of me?"

I felt a diabolical laugh deep inside of me, you sleazy little tramp, here you lie once again in the palm of my hand—instead she was the one who laughed diabolically, leaving me speechless, furious.

"I needed to focus on the exam, you know that," I answered, practically hissing at her.

"I, on the other hand, thought a lot about you," she said laughing, and it was as if she were saying just the opposite, as if she was throwing all her indifference at me.

In any other situation, I would have got up and left, but I thought about her tears, her sweetness, her crazy love for me—and I just couldn't stand the idea that all this would be lost. So, I took her hands in mine, I confronted her face caught between hilarity and sadness, and I whispered:

"Listen, we just need to relax now, and you'll see that everything will go back to the way it was."

"Nothing can be like it was," she said, as it began to rain outside and my world began to cave in on me, and then, almost by accident: "You know, I saw Niso three days ago, right after I got back. He came to visit me at home."

An old waiter approached the table, he asked us something, I don't know what, I didn't hear a thing, I saw her smile at him, I don't know, a purple fog had enveloped me, I saw Angelica's white teeth, so pure, I saw her coral mouth move, and the waiter answer, meek and fatherly, but for me it was all a silent movie, fragments of images parading before my eyes, Angelica's slender neck, the waiter's yellow tail coat, Angelica's languid hands, the waiter's golden cigarette lighter igniting her cigarette, as if we were in a Parisian bistro and she were a mademoiselle or a high-class whore. The waiter left, and I managed to say:

"And . . . and why did he come visit you?"

"Oh, no reason . . . he showed up in the morning unannounced," and she looks away and turns her gaze toward the crowd at the bar, but she doesn't see them, and I know that she is reliving that scene of Niso dropping in at her house, and in her faint smile I see an omniscient malice that tortures me: she sees what took place and I wasn't present, she sees what they shared and she is smiling, look at me, please, look at me, but she seems amused, pleased by those images in her mind—until finally she looks at me again:

"Does it bother you?"

"Why would it bother me?" I replied too quickly.

Angelica took a deep breath, which seemed to last a century, and she smiled at me, a phony naive smile, a phony sweet smile, a derisive smile, and I felt my dry throat, and I hated her, or I would have liked to hate her—and the waiter came back and placed two empty cups on the table with a tea bag for each and a teapot filled with hot water. I watched her as she poured the water in the cups, first mine, then hers, and she was so beautiful, so beautiful and inaccessible, she never missed a gesture, she was perfect. Niso and her nude in each other's arms, she was coming while I was buying tickets for Shakespeare, I felt like throwing up, but I chased the image away, she was in love with me, nothing happened with Niso, then she said:

"I don't know. You seemed upset."

"Upset? That's insane. It's not like . . . no way, it's just that I'm tired from the exam—ouch, this tea is so hot!—But what I mean is, I admit I'm surprised, I thought he hated you."

"Indeed. That's why he came over. To ask for forgiveness. *I came to ask you to forgive me*, he said. *And to show you my most sincere gratitude for allowing me to love you so sweepingly*. You know how dramatic he is . . ."

I perked up. She was making fun of him. She was imitating Niso's stern demeanor, with his pursed lips, his eyes closed, and his mellifluous voice. Damn, she was so beautiful even when she was imitating a guy and I had scalded my tongue on the tea. She scolded me: "Hey! Can't you even crack a smile?!" And this time her smile was sincere, a smile full of love that flooded my heart, nothing had happened with Niso, she loved me. Niso had drawn the short straw and had gone home with his tail between his legs—but once again she looked away as she drank her tea, slowly, and again she stared into the emptiness within the crowd, and I knew that in her mind she was replaying the images, known only to her, and she mumbled, as if she were fessing up:

"We spent the whole morning together."

A punch to the gut. She didn't notice, looked somewhere else:

"We had lunch together. We laughed so much. We had never laughed so much even when we were together. He's always so . . ."

My heart was gripped by a frozen vise. I was waiting for her while she was laughing it up with Niso, and now, at last, I could see them, I could clearly see her laughing with Niso, I was buying her roses and theater tickets and she, placid, was laughing with Niso, I could see them on the couch in her house, peeing their pants laughing, peeing their pants laughing behind my back, I could see them pigging out together while I, oblivious, was contemplating what charming things to say to her, a wave of violent rage came over me, the rage for my betrayed innocence and for her desire to hurt me, and she said *It's been such a long time since I laughed like that,* and I sprang to my feet and told her:

"*You're demented, just like your demented father.*"

I myself felt that horrible remark. An earthquake. Then, silence. I still had time to see her face, livid, devastated, I wasn't sure if she was more furious or shocked, I wanted to take it back and replace it with something less hideous, less definitive, but I knew I couldn't. I ran away.

12. May (two years later)

Just now, Saba called me to tell me Angelica is dead.

It went more or less like this.

I had spent the whole morning roaming around the house, going back and forth, watering the roses, turning on the TV, feeding the cat, making another coffee—anything to avoid opening the book on Dante. I really didn't feel like it. Truthfully, I *never* feel like it, I need to see the exam menacingly stare at me through the window (and if not the exam, then my mother) and have the fire lit under my ass to finally start studying, but with a month left there's no point. My God, how idle I am, how lazy! I'll end up in the *Antinferno*. I felt hungry. I made myself a ham sandwich—that's when the phone rang:

"Hello?"

" . . . Hello . . . Ema . . ."

"Saba?"

I got excited: "Hey, Saba! What a nice surprise!" But she started crying:

"Ema . . . Angelica is dead."

Saba told me all the details. It was surreal—but only for those who didn't know Angelica. I immediately understood what had *really* happened, and I told her so. Saba, almost heartened, was startled: "Yeah, I think so too . . . oh Ema, what are we going to do?" (Ah, that age-old confidence and trust from someone who only says half of my name!)

"Nothing, there's nothing we can do. Try to stay calm, Saba, try to stay calm, I'll see you tomorrow."

I laid the sandwich in the fridge, it didn't seem right. But first, I carefully wrapped it in cling film. (*Angelica is dead*, and I'm busy with the preservation of nourishment.)

I went into my room and lay down on the bed, "Well, I guess studying is out of the question today," I said out loud, relieved, I realized, and I kept on repeating Saba's chilling words *Angelica is dead, Angelica is dead*, as if I wanted to give consistency to an impalpable reality, as if I were looking for astonishment, for horror, for a pain that, despite trying hard to, I wasn't able to feel.

For that reason, I pulled out my journal, a lacquered yellow notebook, brand new, kind of effeminate, truth be told, and I started to write, and through writing, I remembered.

I remembered that fateful meeting in Venice after my first college exam, April two years before: I'm leaving the bar walking in the rain, my leather shoes on the wet cobblestones, dodging mauve umbrellas and gray raincoats, picking up my pace to forget, to erase that distraught and beautiful face that blinds my brain, that bursts in my head, in every cell, in every nerve, I need to flee as soon as possible: and in the meantime, I'm trying to hold on to my rage because it is dangerously slipping away with every step I take, evaporating in the rain, and I'm doing everything I can to cling to it because while it's trickling away, it gets replaced by a void that sucks at my guts, and so I curse at her again in my mind, but it's a fainter and fainter voice and the pain in the center of my chest grows sharper and sharper, and the sky is getting darker and I look back—I look back once, twice, ten times—but she's not there, she's not following me, it's better this way, it's better this way, it's raining on the water in the canals, it's raining on my face, I feel sick, I feel ill, and now deep inside me, there's only a vast white silence in which my words echo ominously, *you're demented, just like your demented father*, and I see her eyes again, and I slow down, I slow down, and then I stop, I stop . . . I go back.

This time, I run. I run, darting through drenched people, I run: a book slips out of my hand, then another, then they all tumble onto the flooded street, flying open, their pages like a poker hand, I pick them up hastily, wet, dirty, then I get up and try to pull myself together, but it's pouring, it's pouring everywhere, I feel my drenched hair and my heart stuck in my throat, I'm at the bar: I look for her, like a maniac, I jump, I look, I see the old waiter, I pounce on him:

"Excuse me . . . excuse me . . ." I look like a bum and I'm out of breath. "The young lady, the girl who was here . . ."

He looks at me coldly. "She left," he says and turns his back on me.

Then that night, I call her. She isn't there. I call again, leave messages, I feel like a fool. I lock myself up in the darkness of my room, and I listen to a heart-wrenching song by a singer specializing in heart-wrenching songs, the end of love stories and stuff like that. I can't wrap my head around the dread that gnaws at me. An unthinkable dread up to a few weeks ago. I think of how superficial she is, I see her naked, wrapped around Niso, I try to remember all the negatives, her hysterics, her rhetoric, her snake—but all that comes to mind are her sweet eyes, her support during my trying times, her efforts to help me with my play, with my work, her trust in me, her unconditional goodwill—I'm trying to hate her, but how can I?

She made me a part of her life, she told me about her father, I recall our encounter on that bench in November, our phenomenal Christmas, the pain I caused her on New Year's Eve, the way she came back to me in spite of everything, the way she believed in me, her love . . .

My heart breaks in two and I love her. I love her to no end.

Oh yes, I had loved her endlessly, I tell myself, and I stop writing. I close the notebook, I look for a cigarette: but I quit smoking. Too bad, I could use one right now. I quit doing a lot of things since then. I quit imitating Paul Newman. I quit seeing my friends. I quit writing. Only lately, I must say, I have felt the urge to write a novel. A fiery, intoxicated, stylistically perfect novel that will win me the Nobel Prize—like Paul Newman in *The Prize*!

Here I go again.

Well, I go to the bathroom, pee, and lean out of the window: the morning air is crisp and clear, the sky is young and blue, and *Angelica is dead*. Nothing. The crystalline splendor of a May morning, the people merrily walking down the street bathed in sunshine, the heady perfume of pastries wafting up from the corner pastry shop—it all seems more striking than the death of the woman you loved.

And yet, I still remember—and as I remember I pretend that I have a cigarette between my index and middle fingers—I remember that at a certain point I stopped leaving messages on her answering machine because being so ridiculous was suffocating me, and so did the ridiculousness of staring at the phone for hours on end, willing it to ring (*now you will ring, phone, now you will ring*). I had let the days bleed into each other, allowing each one to replace the previous one, painstakingly, one blood drop at a time.

Because I was truly losing blood. Drop by drop, a slow, daily ache. I wandered around the city like a starving dog, walking for miles on end, singing children's songs to distract myself. A couple of times, I even tried getting trashed in some third-rate bars to no use. The images of a happiness I had not been able to grasp and had not recognized until then, until it was too late, when it was already irremediably lost, were strung together like bundles of thorns, I had had her love and it maddened me to think that I had not enjoyed it, that I had lost it—a sublime gift thrown to the dogs. So sublime that, when the pain gave me a break, I became emotional: love was softening my heart and I looked at the flowers, the stars, a small child, with a tenderness I had never felt, and this tenderness in turn amplified my immense feelings for Angelica, my deep and painful affection for her smile, for her wounds. Ah, her wounds! How I wanted to soothe her wounds, they burned in me more than mine, how her saddened face hurt me! How I would have loved to take her by the hand and sit for hours listening to her talk about her father!

I had entered my *dolce stil nuovo* phase.

I stop pretending to smoke by the window and go back to my room. I realize that my love is adorned by delicious literary nuances: I had left that bar raging like Guido Cavalcanti—Love is Mars's son and it's deadly to intelligence—then I had been Guido Guinizzelli, *within the gentle heart abideth Love*, and Angelica had become an angel-woman, pure and a vessel for purity, and in fact I thought about her in every way possible except as a sexual being, and I wanted to kiss her, hug her, serve her, look after her, but make love to her, no, I didn't even think about it . . .

And then, Dante recounts in *New Life*, Beatrice had stopped saying hi to him. And with that lost hello, he had lost his health because being met with a smile from Beatrice and saying hello to each other was all that he lived for—Dante had to find another source to satisfy his love, and so he decided from then on he would find satisfaction and peace in just *extolling* the woman he loved. Precisely like me. To anyone, whether it was my mother or a new fellow classmate, I would tell how precious and noble Angelica was.

But then Beatrice had died, and now Angelica, too. At the end of *New Life*, Dante says he would no longer speak of her until he could say something that no one had ever said before—and he writes *The Divine Comedy*.

Good heavens!

I want to write something, too.

After all, books had provided great consolation in those months. I would read them to find answers to the questions that haunted me: if she had loved me, did she really stop loving me? Can love really just end? Not for me, of course, I would love her forever, until the end of time!

And so, I left my house less and less often, I withdrew in absolute solitude and frenetically consulted Ovid's *The Art of Love* (the same way you would consult a medical encyclopedia), and his advice on how to keep love alive reassured me—but nothing could assuage my anxiety over my biggest problem: the diachronicity of our feelings. I aloof when she loved me, she indifferent when I was consumed.

Was it possible to love each other at the same time, to sip happiness from one another, harmoniously hugging like mythological woodland creatures? Oh God, the happiness of being loved by her, now that I loved her so much, seemed so overwhelming as to feel impossible, inhuman. To such a degree that, imagining she finally called me and told me she loved me, I was appalled to realize I wouldn't have believed it, and as much as she could insist, and although I longed for it more than anything else in the world, I would have never been able to get any pleasure from it, because I wouldn't have believed it: I loved her too much.

I make myself another coffee. The kitchen is cold, but outside is a mild spring morning. I sit at the table, the sun streaming in and shining on my coffee cup, and I open the journal from those days. It's a little elementary school notebook, in rather poor condition, worn, the pages with their small squares show their age, interspersed with green ink and my usual girly penmanship, and in it I find a thousand things I had forgotten about that now I remember, I feel all the suffering—but only in my mind because my heart is distracted by the high quality of my prose.

    I find the angst of certain afternoons, of certain nights. Even of certain mornings. I find the description of her perfume on other women in the streets, I find sentences like this one: "I wander through bars that sometimes saw us together, and I can no longer breathe when I glimpse features similar to hers in someone: but it's never her." I find that, compared to the preceding pages and those from my famous play, the style is sparer, crude, and yet very accurate, thought through to the last comma, as if the only consolation for my pain was finding a word to match it, as though, if my heart had to break, at least let it break in music.

    And I find that October evening, six months after our rainy farewell at the bar in Venice: France and I at the movies. Dear France! He was the only one who came looking for me to draw me out of my shell, to do something together, and I would accept—rarely—to go out for a beer or to some other place, more out of politeness than anything else. Anyway, we were eating popcorn waiting for the movie to start, and France, blushing, told me that Angelica had come to the Sbruffon a few weeks before—I pictured her going in, as regal as the first time

I'd seen her, and I got so worked up, as if at that very moment, she had actually come into the movie theater.

"Was she beautiful?" I asked him, hoping he'd say no.

"Hmm, well."

"Was she alone?"

"Yes."

"And Niso?"

"Oh, he was very polite. As if nothing had happened. But I think he was dying inside."

"But aren't they together?"

France looked at me with his famous stunned expression. They weren't together. Angelica, like me, had also dropped out of sight. *Like me*, maybe, she was preparing herself for running into me accidentally, she lived every second in wait, *like me*, probably, she was creating her own solitude to be ready when fate would have us meet again, *like me*, probably, she was going to the gym every day so she'd look beautiful on the day we'd see each other again, *like me*, but of course but of course! She was afraid and craved at every street corner that we'd bump into each other, and that we'd give ourselves fully to one another, and that we'd . . .

"She moved to Stockholm."

I close the notebook, get up, pour myself another coffee, look outside at the garden beyond the kitchen: a brilliant green and gold, red roses that drink in the morning sun, little birds chirping away—Stockholm. From that moment, something changed. I had kept that illusion alive all by myself, nourishing it every day with caution and devotion, like the most romantic and inveterate of botanists cares for a dying plant, I had lived through a desolate, wasted summer to reconnect with her: and she, instead, had gone to Stockholm, to the cold, nullifying any chance of running into each other. She had gone to her mother, whom she hated, rather than to me.

Beatrice had snubbed Dante, and Angelica had gone to Stockholm, and I got angry, yes, I got angry with a bitter rage that I hadn't felt for over six months—I remember that I was watching the movie with

France, but I didn't see anything, only her, indifferent, sipping a cognac in first class while I, oblivious, had a lump in my throat each time I turned a street corner in Mestre in the hopes of running into her . . .

I pitied my innocent heart, my illusions that had been shattered like a swallow eviscerated by the winter cold (by Stockholm's cold), and I felt contempt for the cowardice that had made her leave: to hell with her!

But it wasn't that easy. Rage and the *dolce stil nuovo* took turns intruding into my long days, and beneath it all lingered a silent pain. Rage, nonetheless, has the gift of making you less helpless. I met a girl in college with thick glasses and huge tits, we went out once, twice, and I always talked about Angelica. She held my hand, between glasses of wine at the table in the bar, I felt some consolation and astonishment in the realization that I had become aroused. We ended up in bed together. But then, right in the middle of it, I felt an uncontrollable desperation in the pit of my stomach. Abysmal guilt, physical suffering. I ran away and met another girl. Dyed hair, nice smile. And another, with beautiful legs and a southern accent, and still another . . . Even though I tried to stop myself, I always ended up talking about Angelica, but they held my hand over the table, I got aroused, and we ended up in bed together, and then that desperation, right, but by then I would toss it away like an old rag (running off into the night), and I met other girls, I couldn't help feeling the pleasure of hearing myself talk about Angelica, to feel their admiration, my growing excitement—and even though I knew the price to pay would be a silent ache in my gut, I talked about Angelica as if she were an evil princess who had sucked my blood dry, I described her soft, perky breasts, and I said that she was a slacker who had suckerpunched me, who had stolen my heart because I was distracted—great job, give it back to me, you bitch!

But it was all literature. It had become literature, and I hadn't even realized it. I used to say I was lying in wait for her because I had a knife stashed in the lining of my jacket and I wanted to rip her eyes out and eat them, but it wasn't true, it wasn't true: yet, the girls listening to me were captured by this novel of mine and inevitably yearned to become the new heroines of my heart, the idea of seducing me and leaving me drove them crazy—so that I would go around talking about them too, in the same way. Ah vanity, vanity! Vanity is unstoppable! Vanity had destroyed me, vanity was saving me. I wrote invectives and maudlin letters that I didn't send, I wrote comedic pieces with her as the main character—each time I made my new female friends read them all, and it was only their vanity that would make them console me, and it was out of vanity that they counted on eradicating my suffering, and it was out of vanity that they fell in love with me.

I look at myself in the mirror.

I try to figure out the exact moment when my falling in love had been over and when it had been transformed into a part to play: but I can't pinpoint either the moment or the day or the month. I only know what I felt a year ago, when for the first and last time, I saw her again.

I was going for a stroll around the main square, it was a warm April evening, and I was just about to pass the bench where we had sat together for the first time, one faraway November so long ago. I walked that way daily, and every single time I would imagine her there, just like I had seen her that first time, in her long overcoat, wearing those black stockings, her mascara intensifying even more her strikingly beautiful green eyes, her long hair grazing her face, magnificent, and that thought had by then become an automatic reflex, like shifting gears in a car, by now bereft of emotion—and here she was.

A wave of light. A pink and opaque, dim, indefinite dream, pastel-colored. I had been waiting for that vision for so long that my mind was convinced it was still wandering, but there were details that did not fit and needed to be brought up to date.

A white blouse, a long white skirt with an embroidered hem, cream-colored sneakers, but I would recall these details only later, right now I only saw a figure as if wrapped in an unwavering aura, her copper hair down to her shoulders, and my heart (waiting for my brain to confirm she was real) was so stunned as to remain calm, but then it started to trot faster as soon as I focused on her eyes without makeup, tired eyes, and saw her barely outlined mouth say:

"Hi."

"Hi." I didn't have any breath for anything more. Now my heart was galloping. She was so clear, so luminous, so Nordic. I think she said:

"Do you remember me?"

And she got up. I felt a shudder run through me that made me all tense followed by a swaying tremor. And I was blind, my God, I was blind, she was right in front of me, but I couldn't see anything. I don't know how, but I managed to give her a perfunctory kiss on each cheek. She hugged me. I felt her breasts pressing against my chest. Her perfume. Her velvety, soft skin. I had to tell my muscles, my limbs, and my optic nerves to do their job because it seemed like each one was doing what it wanted. I needed to regain control of myself. From somewhere, her voice reached me:

"How are you?"

Ever so slowly the weakened souls of my senses were returning to their rightful places, my sight was coming back, my hands went into my pockets, my lips followed my command to muster a satisfied grimace. I was afraid I would stutter, instead, clearly enough, I managed to say:

"Not bad. You look good, hmm? Very good, indeed. But . . . what are you doing here, I mean *right here*, I don't know if you remember, but . . . " Now I was exaggerating, I was talking too much, and I had already started with the rigmarole of old memories, what a moron! Luckily she stopped me:

"What a nice coincidence, isn't it? There was a one in a thousand chance that I'd run into you *right here*."

"Well, I actually come by here every day at this time." She laughs. Then she smiles affectionately and says:

"You're still the same, a leopard doesn't change its spots."

"Or its bad habits, right?"

Silence. Her skin is so pale and delicate. It even has a few freckles. I didn't remember she had freckles. It had to be Stockholm.

"How is Sweden?" (In anticipation of this great reunion, I had prepared a slew of wonderful witticisms about moss and lichens: but, alas, I had forgotten them all.)

"Oh, I came back after two months. I couldn't stand my mother. All she thinks about is money."

"She's a businesswoman, what should she be thinking about, reindeer?"

She smiled again and looked at me with eyes lit up by affection. But I was starting to feel better. The April air was gentle, and people were walking by, she and I looked at each other, standing there, and I saw that she was also excited, that a slight blush had flooded her cheeks and that her breathing was tripping, and now my heart was calm, it was a horse grazing in the woods after a frenetic gallop, it was a disenchanted horse that no longer expected treats from men, it was a philosophically bitter horse.

To complete the remake of that ancient November night, we headed toward the bar with the round tables. The guy with the blue eyes and the ponytail was still there and for a change was smiling. We ordered white wine.

She said, "It seems like centuries ago, doesn't it?"

"Or five minutes."

She got excited: "Really?"

"No, you're right, centuries." Silence.

"I was so angry with you . . ." She murmured, staring into my eyes, melancholically. It was my turn, I hit the ground running:

"Please forgive me, *in all sincerity*. I have been a coward, an idiot, a despicable human being . . ." And I owned up to all my mistakes and even a few more, like a boy in a confessional, I heaped insults upon myself, I took potshots at myself, I repudiated myself, anxious to free myself of my shame—because what I had wished for in those months more than anything else hadn't been her mouth or her legs, instead, I had wished to erase my past as a wimp, erase my grandiose thirst for glory humiliated by Guglielminetti, my tears on the telephone during my days as a waiter, my anguish when she had left, my jealousy, that sentence: *you're demented, just like your demented father* . . .

I wanted to change my past. What bound us together was my shame at being so weak, it was only due to my weakness that *she* had stopped loving me and *I* had fallen in love—damn it! I wanted her to know that I knew I had been an idiot, and knowing it meant I no longer was one, I wanted her to love me again and me not to love her, or it didn't matter, I just wanted her to see me again for what I was: Paul Newman.

The guy with the blue eyes came over to bring us some wine and a bowl of saltines. I spent a few more sentences denigrating myself, then I was done, my eyes fixed on her:

"It's just that I was young, and I loved you."

She got nervous. I knew that saying something like that would shake her. She brought the wine glass to her lips and swallowed a substantial sip of wine. Her eyes were sad, and her voice was so low that I could barely hear her:

"So, you too miss our youth?"

She looked at me, profoundly sad, and I felt entangled in her voracious, devouring, ball-and-chain sadness, and I couldn't fathom how in all those months I had felt an unassailable tenderness for that sadness, a nostalgia for that sadness, that sadness as aggressive as a factory whistle, and I now remembered how all of her sadness had always bothered me, nauseated me, and I had the sobering impression that it had been precisely her sadness, as lugubrious as a Portuguese fado, that had prevented me from falling in love with her the first time we met.

"Ema, you know . . . it seems to me that we will never again be as real, as spontaneous . . ." She murmured with such drama that I would have laughed in her face, "It seems to me that I may never again be able to have those absurd dreams, that now it's just a matter of . . . *living*."

"Speak for yourself. I'm twenty-one and I'm so handsome. Eat your saltines."

She smiled and took my hand:

"Are you still writing?"

Old humiliations resurfaced, blood rushed to my cheeks, I pulled on the parking brake of irony:

"Of course. I recently wrote a couple of postcards, very deep, and I'm on the third chapter of a birthday card."

I was joking around too much, but she didn't seem to mind:

"And all the others, do you still see them?"

"No. We're scattered all over the world. A beautiful diaspora."

She looked down and said in a murmur:

"I'm so sorry . . . I feel responsible for that."

"Don't let it go to your head. Besides, losing touch with each other is a relief."

"Losing you was the hardest thing in my life."

I almost laughed. She looked at me, I looked at her, and I couldn't hold back:

"Let's not exaggerate. Harder than losing your father?"

She jumped to her feet, I was afraid she was going to slap me, her eyes filled with tears, and she said, "Goodbye," but she wasn't angry, no, just desperate, she tried to muster a smile, turned around, and walked toward the entrance, I felt the urge to follow her, but something kept me glued to the chair—I could have stopped her, kissed her, made love to her—but I didn't budge—we could have been together again, eaten sushi, watched a movie, gone to the theater—but she left and I remained sitting where I was—we could have gone dancing, *traveled*, taken a cooking class together—but then I saw her walking away from me, her back to me, fast, getting smaller and smaller, and I didn't move, I could have run after her but I was glued to my little table with the bowl of saltines still full and our two empty wine glasses, I watched her as she faded into the horizon like in a French song from the '30s, and now I was sad too, but my sadness was not like hers, my sadness was a cold stew, a cow wandering alone in the Abruzzo mountains, my sadness was knowing that it was definitely over, that there were no more illusions to chase after, that getting back together was possible, yes, and maybe we could even love one another, and maybe it is even possible to love one another *forever*, but being happy is much more complicated, to be happy you must be alone, and therefore, I settled the check with the guy with the blue eyes and the ponytail, and for the first time I saw he wasn't smiling, how strange, and I thought that there had to be a certain sadness in tending a bar, making the same martinis every day, every day bringing saltines and wearing a ponytail and a smile, a slow sadness like a noose, hidden like a back room, inescapable like death . . .

So, this is how I spent the long day *Angelica died*, killing hour after hour: I turned the TV back on. I fed more liver to the cat. I made myself an umpteenth coffee. My mother came home, and I told her everything—my mother was very upset: mom, you didn't even know her! But she even started crying and got worried about me, how are you, honey, tell me, I knew that I shouldn't have told her, and then my dad came home, too, and so, I went out for some fresh air . . .

This is how I spent the slow warm hours kicking pebbles with my sneakers, even kicking an empty Coke can, but on the side to give it a nice spin, and I roamed through the streets of Mestre, young and impudent Mestre on an almost-summer afternoon, I saw men and women and children and basset hounds, I smelled fresh cement and mock orange flowers and exhaust fumes and daisies, I put my hands in my pockets and went by street corners that had seen us together, I went by the famous bench, I went by the usual bar and peeked inside (sitting at the table we had shared that last time was a very large blonde and her black poodle), and I kept walking, I marveled at a rows of rotisserie chickens (fat dripping onto layers of tin foil), I watched the show put on by a pigeon and four swallows fighting over a leftover croissant at an outdoor table of a downtown bar (we had been there, too) and the bullying pigeon was winning, so, I intervened and gave him a tap on his behind, he took off terrified, the swallows looked at me in ecstasy, brimming with gratitude, and then I glanced at the movie posters and at the lemonade-colored sky and at the old antennas on the red and blue buildings. In Piazza Ferretto I bought an ice cream cone because I was hungry. I went to the bookstore. Then to the movies. Then I went back home. I went back home and my dad said, "I'm sorry."

And this is how I spent the night, I tried to read a few pages of an old American novel, I looked for comfort among the old Bentleys and the golf courses in West Egg, usually the old America consoles me, but I needed something even older, I pulled out an old Claudian mythology book, then an illustrated soccer almanac with all the players' pictures from the beginning of the century: Herbert Kaplan, founder and captain of AC Milan, in his knickerbockers and his formidable moustache; Silvio Piola, with his magnificent smile and his gelled hair combed straight back; Valentino Mazzola, holding the hand of his young son Sandro before the start of the match . . .

So beautiful.

Then I turned to Donald Duck comics, Donald Duck never disappoints, and visiting Duckland always lightens my heart, and in fact I felt better reading one story in which Donald Duck urges his nephews to buy string beans, they forget to, but to make up for it, they bake Donald's favorite cake. Then I watched TV. I watched the highest-paid show host sweating like a pig, he had a ruddy nose and was acting his endearing part and cracking lewd jokes, I changed the channel, a small group of young people around a hostess was discussing the thorny issue of a girl and her mother (in the studio) struggling with a father's and a husband's decision to change gender (on an external link wearing a red ostrich boa and a black bowler hat). The story captivated me for quite a while. The most astonishing aspect was that they were all ugly: the small group of young people, the hostess, the daughter, the mother, not to mention the father-husband wearing the ostrich boa. But *really* ugly. I wondered why. The only beautiful thing was the gender-changer's black bowler hat, that was magnificent, grandiose, and it seemed to mock everyone from the top of the crossdresser's head, it seemed to mock the small group of young people, the hostess, the daughter, the mother, and the individual himself who had adopted it as an appendage. I changed the channel. The commercial for a pasta brand showed a little girl, beautiful this time, who had unwittingly slipped a piece of rigatone into the jacket of her young father—also very handsome—and when the young father finds it in his pocket that night and takes it out and *understands*, he is touched. Gee, fatherhood plays some tricks on you, I told myself. So, I turned off the TV and tried to go to sleep. But before that, I said a prayer for Angelica.

I said:

"Good Lord, if you exist, then Angelica probably still exists. That would explain my particular behavior today—but that's another story.

Well, forgive her if she did what I think she did. Let her see her father, let her be happy. And you, Angelica, if you can hear me: well, hi."

A subtle shiver enveloped me, then I fell asleep.

I drive slowly along the Riviera del Brenta, with my elbow out the window, and I can't help but be carried away by the sweetness of the May morning, by the sunrays merrily bouncing on the surface of the river, on the trees and the orange-roofed houses, on the faces of elegant girls going to a bar for breakfast before heading off to the office, on the chrome-plated trunks of the cars I meet, on the bicycle bells of old people pedaling in search of a newsstand. The funeral, Saba informed me, is at nine, in a little less than half an hour. I have butterflies in my stomach, my pulse is racing, and the tie is squeezing my neck. I'm not one to wear ties, but I wanted to look nice. I changed clothes ten times in front of the mirror, neurotically, almost as if I had to go to a party to meet my belle, I practiced all my expressions, I let the sunrays filter through the curtains to illuminate my blue eyes. It is a warm Saturday, the morning air permeates the streets with its gentle touch, the sun shines on the austere facades of the villas, on the green shutters, on the red flowers on the balconies and wraps everything as if in golden silk drapery.

I arrive right on time at the small country church. It's small and white, and now my heart is racing: in the churchyard there's a handful of people. Only three. And about six feet away, there's a fat, black cat purring in the sun. The first one I recognize is France, wearing dark glasses, he comes toward me. He mumbles something:

"The caskets are already inside." The caskets. I feel like I've been punched in the gut. I say: "It's terrible." France purses his lips in a way that I've never seen him do. I know he's suffering more than I. It's kind of absurd, but that's how it is: you can't even say that they were friends, she and he, France barely had the courage to talk to her, and yet his suffering is clearer than mine. Then, Niso. He's also wearing dark glasses. He hugs me. I find it a bit much, it's giving me goosebumps, but I feel its strong and sincere embrace, and just for a moment I feel choked up—Niso, my friend! At last, I feel compelled to speak to him, to tell him I'm sorry—and I realize that I would say to him the same things I had said to Angelica a year ago—then, behind me, I sense someone:

"Hi, Ema."

I turn around. Damn it, she's got dark glasses, too. She's wearing a black pants suit, gloomy, long hair, and I had never realized she was so short.

"Hi, Rebecca."

We hug each other. I smell the perfume in her hair, and her hug also seems sincere—but that perfume, that perfume distracts me, unsettles me, takes me somewhere else. From under her dark glasses, two heavy teardrops streak her face. They also give me goosebumps. I don't understand. Why is she crying? Is it for us because we've lost touch with one another? For Angelica? Now I realize that she's wearing the same perfume as Angelica.

The crunching of our footsteps on the white gravel in the churchyard is the only sound in the cemetery silence of the morning.

"Shall we go in?" Asks France. "What about Alcapone?" Rebecca whispers. "He isn't here, he had to work," Niso mumbles. Their voices are weak and raspy, the voices of weary ghosts, and I recall a long-ago day by the sea, we had just finished our final exams, and on the beach we were playing a merciless soccer match, Brazil-Uruguay in the World Cup, if I'm not mistaken, right, a great game, and I look at Rebecca's black diminutive silhouette, and magically I see her with a lime-colored swimsuit caressing her naked body, I see her splashing around in the water—happy.

We are about to go inside, the four of us. The fat black cat lifts his head up for a minute and opens an eye to make sure that everything is in order and then once again sinks into a deep sleep. The bells are ringing. We go through the small wooden door of the church, a welcome wave of cool air greets us—in front of us, just a few yards away, lie the caskets.

They are next to each other, both made from a pale wood, with bronze handles. A stifled moan: it's Rebecca. She brings her left hand to her mouth. Niso and France on either side support her. I stay behind paralyzed by a shudder that electrifies my whole face, more due to Rebecca's spasm than to the sight of the caskets.

There are only around twenty people, about ten on the right and ten on the left. Scattered, they take up the first three or four rows. All men and women are dressed in black with their heads bent, one takes out a handkerchief and brings it to her face, another one is kneeling, someone else . . . In the first row, on the left, I see a tall woman, long ashen hair almost down to her bottom, a first-rate bottom, a dark gray suit, black stockings, and high heels—she must be the American mother. More than anything else, I wish I had a pair of dark glasses to scrutinize without being scrutinized. Rebecca, Niso, and France sit down in the first empty row behind the others, on the left. Instinctively, I sit a couple of rows behind them, by myself.

The priest arrives, and he starts speaking. I can't follow a word he's saying, I start glancing at the people, catching their profiles, on my right. Then, I turn to my left and I see Saba, magically, next to me. She has lots of curls, white skin, a black jacket, a black skirt to her knees, and no stockings. She smiles at me. I smile back at her. I feel an ancient emotion, of genuine tenderness. I graze her face with a small tap, then I kiss her on the cheek. The priest is saying:

"Two young lives have been cut short" And I ask Saba how she is.

"Better, now. And you?" she whispers.

"Good."

"I have no tears left to cry. You too, eh?"

"Eh . . ."

Then she stares at me with those sparkling eyes I remembered so well, when I knew she didn't want us to see each other anymore, but once again I know what she actually wants:

"Have you thought about it?"

"Of course."

"And you still think we shouldn't say anything?"

"Yes. It wouldn't do anybody any good. Neither to Angelica's memory, nor to the thirty-five year old guy's memory . . ."

"But the truth . . ."

"The two of us alone will guard the truth, you and I."

I look at her knowingly. To tell the truth, I'm not convinced that the two of us alone would guard the truth. In my opinion, the American mother and the thirty-five-year-old's family *knew*. And by some overt or unspoken pact, they had managed not to have any details leaked of such a macabre accident that would have been fodder for the newspapers and TV for days on end, even more so if it were known that it had not been an accident. But I like this detective role I am playing and I like Saba's pale face, the color of peach flesh, and her curls dancing on her furrowed forehead—ah, the truth!—and I remember those long, lethargic afternoons spent between the bed and the kitchen table, between chats and eggplant moussaka, I would love to place my lips on hers, delicately, like a rose petal on another, and I look at her breasts within her black jacket, and I recall her ass, wonderful and moon-like, and I feel a shock of happiness run over my skin.

"The Lord has decided to call Angelica and Tancredi to Him," the priest says.

"His name was Tancredi?" I ask Saba, astonished.

"Yes. But then . . . we're letting everyone think that . . ."

"That they were two lovers killed in a freak accident. It's better than letting them know she was an assassin and he was an old stalker, right?"

"But are you really sure it happened like that?"

"Saba, my love: I've seen every episode of Lieutenant Columbo. She reeled him in, and then threw the snake at him."

"And then?"

"I told you. We could speculate that the snake was so enraged that it bit her, too. But Angelica really knew how to handle that reptile, believe me. And you also told me that he was scarred by the bites, whereas she only had one . . ."

"It's horrible."

"But did they ever find the snake?"

"Yes, they killed it."

I needed to know. I was afraid it might reach me, sooner or later. And anyway, I will forever dream of it. I shuddered. I hear Saba sigh:

"And so, she committed suicide . . . "

"But if you think about it, she was born for suicide. And for quite a suicide. Yes, it all fits, it's consistent with her character, tragic till the end."

"Yes, but then isn't having a funeral together as if they were a happy couple ridiculous!?"

"Oh well, yes."

Furthermore, her whole life had been a ridiculous tragedy, and her love life—a ridiculous love life. First, her father, a pathetic clown. Then, a stalker named Tancredi. And finally, me: the greatest playwright in the world, the fastest waiter in the west—Paul Newman! And out of the fog in my mind, after centuries, Guglielminetti and his black boots, don Faust and his greasy ponytail bound into the limelight, and once again inside me I feel the passion of ambition and the pain of failure, and I reopen my eyes to see France's strong shoulders, I see his arm around Rebecca's thin waist, Rebecca, who roams Venice and Mestre with me, I see the lanky figure of Niso, the poet, I see his serious posing, I see him reciting Baudelaire, and my memories speak, deep inside me, of that terrible and absolute year whose humiliations I thought I would carry forever, the pain of the first love, the warmth of friendship—and instead I realize that in that moment some minuscule spots of color are infinitely more important, the gold and the purple of the priest's cassock, the sun rays that filter through the tall Medieval stained glass windows to sink in a shower of sparkles over the bronze handles of Angelica's casket, and especially, *especially*, the correct phrasing of the words that have been dancing in my head since I first entered the coolness of this small church:

I was twenty.

Twenty, said like that, it sounds so easy.

But it's not true.

It's not that simple . . .

Acknowledgments

Every book is the result of the work of several talented individuals. Heartfelt thanks to my publishers Fred Gardaphe, Paolo Giordano, and Anthony Julian Tamburri, who have once again made my American dream come true; to Giorgio Tarchini, wonderful translator; to Siân Gibby and Nicholas Grosso, splendid editors; to the great Henri de Toulouse-Lautrec for the cover.

This is my first novel. And the first to be translated into English. I remember writing and rewriting it drunk on literature and youth, which are the two central themes of the novel. It has all the hormonal madness of youth, even in the language: it is vital, erotic, politically incorrect, excessive. Perhaps I wouldn't rewrite it like this, yet I wouldn't change a single comma; revising it once again before translation, I resisted the temptation to polish it, to make it "more mature". In 2009, the novel was chosen by Roberto Pazzi, editor of the "L'Isola Bianca" series for Corbo Editore (Ferrara), a novelist and poet translated into almost 30 languages, and a dear friend who left us in December 2023. I dedicate *It's Saturday You Left Me and I'm So Beautiful* to him.

About the Author

EMANUELE PETTENER was born in Venice, Italy, and is Associate Professor and Writer in Residence at Florida Atlantic University (Boca Raton, Florida). He has written novels, short stories, articles, and essays, several of which have been translated in the United States, Spain, and Turkey. In 2014, Bordighera Press published his collection of short stories *A Season in Florida* (translated by Thomas De Angelis). *It's Saturday You Left Me and I'm So Beautiful*, his first novel published in the United States, was also his first novel published in Italy, by Corbo Editore, in 2009.

About the Translator

GIORGIO TARCHINI was born in Lugano, Switzerland. He received his medical degree from the University of Zurich and his MBA from the University of Florida. He's worked as an infectious disease physician and as a Chief Medical Officer for several hospitals in South Florida. His fluency in five languages has led him to pursue literary studies. He is currently working on a short story collection. This is his first professional translation.

CROSSINGS
An Intersection of Cultures

Crossings is dedicated to the publication of Italian language literature and translations from Italian to English.

Rodolfo Di Biasio. *Wayfarers Four*. Translated by Justin Vitello. 1998. ISBN 1-88419-17-9. Vol 1.

Isabella Morra. *Canzoniere: A Bilingual Edition*. Translated by Irene Musillo Mitchell. 1998. ISBN 1-88419-18-6. Vol 2.

Nevio Spadone. *Lus*. Translated by Teresa Picarazzi. 1999. ISBN 1-88419-22-4. Vol 3.

Flavia Pankiewicz. *American Eclipses*. Translated by Peter Carravetta. Introduction by Joseph Tusiani. 1999. ISBN 1-88419-23-2. Vol 4.

Dacia Maraini. *Stowaway on Board*. Translated by Giovanna Bellesia and Victoria Offredi Poletto. 2000. ISBN 1-88419-24-0. Vol 5.

Walter Valeri, editor. *Franca Rame: Woman on Stage*. 2000. ISBN 1-88419-25-9. Vol 6.

Carmine Biagio Iannace. *The Discovery of America*. Translated by William Boelhower. 2000. ISBN 1-88419-26-7. Vol 7.

Romeo Musa da Calice. *Luna sul salice*. Translated by Adelia V. Williams. 2000. ISBN 1-88419-39-9. Vol 8.

Marco Paolini & Gabriele Vacis. *The Story of Vajont*. Translated by Thomas Simpson. 2000. ISBN 1-88419-41-0. Vol 9.

Silvio Ramat. *Sharing A Trip: Selected Poems*. Translated by Emanuel di Pasquale. 2001. ISBN 1-88419-43-7. Vol 10.

Raffaello Baldini. *Page Proof*. Edited by Daniele Benati. Translated by Adria Bernardi. 2001. ISBN 1-88419-47-X. Vol 11.

Maura Del Serra. *Infinite Present*. Translated by Emanuel di Pasquale and Michael Palma. 2002. ISBN 1-88419-52-6. Vol 12.

Dino Campana. *Canti Orfici*. Translated and Notes by Luigi Bonaffini. 2003. ISBN 1-88419-56-9. Vol 13.

Roberto Bertoldo. *The Calvary of the Cranes*. Translated by Emanuel di Pasquale. 2003. ISBN 1-88419-59-3. Vol 14.

Paolo Ruffilli. *Like It or Not*. Translated by Ruth Feldman and James Laughlin. 2007. ISBN 1-88419-75-5. Vol 15.

Giuseppe Bonaviri. *Saracen Tales*. Translated Barbara De Marco. 2006. ISBN 1-88419-76-3. Vol 16.

Leonilde Frieri Ruberto. *Such Is Life*. Translated Laura Ruberto. Introduction by Ilaria Serra. 2010. ISBN 978-1-59954-004-7. Vol 17.

Gina Lagorio. *Tosca the Cat Lady*. Translated by Martha King. 2009. ISBN 978-1-59954-002-3. Vol 18.

Marco Martinelli. *Rumore di acque*. Translated and edited by Thomas Simpson. 2014. ISBN 978-1-59954-066-5. Vol 19.

Emanuele Pettener. *A Season in Florida*. Translated by Thomas De Angelis. 2014. ISBN 978-1-59954-052-2. Vol 20.

Angelo Spina. *Il cucchiaio trafugato*. 2017. ISBN 978-1-59954-112-9. Vol 21.

Michela Zanarella. *Meditations in the Feminine*. Translated by Leanne Hoppe. 2017. ISBN 978-1-59954-110-5. Vol 22.

Francesco "Kento" Carlo. *Resistenza Rap*. Translated by Emma Gainsforth and Siân Gibby. 2017. ISBN 978-1-59954-112-9. Vol 23.

Kossi Komla-Ebri. *EMBAR-RACE-MENTS*. Translated by Marie Orton. 2019. ISBN 978-1-59954-124-2. Vol 24.

Angelo Spina. *Immagina la prossima mossa*. 2019. ISBN 978-1-59954-153-2. Vol 25.

Luigi Lo Cascio. *Othello*. Translated by Gloria Pastorino. 2020. ISBN 978-1-59954-158-7. Vol 26.

Sante Candeloro. *Puzzle*. Translated by Fred L. Gardaphe. 2020. ISBN 978-1-59954-165-5. Vol 27.

Amerigo Ruggiero. *Italians in America*. Translated by Mark Pietralunga. 2020. ISBN 978-1-59954-169-3. Vol 28.

Giuseppe Prezzolini. *The Transplants*. Translated by Fabio Girelli Carasi. 2021. ISBN 978-1-59954-137-2. Vol 29.

Silvana La Spina. *Penelope*. Translated by Anna Chiafele and Lisa Pike. 2021. ISBN 978-1-59954-172-3. Vol 30.

Marino Magliani. *A Window to Zeewijk*. Translated by Zachary Scalzo. 2021. ISBN 978-1-59954-178-5. Vol 31.

Alain Elkann. *Anita*. Translated by K.E. Bättig von Wittelsbach. 2021. ISBN 978-1-59954-170-9. Vol 32.

Luigi Fontanella. *The God of New York*. Translated by Siân E. Gibby. 2022. ISBN 978-1-59954-177-8. Vol 33.

Kossi Komla-Ebri. *Home*. Translated by Marie Orton. 2022. ISBN 978-1-59954-190-7. Vol 34.

Leopold Berman. *The Story of a Jewish Boy*. Translated by Giuliana Carugati. 2022. ISBN 978-1-59954-192-1. Vol 35.

Alain Elkann. *Nonna Carla*. Translated by K.E. Bättig von Wittelsbach. 2021. ISBN 978-1-59954-201-0. Vol 36.

Luigi Pirandello. *Man, Beast, and Virtue*. Translated by Alice Roche. 2024. ISBN 978-1-59954-205-8. Vol 37.

Maria Teresa Cometto. *Emma and the Angel of Central Park*. 2023. ISBN 978-1-59954-157-0. Vol 38.

Alain Elkann. *A Single Day*. Translated by K.E. Bättig von Wittelsbach. 2024. ISBN 978-1-59954-211-9. Vol 39.

Elisabetta Rasy. *The Indiscreet*. Translated by Siân E. Gibby. 2024. ISBN 978-1-59954-212-6. Vol 40.

Joseph Bathanti. *Sempre Fidele*. Translated by Marina Morbiducci and Darcy Di Mona. 2024. ISBN 978-1-59954-224-9. Vol 41.

Sofia Pirandello. *Animals*. Translated by Daniela Innocenti, Contextus. 2024. ISBN 978-1-59954-225-6. Vol 42.

www.ingramcontent.com/pod-product-compliance
Lightning Source LLC
Chambersburg PA
CBHW031435160426
43195CB00010BB/739